Turn Again Livingstone

John Carvel

John Carvel is education editor of the *Guardian*. From 1981 to 1985 he was local government correspondent and covered the story of Ken Livingstone's GLC. His subsequent positions on the paper include chief political correspondent, home affairs editor and European affairs editor. He was Local Government Journalist of the Year in 1985, Legal Affairs Journalist of the Year in 1991 and was commended for his specialist writing in the British Press Awards in 1984 and 1990. In 1995 he won the Freedom of Information Award for exposing official secrecy by the EU Council of Ministers, against which he took a successful action in the European Court of Justice.

Turn Again Livingstone

John Carvel

P

PROFILE BOOKS

First published in 1999 by
Profile Books Ltd
58A Hatton Garden
London ECIN 8LX

Typeset in Bembo by
MacGuru
macguru@pavilion.co.uk
Printed and bound in Great Britain by
St Edmundsbury Press, Bury St Edmunds

A CIP catalogue record for this book is available from the British Library.

ISBN 1 86197 131 1

Contents

To Florence, two Roberts and one Jack

Preface

It would be easier to write a biography of Ken Livingstone after knowing the outcome of his bid to become London's first directly elected mayor. But readers may find it more interesting to learn about him now while the result is still uncertain. I hope this book will help those in charge of the Labour Party to come to a balanced view as they consider whether or not to block his candidacy. And it may help everyone else to judge their decision and its far-reaching implications for Tony Blair's New Labour project.

This book originated in my work for the *Guardian* when I was the paper's local government correspondent from 1981 to 1985, with a ringside seat for the extraordinary battle between the Greater London Council under Livingstone's leadership and the Conservative government under Margaret Thatcher.

In addition to reporting on the subject in the paper, I wrote a fuller account, published under the title *Citizen Ken* in 1984 and updated in 1986 to take the story to the point when the GLC was abolished. By that stage I was political correspondent of the *Guardian* and got another ringside seat when Livingstone became an MP in 1987 and embarked on a period of unsuccessful opposition to Neil Kinnock's attempts to pull the Labour Party back towards the political centre.

This new book draws in part from material gathered during that period. Quotations in Chapters 1–6 are mostly from interviews with Livingstone, his colleagues and rivals during 1983. Similar quotations in Chapters 7–8 are mostly from interviews in 1985. The analysis of that period has been revised to take account of current perspectives, although the conclusions appear to have stood the test of time. The subsequent chapters covering the period since 1987 – and the Introduction and Conclusion – are based on more recent research and interviews over the last six months.

At each stage Livingstone has co-operated by giving answers to my questions. So did many of his political adversaries who indulged my interest in the subject in spite of their distaste for it. Thanks to all of them for helping me to produce a rounded picture. Thanks also to my editor, Alan Rusbridger, for tolerating this distraction from my normal duties and to my colleagues Rebecca Smithers, Donald MacLeod, Annabel McLaren and other members of the paper's education team for their support during this project.

I am assuming that many of the politically active sources who gave me the benefit of their perceptions and information would prefer to remain anonymous. But I acknowledge my debt to them and to the friends and colleagues who have helped at key stages of this project over the last 16 years: in particular Richard Gott, Jo Andrews, Frankie Rickford, Alison Frater, Tony Travers, Seamus Milne and Judy Graham.

Ken Livingstone's mother Ethel raided the family album to provide the pictures of his early life that appeared in *Citizen Ken* and have been widely reproduced since in newspapers and magazines. Sadly Ethel died last year and I would like to thank his sister Lin for the additional early photographs that appear in this book. Thanks also to Eamonn McCabe, picture editor of the *Guardian*, for help in selecting the other photographs and for himself taking the frontispiece picture.

Without the calming efficiency of Nicky White, my editor at Profile, the book might never have been completed. Thanks to her. And to my sons Bertie and Jack who helped me more than they knew by encouraging me when they would have preferred us to be doing other things.

John Carvel
March 1999

Introduction:
Nightmare on Downing Street

Ken Livingstone's popularity jars with almost everything else we think we know about the present political climate. He is an uncompromising left-winger, surviving in a Labour Party that for more than a decade shifted further and further to the right in search of electoral success. Many of his erstwhile allies adapted to this seemingly inevitable trend and were rewarded with ministerial office when Tony Blair swept to power in May 1997 with a Commons majority of 178. But given that huge popular mandate, Blair had no need to accommodate dissidents who would not enthusiastically march to the New Labour tune. So what remained of the left was marginalised. Within the party mainstream, admirers of Livingstone's undoubted talents concluded that he had stuck too outspokenly to principles and tactics of confrontation whose time had passed.

Even in left-wing parliamentary circles, where there was continuing anxiety about how much further Blair's political realignment 'Project' might go, Livingstone was regarded as a loner without a distinct personal following. There used to be Bevanites and Bennites, but there were not Livingstonites. The word did not exist and it seemed unlikely that it ever would.

Yet, by the early months of 1999 in his bid to become London's first directly elected mayor, he was posing a formidable political challenge to Blair. The government had survived a series of potentially damaging blows to its image of invincibility. There was persistent infighting between the rival camps surrounding Blair and Gordon Brown, his chancellor. Disclosure of an unorthodox home loan arrangement forced the resignation of

Peter Mandelson, the trade and industry secretary and inspirer of the Blairite party reforms. Embarrassing revelations by Margaret Cook, former wife of the foreign secretary, added to the mood of discomfiture at the heart of government. But the voters did not seem to mind. These episodes came and went without any significant damage to Labour's rating in the opinion polls.

The Livingstone problem looked as if it could be a lot more serious. Blair and his advisers were perplexed about how they should respond to the persistent evidence of those same pollsters that the cheeky left-winger was more likely than any other politician of any political party to win the mayoral election in May 2000. A man they perceived as a troublemaker who ought to have been consigned to the ashcan of history was so popular that stopping him was going to be dangerous.

The mayoral plan had been a product of Blair's total domination of his party during Labour's final years in opposition. Against the strong advice of Frank Dobson, then front-bench spokesman on the subject, he insisted that the capital needed a strong executive figurehead who would be responsible directly to the people rather than to the political machinations of a group of councillors on an old-style local authority. London had suffered from lack of strategic vision and local democratic accountability since Margaret Thatcher abolished the Greater London Council in 1986. Now, said Blair, it should be allowed to elect a strong individual to give it a clear voice. The proposal went into Labour's 1997 general election manifesto without much thought about who that individual might be. It was a rare form of devolution imposed from the top down without the people to whom power was being devolved asking for it. They wanted a London assembly, but they were given a directly elected mayor as well.

As soon as Blair had floated the idea, the media started asking the obvious question about who might get the job. Opinion polls were commissioned and time after time they came back with the answer that the most popular candidate Labour could put forward would be Ken Livingstone. That view was not just being expressed by left-wing die-hards in the London party, but also by ordinary voters, the same people who thought Tony Blair was doing a great job in Downing Street.

So here was the first paradox. If Blair was certain of anything, it was that his electoral success was founded on refashioning Labour to shed the image of left-wingery that Livingstone personified. Yet Livingstone was emerging as the candidate who could trounce any New Labour loyalist in a party selection contest run on Blairite principles of one member, one vote. What is more, he had the best chance of winning the subsequent election among the public at large. What did that say about the people's commitment to New Labour?

The notion that Livingstone might be popular was not in the official party script. He had come to fame as leader of the Greater London Council from 1981 to 1986 when he broke the mould of local government by turning it into an absorbing spectator sport. The left-wing coup that brought him the leadership on the day after the 1981 municipal elections, when he deposed the moderate who led the party to the polls, made him the instant bogeyman of the right-wing tabloids. They revelled in reporting and condemning his comments about the need for a negotiated peace in Northern Ireland, recognition of gay rights and other topics that would not have caused outrage in other countries or at other times. The rough and tumble can be left to later chapters of this book, but the upshot was negative publicity for the Labour Party. In 1981 the *Sun* called him 'the most odious man in Britain'.

Livingstone used the GLC as a platform to mount a sustained campaign against the Conservative government under Margaret Thatcher. He managed to do this with a piratical flair that could not be matched by successive Labour party leaders Michael Foot and Neil Kinnock. He left them in no doubt what he thought of their failings. For lots of ordinary party members slogging through long years of opposition, he provided a tonic of optimism and a bit of a laugh. He ran rings round Conservative ministers and drove a coach and horses through their public spending controls.

Thatcher's decision to abolish the GLC, and with it the whole tier of strategic government in England's other metropolitan counties, was the direct result of his brazenly effective resistance.

The approach taken by Livingstone's GLC was a left-wing version of New Labour modernisation. His supporters wanted to break decisively with the past. They thought that too many Labour politicians at national and local level had been too ready to abandon their principles and betray the people who voted for them by cutting services at the first sign of financial difficulty. They were determined to clean up the sleaze of local-government contracts and planning permissions being traded for back-handers. They wanted to be accountable to their constituency members rather than to trade union barons or string-pullers in the national party. In those days nobody talked about Old Labour because the New Labour terminology against which the concept is juxtaposed had not yet entered the political vocabulary. But if you had mentioned the words 'Old Labour' at the GLC during Livingstone's leadership, it would have been assumed that you were attacking the Tammany Hall tradition associated with the party's right wing.

Livingstone and his collective leadership group at the GLC were also open to new ideas. For example, they borrowed policies from the Democrats in the United States for combating racism and sexism in employment by requiring their contractors to offer equal opportunities. They introduced a coherent public transport policy, lowering the fares on the buses and Underground to provide an incentive for people to leave their cars at home and reduce congestion. (The policy made sense at the time because the public transport infrastructure was underused.) They solved social problems by giving grants to voluntary bodies, instead of allocating the work to more expensive and less committed bureaucracies. They pioneered techniques of political propaganda that were subsequently adopted by Labour to refashion its image.

During the run-up to abolition in 1986, Labour was improving its poll ratings in London faster than in the country at large. But the party's high command put this down to the professionalism of the council's advertising consultants, rather than the campaigning skills of Livingstone or the popularity of his policies. They recognised that he had a showman's talent and an appealing cheeky-chappy style. His south London nasal tones were instantly recognisable and his strange interest in salamanders and other more exotic amphibians was a memorable idiosyncracy. But it was assumed that his policies of increasing local taxes to improve services were deeply unpopular with the middle-class voters that Labour needed to attract, while his support for gay rights and sympathy for Sinn Fein alienated the party's core working-class vote. When he became an MP and member of the party's national executive in 1987, he embarked on a period of opposition to the party reforms being pushed through by Kinnock to make Labour more electable. By 1989 Kinnock had effectively won the internal party battle and Livingstone was voted off the NEC with what looked like a one-way ticket into the political wilderness. When John Smith succeeded Kinnock after Labour's defeat in 1992, there was a chance that Livingstone might be rehabilitated. But Smith's untimely death left him powerless in the margins.

So there was considerable surprise in the Blairite camp when opinion polls put Livingstone at the top of the list of Labour candidates most likely to win support at an election to become London's mayor. The first of these polls was in November 1996 and the popular verdict in favour of Livingstone became stronger as time went by. The party spin-doctors' response was a clear message to political correspondents that the polls were irrelevant because he would never be allowed to become the Labour candidate. In April 1998 a poll by NOP for the *Evening Standard*★ showed that three-quarters of Londoners thought stopping Livingstone in this way would be wrong. By November 1998, 91 per cent of Londoners polled by Carlton TV were saying he should be allowed to stand.

★London's evening newspaper changed names four times during the period covered by this book. For clarity, it is referred to throughout as the *Evening Standard*, the name it held from 1849 until the early 1980s and again since 1986.

Later chapters of this book, describing Livingstone's fierce criticism of successive Labour leaders, explain why Blair could not reasonably have been expected to feel enthusiastic about having him as mayor. In effect, the prime minister was being confronted with two equally preposterous propositions. Would he stand idly by while London party members selected as Labour candidate an unreconstructed and skilful left-winger, who might be expected to use the megaphone of mayoral office to challenge his vision of where the party should be heading? Or would he intervene to block the candidate best able to stop the prize falling into Tory hands? A Conservative victory in the mayoral race could provide not only a springboard for the revival of that party's electoral fortunes, but also a platform for constant high-publicity attack on the government of the sort that Livingstone had deployed so effectively against Thatcher.

Blair did not have to make up his mind in a hurry and it would be wrong to suggest that he spent much time agonising about these questions during his first 18 months in office. There was plenty to do. Making peace in Northern Ireland, bombing Iraq, pushing through reforms of the education and health services, and supervising a wide-ranging programme of constitutional change – these were urgent priorities. A decision on whether to block Livingstone did not have to be taken until the late summer or autumn of 1999. There had to be a procedure by which the left-winger could be stopped if need be, but the signal about whether it should be used to do so could wait a while. Perhaps in the meantime something would crop up to make the Livingstone challenge self-destruct.

There was no personal animosity between Livingstone and Blair as there had been between Livingstone and Kinnock. According to a Downing Street source close enough to Blair to know his mind in this matter, there had been a distinct chance that Livingstone could have been offered ministerial office if he had kept his nose clean during the early months of the Labour government. 'Tony always hoped that Ken would come on board when we came into power. I think he would probably feel that he had indicated that was the case to Ken.' Nothing specific was offered, 'but there were discussions ... There was a reasonable chance that, if Ken had not behaved in the way he did for the first spell in government, things would have come together.' This reference to Livingstone's misbehaviour related particularly to his coruscating criticism of economic policy and call for the chancellor's dismissal.

In otherwise frank interviews for this book, Livingstone has refused to discuss whether there might or might not have been private discussions with Blair before or after the election. It is the clearest signal possible that he did not want to prejudice the possibility of a political deal letting him run for the mayoralty by breaking the confidentiality of previous contacts. But the account from Blair's side of the fence is revealing. If the prime minister was open to the possibility of giving Livingstone ministerial office at some time after the 1997 election, he could not rule him out of the mayoral contest on the grounds that his political behaviour before 1997 was in some way beyond the pale. Nor did Blair feel slighted by Livingstone's apparent rejection of the olive branch. 'Tony likes him. They can have an amiable chat ... He will always have regard for somebody who is a good communicator. He feels it is a terrible waste. He is rather depressed about it,' the Downing Street source said in an interview to give Blair's side of the story in January 1999.

That mood of sorrow rather than anger was no doubt an accurate description of the prime minister's attitude, but it should not be taken as a signal that Blair was preparing to let Livingstone run as mayor. It certainly did not reflect the loathing of Livingstone among the Blairites on the Greater London Labour Party board who thought they were doing their leader's bidding. Perhaps they were over-interpreting his desire to be rid of a turbulent priest, but more likely they were preparing the ground to strike the blow against Livingstone whenever he gave the order.

Skirmishing centred on the procedure to select Labour's candidate. There was never any doubt that the ultimate decision would be made by a ballot of all the members of the London party. The question was how the shortlist of candidates would be drawn up from which the members could choose.

Livingstone's supporters landed the first punch. At a regional conference in June 1998 they pushed through a resolution including a demand that any candidate nominated by at least ten London constituency parties should automatically be shortlisted. That would have passed the initiative to the grassroots and would have virtually guaranteed that Livingstone's name went on to the ballot paper. But party rules did not let regional or local parties make up their own rules about candidate selection. That was the prerogative of the National Executive Committee, which was under firm Blairite control.

Since the mid-1980s machinery had been in place for national party supervision of the selection of candidates for parliamentary by-elections. It was justified by the need to avoid picking people whose views, personal lives or inability to withstand pressure might disgrace the national party during a high-profile campaign. After the 1997 election, the arrangement was extended to cover candidate selection for the European Parliament, the Scottish Parliament and the Welsh Assembly. In the case of the European elections, intending candidates were left free to seek nomination from constituencies and those who passed that hurdle were vetted by panels of NEC and regional party representatives. The panels, dominated by Blairites, then decided who got through on to regional candidate lists, and in what order. Under the system of proportional representation that was to operate in the Euro-elections, they effectively chose who would be a Labour MEP and who would not. In the case of the Scottish and Welsh elections, the mechanism of control was reversed. Shortlisting panels decided who was suitable to go forward as candidates and party members were then allowed to pick from this pre-vetted field.

It was always likely that the procedure to select Labour's candidate for mayor, and members of the London assembly being set up to share power and monitor the mayor's performance, would follow the Scottish and Welsh pattern rather than the European. That way there would never be an opportunity for party members to express a preference for 'unsuitable' candidates who would then have to be weeded out in a process that would look seriously undemocratic.

Although Livingstone had the backing of the public opinion polls and delegates at the Greater London Labour Party conference, he commanded little support on the regional party board which was charged with making the initial recommendation about how the new system would work. In November 1998 the board agreed that all party members should be eligible to nominate themselves for mayor. A panel of representatives from the region and the NEC would then select a long list of possible contenders before interviewing the candidates to produce a shortlist for a ballot of all London party members. A parallel recommendation for the selection of candidates for the London assembly was approved by the NEC in January 1999 and there was little doubt that it would agree the regional board's suggestion for a mayoral selection procedure at a subsequent meeting. Longlisting would probably take place in the early summer of 1999 and shortlisting in the late summer or early autumn, leaving the candidate at least six months to prepare for the election in May 2000.

The shortlisting panel would be entitled to ask searching questions about contenders' general record of loyalty to the government and about specific support for the mayoral plan. On both counts, Livingstone was vulnerable. On the first, the panel could ask why a loyal Labour MP would write an article in June 1998 saying: 'Unfortunately, Gordon [Brown's] economic misjudgements are the major factor threatening our chance of gaining a second term in office ... Quite clearly, Gordon is not on top of macro-economic policy ... In the coming Cabinet reshuffle the one move that most urgently needs to be made is the one that Tony Blair's bizarre prenuptial arrangement at Granita [a restaurant in Islington] prevents him from doing: moving his chancellor to another job' (*Independent*, June 10th 1998). Other choice indiscretions included criticism of the government's 'ill-judged and lethal support for Bill Clinton's reckless gamble' in ordering the bombing of Iraq. As Livingstone put it: 'Once again the unedifying spectacle of Britain running along behind America, yapping like a demented poodle, has shown the complete absence of any long-term strategic thinking in the Foreign Office about Britain's position in the world' (*Independent*, December 23rd 1998). The panel could ask whether a loyal Labour MP would have said that the prime minister was surrounded by 'a lot of ghastly people ... like lice on the back of a hedgehog' (*Guardian*, October 9th 1997). Or that Peter Mandelson was 'just an apparatchik, just obeying orders. He is the sewer, not the sewage. Anyway I like him, he's full of witty gossip' (*Daily Mail*, October 25th 1997).

Specifically on the mayoral issue, the panel could ask why the job should go to someone who said in October 1997 that most Labour MPs thoughts the idea of creating that post was 'absolutely barmy.' Livingstone would have answers. In October 1997 most London Labour MPs probably did oppose having a directly elected mayor, because at that stage they still agreed with Frank Dobson's original preference for the mayor to be the leader of the largest party group on the assembly. But no answers would be effective if the message had been handed down from Blair that a Livingstone candidacy was unwelcome. Popularity among party members, ability to win the election for Labour and capacity to do the job would count for nothing if the leader decided that he wanted Livingstone to fail this suitability test. A system invented to stop the selection of parliamentary by-election candidates who were likely to get too little electoral support could be used to block a mayoral candidate who was likely to get too much.

But would this procedure be used to stop Livingstone? Blair might feel threatened with Livingstone as mayor, but he was also well aware of his vulnerability to the allegation that Labour was run by control freaks. One of the by-products of the government's

Mark Seddon, editor of *Tribune*, and Ken Livingstone at the Labour Party
conference, Blackpool 1998 (*Fred Jarvis*)

massive parliamentary majority was a perception that it was largely
composed of yes-men and yes-women, obeying instructions
relayed by pager message from the party's Millbank headquarters,
where policies were fashioned according to their appeal to focus
groups, without much attention to political principle. The success
of left-wingers, including Mark Seddon, editor of *Tribune*,
fighting under the Grassroots Alliance banner in the 1998 elections
for the constituency section of the NEC was a warning signal that
party members wanted to resist the central control of what
Livingstone called the 'Millbank Tendency'. Another came during
the contest over who should become Labour's candidate to lead the
Welsh assembly. Alun Michael, the Blairite minister, won the
nomination thanks to union block votes, but his challenger Rhodri
Morgan secured two-thirds of the votes of rank-and-file party
members. That was controversial enough, but at least Morgan's
name was allowed through on to the ballot paper. Blair knew that
fixing the mayoral selection had the capacity to provoke huge
dissent in the party and distaste among the general public.

Everybody knew that Blair was well to the right of the centre of gravity of his party, but was embraced as its leader because he had the capacity to win elections. What would happen if he allowed a perception to grow that he was not prepared to tolerate the Labour candidate most likely to win the London mayoralty because that candidate was too far to the left? The contest in May 2000 was to be fought under an unusual system of proportional representation in which the winner was likely to be decided by the second preferences of Liberal Democrat voters. There was a clear danger that a decision to block Livingstone could hand the mayoralty to the Tories. What would the party and the people think of a Labour leader who preferred victory for the Conservative enemy to an arrangement with his own man?

And there was another paradox. Blair spoke passionately in support of devolution of power from Whitehall. His plans for London were part of a wider commitment to devolution for Scotland, Wales and eventually the English regions. Yet he was caught up in a mindset that Labour could only achieve electoral success if it maintained clear discipline from the centre. Blair wanted the mayor to be a strong independent voice for London, but how independent would it be if it had to pass the test of being acceptable to the prime minister? Might not many people think that Livingstone's tendency to go off-message was an essential qualification for the job description Blair himself had invented?

Blair's view was that there was a huge difference between a Labour candidate who would fight hard for London to strike the best deal with the government and an oppositionalist who would use the job to score political points. He was said to be obsessed with the need for a successful mayor who could deliver real improvements for the capital. He feared that Livingstone would feel he had to take the government on to achieve anything, behaving towards it in much the same way that the SNP would in Scotland. But he also recognised that he could be damaged by the allegation of control-freakery that would be used against him if he blocked Livingstone. 'That would not be a two-day wonder. It would be significant. No one underestimates the fall-out. It's wider than just the party. Ken is more popular among the public than in the party. They see the jolly side ... This feeds outside London as well,' said the Downing Street source.

So was it conceivable that Livingstone could resolve this dilemma by striking a deal, getting a chance to run if he would promise to behave himself? 'Not inconceivable, but unlikely,' the source said. 'So little thought has been given to it. There's been chatting about it and talk among London MPs and whips. London MPs think it could not be a runner, but Tony will explore anything. That sort of discussion has not in any real sense been had.' But the outcome was not likely to take the form of a crude deal. 'It's not the way Tony would work. He'd tend to reach a fairly clear political view – not on the basis of a deal that may or may not work. He'd think: yes he'll be OK – or not.'

During the winter of 1998–99 Livingstone often seemed to be in two minds about whether to rage against the undemocratic injustice of the proposed selection procedure or keep calm and try to strike a deal with Blair. Towards the end of January 1999, he chose the latter. In an open letter in the *Guardian*, he gave Blair:

> a categorical assurance that, if Londoners voted for me to be their first elected mayor, I would work with your government, not against it ... I am convinced that your administration has the potential to be a great reforming government on a par with those of 1906 and 1945. I also know that if your government fails I may never see another Labour government in my lifetime. There is simply no question whatever of my seeking to use the mayorship as a platform to wage political warfare against this government ...
> To those who claim my assurances cannot be relied on, I would point out that in 30 years as a Labour Party member, I have never given such a commitment and failed to honour it.

He offered to take on a New Labour running-mate as deputy

mayor, suggesting the name of the broadcaster Trevor Phillips as a possibility. Control of the mayoral campaign should be under the control of the Labour Party's election unit. 'It would be a tragedy if the new system of government you are creating were to fall into the hands of a Tory mayor because of a backlash among Londoners resentful at being told who they could or could not vote for,' he said. (*Guardian*, January 29th 1999)

This message of sweet reason was muddled when the *Evening Standard* chose that day to publish another article by Livingstone attacking John Prescott, the deputy prime minister, for allowing faceless bureaucrats in his department to impose devastating cuts on Labour-run councils, including his own borough of Brent. It was inexplicable that 'the poorest councils in London have had a whacking from the government', he said. Jim Fitzpatrick, the Blairite chair of the Greater London Labour Party, retorted: 'If Ken cannot keep his word for a mere 24 hours, how can anyone believe he would stick to his promises over a four-year mayoral term? His letter to the *Guardian* has been exposed as a publicity stunt and an attempt to dupe party members into thinking he could be loyal to a New Labour government.'

At the time of writing, it is too soon to say whether sweet reason would have any effect on Blair. Livingstone left unstated the mayhem he could cause if it did not. He could organise a legal challenge against a decision to leave him off the shortlist. He could launch a write-in campaign to persuade London party members to spoil their candidate selection ballot papers by crossing out all the shortlisted names and substituting his own. Beyond that there was the ultimate subject of speculation. If he were to be spurned by his own party, would he stand as an independent? The Downing Street source thought it was improbable. 'It would be a huge mistake. He would lose a lot of support in the party. It would be such an egocentric thing to do.' He might think that letting the idea float would put extra pressure on the party to let him stand. But that would not work and he would not do it. 'It's not part of the equation,' the source said.

But around Livingstone there are voices hoping for just such an outcome. The organisation he was setting up to fight the selection battle if he got on the Labour ticket could so easily be turned into an independent campaign team if he did not. Assorted stars were being assembled for a Luvvies for Livingstone fund-raising drive. A rudimentary organisation was being formed to secure nominations in the 14 super-constituencies on which the assembly elections would be fought. Friends of Livingstone thought that, if he were to be kept off the shortlist, he would sniff the political winds around January 2000 and decide whether he had enough support to make it worthwhile contesting the election as an independent. That would be the ultimate nightmare on Downing Street. It would be a sad outcome to his 30 years' service in the Labour Party and the consequences will be explored in the Conclusion.

This book will not say Livingstone is the best candidate to be mayor of London. It will not try to compare the merits of his possible Labour rivals, let alone their Conservative or Liberal Democrat opposite numbers. But it does start from the premise that this experiment in London government is based on principles of devolution and democracy. Livingstone fought against abolition of the Greater London Council under the slogan 'Say No to No Say'. It would be ironic if Londoners were to be denied the opportunity to say either yes or no to him now that he is the most popular contender for office in the new Greater London Authority. This book contains plenty of ammunition for those wanting to argue that Livingstone would be a disaster as mayor, as well as plenty of evidence to encourage his supporters. People can weigh up the pros and cons. That is what elections are for. Local party members are entitled to come to the same conclusion as their national leader, or a different one. That is what devolution is for. The information is available to help them make up their minds. That is what books are for.

1 Spawning Grounds

Livingstone's early life gave few clues that he was going to become one of the best-known socialists of his generation. He was a slow starter, both academically and politically. He failed the 11-plus, truanted from secondary school and left with only four O-levels, not including maths. As a teenager, he did not have firm political allegiances and he did not become a member of the Labour Party (or any other) until the age of 23. When he joined in 1969, his future left-wing comrades were quitting in protest at what they perceived to be the ineffectual pragmatism of Harold Wilson's government. As they headed for the more intoxicating fringes of revolutionary politics, he became a Labour borough councillor, regarded at first by the left-wingers in his group as a bit of a centrist. This was an uninspiring start to the career he chose for himself and he served a long municipal apprenticeship before discovering his political self-confidence. But, once acquired, this quality never left him.

His political loyalties cannot easily be explained by his upbringing. He was born into a working-class Tory home. By dint of hard work and Victorian values, his parents advanced themselves to become owner-occupiers with a better standard of living than previous generations of their families. The formative years of his childhood in south London were under the governments of Harold Macmillan, who won re-election in 1959 by telling the people that they had 'never had it so good'.

So the development of Livingstone's socialism did not follow any of the usual patterns. It was neither a working-class response to the personal experience of poverty, nor an evangelical middle-class reaction to the discovery that other people were living in unacceptably bad conditions. He was not initially won over to socialism by books or the teachings of a political mentor, although both of those came later. Nor can it seriously be suggested that his progress towards left-wing activism was a form of rebellion against his Tory parents. They were a close-knit family and he loved them deeply.

This is the story of the slow political awakening of a solitary young man with a social conscience who became angry at the failure of Labour politicians to do as much as they should have done to look after his local community. It is a left-wing version of New Labour's break with the past. Livingstone moved to the left in protest at the performance of Old Labour – and held his ground when the party moved dramatically to the right.

He was born on June 17th 1945, just after the Allied victory in Europe, but before the Second World War ended in the Japanese theatre with the nuclear explosions at Hiroshima and Nagasaki. His mother, Ethel, was an acrobatic dancer who had gone on the stage at the age of 14 and toured the provincial music halls, mostly in a three-woman act called the Kenleigh Sisters. They did many of the tricks now associated with gymnastics competitors, back-flips, splits and balancing acts, often followed by some tap dancing and perhaps a little ballet. She also performed in circuses in an act that involved skilful balancing tricks on ladders on the top of elephants. In spite of frequent offers, she always turned down speaking parts.

His father, Bob, was a merchant seaman who survived several days adrift in the Irish Sea after being torpedoed on a wartime run to Murmansk. They had met on a Tuesday night in April 1940 at a music hall in Workington where Ethel was performing alongside the Great Lyle, an illusionist who purported to saw people in half. Bob was with two of his shipmates in the front row during the performance. They were on shore leave and, after a few drinks, were making rather a nuisance of themselves waving and winking at Ethel and her two fellow artistes as they went through their act. At the interval the men slipped a message through to them via one of the show's comedians, inviting them out for a meal afterwards. Ethel had only recently broken off another relationship and was feeling rather hostile towards men in general; but the others were keen and so she went along to make up the pairs. It was during the black-out and the only place to eat in Workington was a fish-and-chip shop.

Ethel and Bob hit it off instantly. In later years she recalled: 'We were chatting away and then he started singing and he had a voice very much like Bing Crosby. He sang "I have eyes to see with, but they see only you". It was a lovely number. And he really meant it. We were meant to meet.' With Bob away at sea and Ethel on tour, they saw each other only three times over the next three months and then got married.

Ethel's father had been killed in the First World War and she and her brother were brought up by her mother in a succession of private rented flats in south London. Bob was born in Dunoon in western Scotland. His family had emigrated to Argentina, but came back to Scotland for the birth so that he would not be obliged to serve in the Argentinian armed forces when he grew up. He was brought up in Argentina until the age of seven and then returned to Scotland, where his mother died when he was 14. The family disintegrated and he went to live with his sister until he was 16, when he joined the merchant marine. Ethel and Bob were both 25 when they met. The stability of their marriage gave their children the background of two-parent domestic harmony that they themselves had lacked. Ken Livingstone says: 'Most of my contemporaries at school had parents who seemed to have fallen into a state of either armed neutrality or resigned boredom. Mine were quite unusual in the sense that they were still very much in love. They met and clicked instantly.'

Ken was their first child. He was born in Ethel's mother's flat at 21b Shrubbery Road, opposite the police station in Streatham. By strange coincidence, he suffered from the same post-natal condition as Herbert Morrison, Labour leader of the London

Ken as a young baby with his mother, Ethel, 1945 (*from the late Ethel Livingstone's family album*)

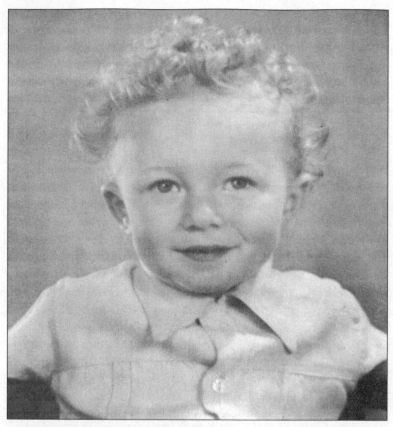

Ken on his first birthday (*from the late Ethel Livingstone's family album*)

County Council from 1934 to 1940 and the only local government politician before Livingstone to become a national household name. Both Morrison and Livingstone got eye infections at birth. In Morrison's case it caused the permanent loss of one eye. By the time Livingstone was born, medical science had advanced and the doctors prescribed drops, which cleared up the mass of yellow pus disfiguring his infant features.

Ethel recalled that he looked so awful as a new-born baby, with his bad eye and total lack of hair, that she covered him up when

Bob, Ethel and Ken Livingstone, Butlin's, Skegness, summer 1947 (*from the late Ethel Livingstone's family album*)

she took him out for walks. 'I thought he looked ugly, so I used to put the blankets over his head and tell people not to disturb him. He looked terribly ill for the first few weeks, but he was lovely by the time he was six months.' The baby was christened Kenneth Robert. His sister Lin was born two and a half years later.

Their father Bob went back to sea as a trawlerman and was away for long periods. Much as he loved Ethel, he could not take living with her over-possessive mother. Livingstone recalls: 'My

Ken, 6, and his sister Lin, 3½, 1951 (*from the late Ethel Livingstone's family album*)

mum started pestering the old London County Council for a home of her own, because living with us in one room at my grandmother's place was no joy. And eventually about 1950 they got an offer on the new Tulse Hill estate and moved in there.'

Although the estate was to deteriorate badly in the 1970s, it was initially very attractive. The Livingstone family stayed there until 1957, when they managed to buy their own house in West Norwood. 'My parents really had to struggle to get the deposit and the mortgage. After my father stopped doing the trawler fishing, he used to be a window cleaner during the day and in the evenings he worked on shifting stage scenery at the Streatham Hill Theatre when Streatham was still suburban enough to sustain an arts theatre. My mum usually worked serving at the bakers, Broomfields – she eventually became manageress – and in the evenings she used to work at the cinema as an usherette. My gran used to stop with us and look after us as kids. They really worked hard all the time.'

From 1955 Ethel started saving all her £4-a-week wages to

provide the £400 deposit they needed for a house of their own. By the time she had saved the money, the cost of the deposit had risen to £500, but the estate agent lent them the extra £100 out of his own pocket. They moved into a big old three-storey house at 66 Wolfington Road, West Norwood.

The young Ken was always an outgoing child, with a desire to hold the centre of the stage. When his mother collected him from his first day at St Leonard's Infants School, the teacher reported that he had kept the whole class amused all afternoon by talking and singing and doing little acts.

The Livingstone family almost always earned enough money to go on annual holidays to the south coast, to the Isle of Wight, or north to Dunoon to stay with relatives. They went to the cinema two or three times a week and got their first television in 1956. Livingstone's first political memories are of cinema newsreels of the Korean war, but at that stage there was little political discussion in the home. Both his parents held Tory party cards and his father used to man a polling station for the Conservatives on election days, but they were not activists. Livingstone recalls: 'They were part of the generation of Tories who thought Churchill was excellent and have been progressively more disillusioned with each successive Tory leader.' His uncle was active in Streatham Conservative Association. 'But he resigned in protest when old Shrunken Glands [Duncan Sandys, Winston Churchill's son-in-law] was imposed on them as the Tory candidate in preference to his local employer.'

Livingstone's political perceptions began to develop during the Suez crisis and Hungarian uprising in 1956 when he moved to secondary school. He had failed the 11-plus, an exam that supposedly identified the ablest children so they could be creamed off into grammar schools and the rest consigned to secondary moderns. Although he did tolerably well in the general knowledge paper, he did badly at English and maths. But he did not get sent to a secondary modern because London was going

The Livingstones and friend, Battersea Park Fun Fair, 1955 (*from the late Ethel Livingstone's family album*)

through the early stages of secondary education reform. He was given a place at Tulse Hill School, a brand new comprehensive that took children of all abilities. At the outset it retained some aspects of the selective system by segregating the high-flyers. Livingstone recalls that 11-year-olds were divided into 13 entry forms. 'There were three forms that were considered academic, three forms that the school thought were worth worrying about, and the rest which were largely ignored.' Livingstone was put in form six at the bottom of the middle category.

In his first year there he was exposed to an influence which he thinks had a dramatic effect on his political development. His form master was Philip Hobsbaum, an inspiring teacher who went on to become Reader in English at Glasgow University (and was a distant relative of the Marxist historian Eric Hobsbawm). 'In terms of 1956, he was positively revolutionary. He put newspapers on the classroom wall. He'd move all the desks out to the edge and we'd have an impromptu play. We'd stage a mock trial and things like that ... For 11-year-old kids he was incredibly larger than life, dominating, with a great beard. We'd all look up at him and he'd do outrageously exciting things – as opposed to all the other boring teachers. So we all loved him greatly. He got us to debate Suez and Hungary. We were never aware of what his own politics were, but he made us discuss politics.'

Hobsbaum remembers Livingstone as one of four exceptional boys in the class whom he expected to hear about again in later life. 'He was highly articulate and very friendly, a marvellous communicator. I thought he would have a future in journalism or advertising rather than politics. At the age of 11, he had great ability to get his points across and he was unflappable. He would always turn aside any aggression from the other boys with a joke.' Hobsbaum recalls taking the class to visit the House of Lords. 'He was completely at home there, not at all in awe of institutions or being on strange territory.'

Hobsbaum taught Livingstone only for a year. 'They shuffled round the form teachers each year, which was a real pain. But he

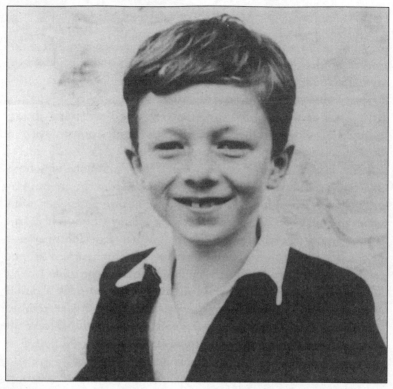

Ken, 10, while at St Leonard's Church of England Junior School (*from the late Ethel Livingstone's family album*)

started me arguing about politics. I then found it was a subject of endless discussion and argument at the dinner table every night, because my father had strong political views. From then on, right the way through, the amount of time I spent discussing politics built up and up ... Yes, I became an argumentative cocky little brat.'

After the first two years, Livingstone moved, in more ways than one, into a different class. 'It was a jump I never adjusted to, because virtually all my friends in the sixth grade were working-class. I then moved up into the second grade and into a form which was overwhelmingly middle-class. I didn't find it a happy transition and I kept most of my friends from the sixth grade. So I was aware of class and I really didn't perceive myself as middle-class. It was a gut reaction. I suppose I perceived myself as working-class without really being aware of the terminology.'

By his fifth year, political discussion at school was becoming more vitriolic. 'It was the time that Colin Jordan was stomping around in jackboots. There was a large block of fascist supporters at school and another block of kids who were in, or claimed to be in, the Communist Party. I used to argue with virtually everybody and never joined anything … Why not? Because my primary interest was natural history.'

At that stage Livingstone was spending his pocket money and the income from a paper round on building up a collection of increasingly exotic reptiles and amphibians. His mother recalled that his bedroom came to resemble a reptile house at the zoo. The family favourite was a South American bullfrog, *Leptodactylus Pentodactylus*, which they nicknamed Black Joe and which the young Ken took for walks on his shoulder, often calling in at his mother's shop to frighten the customers. As time went on he acquired two monitor lizards, each a metre long (one of which terrified the household when it escaped and hid behind a chest of drawers). He also kept salamanders, snakes and a baby alligator which his mother unsuccessfully tried to ban from the house on the grounds that when it grew up it might eat the dogs. Once a friend lent him two extremely poisonous Formosan vipers while he went on holiday, thoughtfully providing a serum which, in the case of bites, had to be injected within two minutes to avert death.

The teenage Livingstone was a solitary young man, rarely going out after school except in the dead of night to dig up worms from neighbours' gardens to feed to his pets. He hated sport, never took to religion and seemed to have little interest in girls (except for his sister Lin's friends, whom he would lure up to his room for close encounters with his frogs).

Lin remembers his love of shocking people as one of the banes of her childhood, like the time when he left her unawares on a bus after firmly tying her plaits around a metal pole. 'You could never get your own back if he decided to show you up. Nothing embarrassed him,' she says. It was a lesson that Livingstone's future political opponents were in time to learn without the compensations of close family love. Lin also dates her brother's pro-feminist perceptions from this time, in spite of what he did to her girlfriends with his frogs. 'We were always brought up as equals. There was never any question that Ken was more important than I was because he was a boy. Mum's opinion was never any less important than Dad's and Dad always did the housework. I don't think Ken has ever felt superior to women, the way a lot of men do.'

The equality was less obvious between mother and son. The young Ken often refused to eat what the rest of the family were having for dinner and made his mother prepare special homemade fishcakes or beefburgers – he would not touch ready-made versions available in the shops. It was always a toss-up whether the dinner-time row between Ken and his dad would be about his exacting culinary requests or his tendency to come out with provocative political remarks designed to rile his father's Tory sensibilities.

Livingstone says that his interest in politics 'became really acute in 1960 with the American presidential election. Also the election of Pope John XXIII had quite an impact because he was one of the first public figures to come over via the medium of television as a really decent person. He made a strong impact on me. His death was the first time I cried for someone that I didn't know.'

Livingstone left school at 17 at the end of his first year in the sixth form, with O-levels in English literature, English language, art and geography. Tulse Hill had awakened the two enthusiasms which were to dominate his life: politics and natural history. But it had failed to win his affections. 'I was a bad kid at school ... I didn't find it a happy place after that first year with Hobsbaum.

And I wasn't then happy until I left. I didn't like the restrictions. I used to bunk off quite a lot. Two or three of us would mooch around the streets for the afternoon. Or I'd go to the library and read natural history books, political books, things about China ... The real problem is that a school with 2,100 kids cannot know where they are. I managed to avoid a whole range of things I didn't like doing at school just because I was sufficiently cunning.'

When Livingstone left Tulse Hill, he says he was politically aware, but still uncommitted. That changed when he started work in 1962 as a lab technician at the Chester Beatty cancer research unit in Fulham Road for just over £6 a week (worth about £70 in 1999). 'There were about 14 of us technicians, all men. I suddenly dropped into an environment where everyone except me was a committed socialist from a committed Labour background.' It was the time when the Macmillan government was creaking towards its close and Harold Wilson, a fresh Labour leader, was promising to end government from the grouse moors and regenerate Britain's economy 'in the white heat of the technological revolution'.

'It was then that my political allegiances firmed up solidly on the Labour Party side with all that naive belief that Wilson was actually going to do something.' Livingstone says he felt a 'trembling of excitement' when Wilson won in 1964, followed by a growing disillusionment over the next two or three years.

He could at this stage have become just another disaffected Labour voter, but in the winter of 1966/67 he went on a six-month hitch-hiking tour of West Africa which sharpened his political awareness. With Mick Towns, a fellow worker at the Fulham Road laboratory, he travelled through France, Spain, Morocco, Algeria and then due south to Niger and Nigeria, arriving in Lagos as the Biafran war was developing, and then on to Togo and Ghana. The trip was designed to pursue their mutual interest in natural history; and indeed for about 1,000 miles of it Livingstone nursed a baby ostrich that he had saved from certain death in a local cooking pot. He hitched with it wrapped in a towel under his arm and got severe gastric problems from pre-chewing its food. The ostrich was left behind in Lagos children's zoo. But in the course of the tour Livingstone picked up a lot of less tangible experiences that changed his perceptions. It was a time of political ferment in West Africa, with massacres in Nigeria, a coup in Togo and recent upheavals in Ghana and Algeria.

'My six months hitch-hiking abroad had very much the impact on me that national service must have had on some other people, or going to university. It suddenly dramatically expanded my horizons. We kept meeting Peace Corps and VSO [Voluntary Service Overseas] people, young people who were leftish, or at least argued a lot about politics. It gave me a lot more self-confidence.'

Livingstone had given away his reptile collection before making the African trip. (His mother put her foot down at taking on the job of feeding the snakes with live mice while he was away.) By the time he came back, his interests had become focused almost totally on politics. In Africa he had met a group of American Peace Corps workers who wanted to avoid the draft for the Vietnam war. Livingstone got involved in trying to get them into Britain. He lobbied his local MP, John Fraser, and for the first time became a political activist in the British campaign to help the US draft resisters.

A second influence was the attitude of the Norwood Conservative candidate on race. 'My father's major philosophy had always been strongly anti-racist. As a merchant seaman he'd been around the world several times and had worked with people of all races. It's something he drummed into me all the time.' Livingstone was propelled closer to the Labour camp by the local Tory calls for repatriation of immigrants. He also became involved in trade unionism when he helped to organise a branch of the Association of Scientific, Technical and Managerial Staff (ASTMS) to oppose redundancies at the Chester Beatty research unit.

And so, at the age of 23, Livingstone became motivated enough to join the local Norwood branch of the Labour Party. Although he had attended the occasional anti-Vietnam war march and had subscribed for a year to an anarchist group called Solidarity, it was his first firm expression of political alignment. He joined in February 1969, at a time when almost every other socialist of his age was deserting Labour for the headier comradeship of Trotskyism and other brands of insurrectionist politics.

> What I didn't realise when I joined the Labour Party was how totally debilitated it had become. I suppose 1968–69 must have been the absolute nadir in terms of active party membership. Half the people had resigned in protest about what Wilson was doing. They'd gone off to join other left-wing groups like IS [International Socialists] or just devoted themselves fully to trade unionism ... I recognised that you weren't going to achieve social change other than through the Labour Party. No outside grouping was going to replace it.
>
> I joined thinking that there would be a really good chance in about ten years of getting on the local council if I worked really hard. By the time I went to my second branch meeting, I was chairman and secretary of the Young Socialists and on the local government committee. By the time I went to the third, I was membership secretary of the party and on the executive committee. There was simply no one else around to do those things. Everybody else had left. It was incredible. At general management committee meetings in Norwood there were only about 25 people present.

So Livingstone was ensconced in Norwood Labour politics before the left-wingers came streaming back from their various sects to give the local party its reputation for militancy. In May

1971 he took his place for Labour on Lambeth council, the London borough of which Norwood forms part. (His father worked for him on polling day, but still voted Tory in a neighbouring ward.)

This timing was to be a crucial feature of Livingstone's political development. Although by that stage he had read widely, especially political biography, and had become fascinated by the study of voting behaviour, he had never undergone the rigorous ideological training through which contemporary recruits to Trotskyist parties and tendencies were passing. He had not studied the works of Karl Marx and, by the time he might have wanted to start, he was immersed in the minutiae of council agendas and the daily business of practical politics. He was more concerned with policies and the exercise of power than with theoretical analysis.

The issue that most concerned him at the time was Lambeth's serious housing problem and the failure of previous Labour councils to tackle it. 'During the 1960s Lambeth had been one of the real deadhead-type Labour boroughs,' he says. 'It had been run by a guy called Alderman Archie Cotton. There were two or three competent but not very imaginative old working-class right-wingers and about 50 lobby-fodder supporters behind them. Each year they would work out what the rate increase should be and then decide how many houses they could afford to build – perhaps 200 in a good year. So Lambeth had a pretty mediocre housing programme.'

In the borough elections in 1968, when the Wilson government was at its most unpopular, the Conservatives won Lambeth from Labour with a huge majority of 57 seats to three. The Tories had promised to cut the housing programme to reduce expenditure, but within a few weeks of taking office their leaders had a complete change of heart. 'The housing director, Harry Simpson, went to work on them. By taking them round some of the most appalling deprived housing in Brixton where there was a black family to every room, he really shook them rigid.' The result was that the Conservative administration quadrupled the housing programme left by Labour. 'So the whole of the Labour Party in Lambeth, having generally complained about the council for years, was horrified to see the Tories suddenly doing better, and dramatically so. The Tories set up a proper campaign against bad landlords and brought in multiple occupation controls. By 1970 the whole country was aware that the most dynamic housing area was Lambeth.'

One of the Conservatives who played a prominent role in developing that policy was John Major. The future prime minister became a Lambeth councillor in 1968 and was quickly talent-spotted by the leaders of the Conservative group who liked his diligence and lack of racist views. They made him vice-chairman and then chairman of the housing committee, with responsibility for running the building programme and cracking down on rogue landlords. By a strange coincidence, Major had gone travelling in Africa at about the same time as Livingstone's hitch-hiking expedition and their paths almost crossed at Kano in Nigeria in the winter of 1966/67. After Major became prime minister he acknowledged the importance of his political apprenticeship in Lambeth, paying particular tribute to the lessons he learned from Harry Simpson. 'He was the first person who showed me how bureaucracy can be used as a force for good rather than a force for interference ... [and how] you could achieve more by persuasion than by bludgeoning', he told his biographer Edward Pearce (*The Quiet Rise of John Major*, Weidenfeld and Nicholson, 1991).

The lesson learned by Livingstone and other younger Labour Party members on both left and right, was that they must never again be shamed by being outperformed on social policy by the Conservatives. They organised to clear out the council old guard during selection of candidates for the 1971 borough elections. When Labour won with a majority of 51 to 9, there was new blood, but by no means a left majority. Livingstone became vice-chairman of housing responsible for estates management. He was remembered for changing the council's policy towards so-called problem families. Until then they had been corralled by housing department officials into three blocks of indescribable horror at the north end of the borough. Livingstone dispersed them into better accommodation and persuaded the Labour group of councillors to make compulsory purchase orders on large numbers of private-rented properties by drawing attention to slum conditions and landlord racketeering. This covert municipalisation programme was to cause major difficulties for Lambeth's housing department, which never had the money to refurbish Livingstone's acquisitions.

In August 1973 he threatened to resign his vice-chairmanship if the council failed to honour promises to re-house families from three other Dickensian council blocks which were only slightly less appalling than the first three. He told the *South London Press*: 'Although I cannot give them a specific date, they have been let down in the past. So as a reassurance to make them feel better, I will resign if the council don't get moving this time.' The council did not get moving and, after rows with the housing chairman on a range of issues, Livingstone resigned his office in December 1973. From then on he remained on the back-benches until he left Lambeth council in 1978.

Although Livingstone was clearly at the radical end of the Labour group on Lambeth council, he was not in the early 1970s a fully-fledged left-winger. Ted Knight, who was later to become Labour leader of Lambeth council and for several years one of Livingstone's closest political allies, remembers meeting him for the first time in 1970 and regarding him as a centrist member of the Labour Party. 'I viewed him as basically a Harold Wilson supporter, probably with some influence from people like [Tony] Crosland, if he was actually ever considering what Crosland was writing, which I doubt.'

Knight had been expelled from the Labour Party in 1954 and joined the Socialist Labour League, the Trotskyist forerunner of the Workers' Revolutionary Party. He worked for the SLL as an organiser before leaving it in the mid-1960s and being re-admitted into the Norwood branch of the Labour Party in 1970. Under Knight's influence, Livingstone began to develop left-wing perspectives by a process of debate over issues rather than by any more theoretical schooling. Knight remembers that Livingstone initially supported British troops going into Northern Ireland and tended to 'see the good points' in the Tory government's 1972 Housing Finance Act, generally reviled by the left for forcing up rents and leading to the Clay Cross councillors' rebellion. On both issues Livingstone changed his mind.

Knight observed: 'I think it was quite useful for Ken to have somebody closely arguing with him who had very clearly defined views on matters of Labour Party and socialist policies, someone who had actually gone through the schools of Marxist training.' In return, Livingstone taught Knight the value of building alliances across as broad a section of the left as possible. As Knight put it: 'He was able to win wider support and was prepared to seek looser alliances than I would have been. That was his strength and my weakness; and that was why the team was a good one for the period.'

Livingstone had opposed Knight when he stood for the chairmanship of the Norwood Labour Party in 1972, but by the end of that year they were starting to work together. They organised a purge to de-select all the Labour councillors representing Norwood who had not voted to defy the Housing Finance Act rent increases. (Livingstone's mind had changed in time for him to remain safely unpurged.)

So at the local elections in May 1974 Norwood returned a solid block of left-wingers who joined with a scattering of other leftists from other parts of the borough to form a disciplined group on the council, in conflict with the majority Labour administration. Knight and Livingstone jostled with each other for the leadership of the left minority and it is a moot point which of them would have emerged on top when the left took power in Lambeth after the 1978 local elections. But by then Livingstone had moved on to new struggles in a different part of London.

During the 1960s Livingstone had been living at home in Norwood with his parents. They bought a cottage in Lincoln with the idea of retiring there, but in October 1971, just before they were ready to move, his father died of a heart attack. His mother stayed on in London for a year and, when she eventually moved up to Lincoln, Livingstone went into lodgings. For the first time, at the age of 27, he started living on his own.

While he had been working at the Chester Beatty research institute, he had gone to evening classes and gained a fifth O-level (in human anatomy, physiology and hygiene) and an A-level in zoology. This helped him get another technician's job at the Sutton branch of the Royal Marsden hospital. But by 1970 he was becoming disillusioned with the work, which involved experiments with live animals. He says he began disagreeing more and more with the doctors about when experiments should be terminated and would often stop them without the doctors' agreement. It was the technician's responsibility to ensure that the animals did not suffer, but his frequent interventions caused considerable friction. 'At the same time I wanted to work with people rather than animals. Often it was a question of working for hours and hours on your own in a room in complete isolation. It was one of those units where you try and cut down the disease coming in. You had to step in troughs of disinfectant walking into the animal unit. The disinfectant was green. You'd end up with these brilliant green feet as it soaked through the canvas shoes you wore. People would occasionally see those feet and fall around in hysterics. They thought you were being treated for some rare disease.'

And so in 1970, after being out of school for eight years, a green-footed Livingstone gained a place on a teacher training course at Philippa Fawcett College in south London. It was filled predominantly by well-spoken young women from the home counties. Livingstone remembers them gasping in amazement on the first day when the lecturer mentioned there were class differences in society. 'I thought: my God, I've made a terrible mistake coming here.'

The course lasted three years and Livingstone says he probably had one of the worst attendance records. 'I got elected to Lambeth council at the end of my first year. I spent an awful lot of time at the council and very little time at the college. It was everything that was rotten with teacher training. You were told when you came that you would be assessed on your teaching practices in the third year, on 12 written bits of work and on the final exam which no one ever failed. I did the 12 pieces of work and not a stroke more, did the exam and got my qualification. But there was no pressure. It was a complete waste of three years.'

It was at teacher training college that he met his wife Christine. She was a year ahead of him and was president of the students' union when he was secretary. He left college in June 1973 and they married the following December. In May 1974 Christine joined Ken as a Lambeth Labour councillor.

At the time the borough council was still the main focus of Livingstone's political attention. But in May 1973 he had also won the election to be Norwood's representative on the GLC and Inner London Education Authority (ILEA). For anyone interested in housing the GLC then offered the best chance of solutions to Lambeth's problems. In 1973 there were 12,000 families on the Lambeth council housing waiting list and another 40,000 families living in property due for demolition within 15 years. It seemed impossible to meet this public housing demand unless the GLC's resources of land and money could be mobilised.

Ken and Christine made a joint decision that she would work as a teacher, allowing him to devote himself full-time to politics at Lambeth and the GLC. 'We decided that I would do four years on the GLC and then see what happened at the end of it. Initially we thought I'd go back to teaching. But as my time at the GLC progressed I became more and more involved in it. Gradually the prospect of ever going into a teaching career faded away.'

At the start Ken supplemented Christine's income with work for the local Labour Party: he was a paid deputy agent in the 1974 general election. But the couple's financial position was assisted by one of the last decisions of the Conservative government under Edward Heath, introducing attendance allowances for local councillors. At the outset the maximum was set at about £2,000, equivalent to the national average wage. 'They didn't increase it for about six years. So each year my income went down in real terms while Christine's went up as she got promotion. I thought that, with the introduction of the attendance allowance system, it was possible to have a full-time local government career. I thought I could achieve far more as a full-time politician in local government than I could as a back-bench MP. It wasn't until 1975 when the government started to centralise a lot of decisions that I began to have ambitions in Parliament. Before then it seemed in local government that you had a chance to involve people in the running of their lives, to break up the concentrations of power – the themes you have heard me rabbit on about ever since.'

This view was idiosyncratic at the time. Most activists on the left were concentrating their energies on the industrial side of the Labour movement, on single-issue politics, or on the drive to increase accountability within the Labour Party which began with the formation of the Campaign for Labour Party Democracy in 1973. Livingstone virtually ignored these mainstream pursuits. He spent his time moving between Lambeth council and the GLC, making trouble for their right-wing Labour leaders and organising for future victory by the left. In a memorable phrase, Lambeth councillor Elsie Horstead attacked him in 1976 for rubbishing the Lambeth leadership when he was at ILEA and rubbishing the ILEA leadership when he was at Lambeth. 'Here you have a waltzing mouse,' she said, 'who goes around from one group to another vilifying the other' (*South London Press*, March 26th 1976).

In his early days on the GLC, however, Livingstone was not perceived by other members of the Labour group as being particularly left-wing. That recognition came when he took part in a revolt against spending cuts pushed through by the ruling Labour administration in 1975. This revolt and its subsequent consequences for the London Labour party formed the basis of the campaign that brought victory for the left in 1981. Before picking up this strand, it will be useful to see what it was that the GLC did and describe the old-guard Labour leaders against whom the left reacted.

2 County Hall

The Greater London Council was always controversial. It was established in 1964 to provide strategic direction of a city that had long since sprawled beyond the boundaries of its urban core. It was not meant to involve itself with the delivery of local services: that was the job of a second tier of borough councils. But the GLC never managed to prise enough strategic power from the hands of civil servants and ministers in Whitehall and so its councillors were always tempted to interfere too much with the boroughs' business. When Margaret Thatcher's government decided to move against the GLC in the mid-1980s, she was able to identify many shortcomings that might not have existed if the council had been properly set up in the first place. Her mistake was to abolish local democratic control over the city's strategic affairs instead of making it work better.

The origins of local government in London stretch back to Saxon times when the boundaries of the Square Mile of the City of London were established. The City Corporation, which appointed its first mayor in the late twelfth century, refused to extend its elitist jurisdiction to the urban area that grew up around it. As a result, most of London was governed until the end of the nineteenth century by scores of separate parishes, administered by vestries elected by the ratepayers. This framework was unsuitable for the management of nineteenth-century social reforms such as the establishment of a police force, sewerage, paving, street-lighting and universal education. So separate, indirectly elected boards were set up to manage these services, notably the Metropolitan Police Force (1829), the Metropolitan Board of Works (1855) and the London School Board (1870).

The first real effort to package these new responsibilities into a proper democratic system came with the establishment of the London County Council in 1889. This was a directly elected body covering an area that extended to what was then the urban fringe, but now corresponds to the inner London boroughs. At the outset it had complete control of local services in this area. The Local Government Act of 1899 reduced its power by setting up a lower tier of 28 metropolitan boroughs, but the LCC retained the leading role in the provision of public services, including housing and education.

This system worked pretty well through the early years of the twentieth century, reaching its heyday in the Labour administrations of Herbert Morrison after 1934. Morrison consolidated his position as a leading figure in the Labour Party through his mastery of London's administrative machine. He lifted Labour's morale after the Ramsay MacDonald crisis of 1931 by pushing through major programmes of slum clearance and school-building. And he demonstrated the power and independence of the LCC when he refused to accept a government veto on plans to build a new Waterloo Bridge and completed the job by putting the cost on the rates.

By the 1950s the city had expanded to cover all Middlesex and large swathes of Surrey, Kent and Essex. A Royal Commission on Local Government in Greater London, set up under Sir Edwin Herbert in 1957, concluded that a single metropolitan authority was necessary to organise planning, traffic management and highway construction over this wider area. It recommended that the administration of non-strategic services should be passed to a lower tier of borough councils, more closely in touch with the people they served.

Herbert's arguments were sound and they had political appeal for the Conservative government of the day under Harold Macmillan. The old LCC had a permanent Labour majority, but the new wider London area proposed by Herbert could almost be guaranteed to produce a Conservative administration in County

Hall. For Labour, Morrison fulminated against the creation of a Greater London Council on the grounds that it would be far too large for efficient administration. 'I will stump London and we will fight in London to denounce the government for this piece of political jobbery,' he told the House of Lords in March 1962.

It turned out, however, that the GLC did not become such a Tory bastion. Nine true-blue Conservative districts on the fringes of the proposed GLC area fought a successful rearguard action to stay outside it. Their leaders feared that their inclusion in London might lower the tone of their neighbourhoods and add to the financial burden on their ratepayers. Their departure left the GLC on a political knife-edge. It went Labour in 1964, Conservative in 1967 and 1970, Labour in 1973, Conservative in 1977 and Labour in 1981.

Other changes were made to the Herbert proposals, notably the devolution of responsibility for education to the borough level (except in the original LCC area where an Inner London Education Authority of GLC and borough representatives was created to retain a unified education system in the centre). The 1963 London Government Act set up 32 borough councils, each with a minimum population size of 200,000. They were given responsibility for personal social services; refuse collection; environmental health; most licensing functions; libraries and swimming baths; weights and measures; food and drug standards; noise and smoke control; consumer protection; registration of births, marriages and deaths; allotments; cemeteries; street cleansing; working conditions in shops and offices; and many other services. They also had first-level responsibility for a range of other functions that were shared with the GLC, including housing, planning, roads and parks.

This left the GLC with strategic responsibility for planning across London as a whole; control of about 880 miles of the main metropolitan roads; traffic management; housing for the needs of London as a whole; refuse disposal; Thames flood prevention; land drainage; the fire brigade; and (until they were transferred to regional quangos in 1973) the ambulance and water services. Although the council was weaker than its LCC predecessor, it inherited all the appurtenances of power including the splendid Edwardian classical edifice of County Hall on the south bank of the Thames opposite the Houses of Parliament, with its ornate marbled council chamber, 7 miles of corridors and 35,000 staff. It became the biggest council in Europe, responsible for 610 square miles of territory and nearly 8 million Londoners.

Livingstone was first elected to the GLC in 1973 on a Labour manifesto drawn up by the London party's old-guard right-wing leadership that was more ambitious than anything the left would have dared to suggest in later years. The 10,000-word *Socialist Strategy for London* was the final flowering of an era of post-war municipal expansion in which both Labour and Conservative governments encouraged local authorities to spend what was needed to solve Britain's social problems.

Its content was influenced by 1971 census findings that 21 per cent of families in inner London shared their homes with other families (compared with 4 per cent nationally) and 37 per cent lacked exclusive use of a bath, hot water and a lavatory (compared with 18 per cent nationally). Labour proposed a huge programme of public-sector house-building and the purchase of private landlords' property to bring it into council management. It called a halt to grandiose road-building schemes, notably an inner motorway box, in favour of increased spending on public transport. The manifesto promised to freeze London Transport fares as a first step towards their eventual abolition. It also pledged to improve pay and conditions for LT employees to eliminate the labour shortages that were causing gaps in the service, in spite of LT's efforts to recruit more staff from the West Indies.

Labour won the 1973 GLC election under the leadership of Sir Reg Goodwin, who, at the age of 64, was nearing the end of his career as general secretary of the National Association of Boys' Clubs. He was the last of the political heirs of Herbert Morrison – men and women such as Sir Isaac Hayward, Lord Fiske,

Sir Reg Goodwin, GLC Labour leader 1973–77, cuts a dash between County Hall and Parliament (*Guardian, Kenneth Saunders*)

Baroness Serota and Dame Evelyn Denington, who fitted comfortably into the nation's ruling establishment. His long career in local government included leadership of Bermondsey council from 1947 to 1965 when he was responsible for municipalising almost all the borough's housing.

Goodwin was firmly committed to the 1973 GLC manifesto. Indeed he had written much of it himself. So when Labour was returned with a majority of 57 seats to 35, he gave no hint of backsliding. Fares were frozen and the first London-wide system of concessionary fares for pensioners was quickly introduced. Although LT was no longer experiencing serious staff shortages, an £80 million package of improvements in pay and conditions was introduced without extracting productivity concessions. Gladys Dimson, as chairwoman of housing development, started municipalising large tracts of London and acquiring land for the enhanced building programme. In February 1974, Labour's first

Livingstone on the march, April 1st 1973. The occasion was a protest against GLC proposals to enclose the Crystal Palace lakes and monsters and charge admission (*Patrick Smith Associates*)

budget increased the rates by 46 per cent. As the Conservative opposition was quick to point out, it was really an 85 per cent increase once you allowed for the fact that ambulance and water responsibilities had been removed from the GLC with the setting up of regional water and health authorities in 1973.

Livingstone played a modest part in these developments. When he arrived as a new councillor, they made him vice-chairman of what was nicknamed the filthy films panel, the Film Viewing Board, which still in those days vetted films to check their suitability for the London public. But within a year he was promoted to deputy chairman of housing management and was poised to become a key player as the Goodwin administration moved into a financial crisis.

This was the period when Britain's annual rate of inflation began to spiral almost out of control, reaching a peak of 26 per cent in July 1975. The council had debts of around £1.6 billion, mostly borrowed many years before to build houses, roads and other capital investments at fixed interest rates of 3 or 4 per cent. As these loans matured, the money had to be re-borrowed at 12 or 13 per cent. Inflation also dramatically increased the cost of the fares freeze commitment. LT balanced its books from 1969 to 1973, but by the autumn of 1974 it was warning of an impending deficit of £120 million because it could not recoup the cost of pay settlements by raising fares.

If Labour had gone ahead with its full manifesto programme, the GLC rate in April 1975 would have had to increase by 137 per cent at a time when the Labour government was pleading for rate rises to be held down to 25 per cent. Further big increases would have been required in the run-up to the next GLC elections in 1977.

Goodwin was also being warned by Maurice Stonefrost, the council's Comptroller of Finance, that its borrowing needs over the next 3–5 years would not be met by the money markets unless there were cuts in the investment programme. Inflation was having a devastating effect on other big cities around the world:

for example, New York narrowly avoided bankruptcy in 1975 when it could no longer borrow to pay its staff wages. Local authorities in England were protected from the worst of the storm because they had never been allowed to borrow to finance current expenditure. But Stonefrost convinced Goodwin that the financial name of London was at risk if the Labour administration stuck to its commitment to increase borrowing to fund its burgeoning house-building and municipalisation programme. About a year before the Labour government, under pressure from the International Monetary Fund, forced councils to cut their capital programmes, the GLC leadership was preparing for retrenchment.

As the financial crisis developed through 1974 and early 1975, the Goodwin administration pushed through a series of cuts that went down in the folklore of the London Labour left as a gross act of betrayal. Livingstone's role in opposing these cuts became the basis of his credibility on the left as a contender for high office in the council.

The process started in May 1974 when leading committee chairmen went to a hotel at Aldermaston for a weekend of discussions with the GLC's chief officers. Livingstone recalls: 'Goodwin and the others came back from Aldermaston committed to the idea of ending the massive fare subsidy. The argument was that if we carried on subsidising fares at this rate we would have to increase rents or cut the house-building programme, because otherwise the rate burden would be too enormous.'

Goodwin's proposals were rejected by the Labour group in May 1974 on the grounds that it would be political folly to raise fares ahead of the general election, expected in October. The leadership resubmitted the plan a few weeks later. 'They claimed that London Transport had produced new financial projections which were even worse than before,' says Livingstone. 'I managed to block that by arguing it was a rescinding motion that needed a two-thirds majority. By that time they had the votes for a simple majority, but not two-thirds. There were incredible speeches. I was accused of intimidating the group. It was the first time there was a real wave of hatred in my direction.'

So the fares, for a while, stayed down. But after the October general election Goodwin's lieutenants put pressure on members of the Labour group to secure support for a 36 per cent fare increase in the following spring. 'Everyone was told that if it didn't go through Goodwin was going to resign and the administration would collapse. We ended up with a total crushing of the left.' The necessary votes were put through without discussion and the package was announced by Goodwin on October 31st 1974.

The fare increases were justified on the grounds that they were essential to save the house-building programme and avoid rent increases. 'But after a few more weeks had passed, they came back and said there had to be a rent increase too [adding 50p a week to average GLC rent levels of £4.90]. We picked up quite a respectable vote against that one in the Labour group because people felt they were really being messed about.'

These increased charges helped to keep the GLC rate rise announced in February 1975 down to 80 per cent (nine-tenths of it attributable to inflation). By April, however, Goodwin came back to the group with proposals for £50 million cuts in the housing investment programme. This was the period when Tony Crosland, as environment secretary, was fighting in the Cabinet against the Treasury's demands for public expenditure cuts. His political adviser, David Lipsey, rang round selected members of the GLC Labour group pleading with them to stick to the existing programme in support of Crosland's economic stance in the Cabinet debate.

These conflicting signals threw the Labour group into confusion. Stephen Haseler and Douglas Eden, prominent right-wingers who were later active in getting the Social Democrat bandwagon moving, made an abortive attempt to depose Goodwin. They argued that he had done too little too late to raise fares and rents to save the housing investment programme.

Livingstone and the left argued fiercely against every kind of cut. But Goodwin beat off the challenge from both wings and, on April 30th, the group approved the housing cuts. In a memorandum to the meeting, Goodwin explained: 'It should be borne in mind that these cuts are necessary because of the rising cost of servicing capital debts, and if they are not made now more severe cuts will need to be made in election year 1976/77. Cuts now would mean greater room for manoeuvre and less of a rate increase in the run-up to the GLC elections. This could mean the difference between a Labour win in 1977 with a modified housing programme or Labour losing with a higher but unacceptably expensive housing programme.'

Five members of the administration were sacked or resigned their posts: Haseler (chairman of the general purposes committee) and Eden (vice-chairman of housing development), representing the right; Livingstone (vice-chairman of housing management) and David White (chairman of the southern area planning board), representing the left; and Gladys Dimson (chairwoman of housing development), representing neither left nor right, but a passionate supporter of the housing programme that was being squeezed.

Goodwin admitted to the *Sunday Times* (May 18th 1975) that Labour's manifesto, written in 1972, seemed to have been conceived in 'virtually a different era'. He never earned the intended benefit of sacrificing his promises. Although the GLC did not increase its tax rate in February 1976 and 1977, he crashed to a 64 seats to 28 defeat in the 1977 GLC elections.

The story of the Goodwin leadership is essential background for understanding the Livingstone administration of 1981. Reaction against the budgetary cuts provided a focus for the mobilisation of the left. Reaction against Goodwin's non-participative style of leadership provided the motivation for the older-guard members of the centre to support the left when it came to a choice between Livingstone and Andrew McIntosh for leader.

The left's fight back against the Goodwin cuts started at the council meeting on June 10th 1975. Livingstone, Tony Banks and seven other Labour members issued a statement condemning measures 'which are diametrically opposed to the election manifesto on which we were elected in April 1973'. They criticised investment cuts in which 'housing has been singled out for the most destructive attack since before the last war'. The fare and rent increases were 'an attack on the living standards of ordinary Londoners for the benefit of the large commercial ratepayers of the City'. The 50p a week rent increase would save the average domestic ratepayer a mere 1p a week and the 25 per cent fare increase only 9p a week. 'It seems to us to be a total rejection of the social contract to implement policies of this nature at a time when trades unionists are being pushed by the government to take wage increases which do not keep pace with price increases,' they said. The statement called on the government to end the GLC's crippling debt charges 'as part of an overall socialist economic strategy to solve present economic problems'.

The rebels formed a campaign called Labour Against Housing Cuts to fight their case through the party. Its inaugural conference in July 1975 established three main demands: councils should be given powers to requisition all empty property; there should be no cuts in investment in public housing; and the GLC and government must return to the policy of the manifestos on which they were elected. The campaign never tried to mobilise mass support, but it provided a rudimentary organisation to push for change in the London Labour Party.

Resolutions attacking the cuts and establishing mandatory reselection for GLC candidates were passed by the regional party conference in March 1976. But the left failed to make any ground in elections for the regional executive in that year. As a result Goodwin was able to push through what Livingstone regarded as an 'appalling' GLC manifesto which he and others publicly condemned as 'anti-party' on the day before its publication. The left subsequently won control of the regional executive in March 1977 (the month when the Lib–Lab Pact allowed the Labour government to prolong its hold on office in return for the abandonment of socialist measures).

By mid-1976 Livingstone had given up hopes that Labour could win the 1977 GLC elections, which showed every sign of becoming a Tory landslide. 'I decided, after discussing it with my local party, that I should try to find a safe seat. We needed to have a left-wing element in the rump to organise and pull it together for the next election four years later.'

So Livingstone switched from Norwood to Hackney North, where he succeeded the retiring GLC chairman, Lord Pitt. He told the *South London Press*: 'You cannot just have a socialist revolution in Norwood and nowhere else.' This was the first of Livingstone's frequent changes of constituency, which caused him to be criticised as a carpetbagger. But his reasoning at the time was sound. 'I was the only one of the old Labour lefties to survive.'

The 1977 defeat was Labour's worst GLC result since 1967, although probably due more to the mid-term unpopularity of a Labour government than Goodwin's performance. Even if Labour had won, insufficient left-wingers had been selected to produce a left GLC. In that sense Livingstone's campaign had failed. As a Conservative administration under Sir Horace Cutler got down to the job of slimming down the GLC, the attentions of the left switched away from County Hall to prepare for the next parliamentary election. Livingstone's ideas for a left-led GLC were put on ice while he got down to the serious business of trying to become an MP.

A year before Labour's GLC defeat, Livingstone narrowly won selection as the party's prospective parliamentary candidate for Hampstead. With his wife Christine, he moved house to live in the constituency, arriving just in time for him to qualify for election to Camden borough council, which he joined in May 1978.

Livingstone as Labour parliamentary candidate for Hampstead, June 1977
(*Canton Studios*)

He was already by then becoming known to readers of the local paper, the *Hampstead and Highgate Express*. In August 1977 he had been made to pay £250 in costs after bringing an unsuccessful legal action against a Department of the Environment planning inspector who was holding a public inquiry into proposals for a motorway at nearby Archway. Livingstone claimed the inspector had hit him in the mouth; the magistrate concluded that although it was possible that the inspector's hand had come in contact with Livingstone's face, there was no proof that it was done aggressively.

In September 1977 Livingstone caused more controversy by promising that if he were elected to Parliament he would do all he could to get the age of consent for gay men reduced from 21 to 16. And in March 1978 he launched a blistering attack on

Camden council's Labour leadership: 'I have been to group meetings and I was shocked at the way they are run. The leadership tries to rush things through and stop back-bench councillors from raising important matters,' he told the *Ham and High* reporter. 'Some members even have to raise issues in the council chamber in the hope of inducing the Tories to side with them because they couldn't even discuss it with their own group. It's near-anarchy.' This is not the sort of thing new candidates for a council usually say less than two months before the elections.

In spite of these warning signals, Camden council was not prepared for Livingstone's impact on arrival. He won a surprise victory in a contest to become chairman of housing, largely because he persuaded the group to allow the candidates to make speeches and as usual made a good one himself. The *Ham and High* reported on May 26th: 'Mr Livingstone has followed up his capture of the plum post by announcing a whirlwind of controversial policies which he hopes will bring radical changes in the council's housing department from top to bottom.' At the first meeting of the new housing committee in June, Livingstone 'amazed his colleagues and opposition alike by abandoning the usual staid formality of council meetings, accepting comments and discussion from the public and committing the council very much more to the principle of tenant consultation. And his almost presidential-style handling of the meeting underscored his reputation as an uncompromising left-winger.'

By the time the public part of the agenda finally ended after four and a half hours of lively debate, the committee had decided to freeze rents for a year, reform the system of rate collection, slash rents on houses undergoing repairs, change rent arrears procedures and put through some compulsory purchase orders (following personal representations at the meeting by a tenant).

This was the approach Livingstone had been thinking through on the back-benches at Lambeth council. He recalls: 'I knew exactly what I wanted to do because I'd been criticising everybody else for not doing it in Lambeth borough for the previous seven years.' He took the unprecedented step of setting up his own office inside the housing department and dealing directly with its middle management, bypassing the housing director except for a meeting once a week. When officers failed to produce a report on time, he wrote his own on a couple of sides of paper and pushed it through committee. Grandiose building schemes were abandoned and resources channelled into modernising existing council homes and bringing large numbers of private properties into municipal ownership. Homes were let on short-term contracts to squatting organisations, fuelling allegations that Livingstone was deliberately bringing left-wing activist supporters into the borough and on to the electoral register. In October 1978 Livingstone lost a censure motion in Camden council when five Labour members refused to support him against Tory allegations that he was housing single homeless squatters in preference to people on its waiting list. He said they had got their facts wrong and refused to resign.

Gerry Isaaman, editor of the *Ham and High*, said: 'What we first noticed about him was that here was a man who could, unplanned, get up in the council chamber and wipe the floor with the opposition. He wowed them.' But his style of administering housing inevitably led to chaos. Livingstone would promise everyone that he would solve their personal problems with every intention of doing so, says Isaaman. 'He gave tenants his home phone number and would get calls in the middle of the night. He tried to play the role of the magician. So he created around himself a mound of work so big that no one in the world could cope with it. Camden's housing was always in a mess, but he significantly increased the logjam.'

Roy Shaw, Labour leader of Camden council at the time, was less charitable. 'He was a lousy chairman of housing. He was totally in the pocket of the officers. His main concern was using the position as a platform to get publicity for himself. Housing committees were an absolute bear garden.' According to Shaw, Livingstone's successor realised within three months that the department needed a complete management overhaul. 'Ken was prepared to accept the old position. He gets bored with administration. He doesn't like detail.' It is a charge that was to arise again when Livingstone took power at the GLC.

But Shaw, 20 years Livingstone's senior and part of the older Bevanite left of the Party, had more serious allegations about Livingstone's behaviour. 'One of his tricks when he was on Camden council was that he played to the gallery: the left-wing gallery, the trades union gallery, whatever gallery would help him at any particular moment. His ploy was to put forward an outrageous proposition, knowing full well that it would not be accepted – not really believing it himself. It would be defeated in the [Labour] group. He could then turn round and say: it's all the fault of those right-wing bastards; if it had been left to me, I would have done so and so. Thus he became the hero of a trades union group or whatever group he was particularly interested in at that moment. He did this on several occasions. Sometimes he did it so blatantly that, in speaking to the motion, he would say: I fully appreciate that there may well be members here who cannot support this motion, people who own their own homes, with families, who can't risk surcharge [a fine on councillors for unreasonable spending]. He was more or less saying: for heaven's sake don't vote for this. And of course it would be defeated. Now there was one occasion when he did this and something went seriously wrong.'

In February 1979, during the so-called winter of discontent which defeated the Callaghan government's claim to have a workable incomes policy, Livingstone proposed a local settlement with the National Union of Public Employees which was engaged in a national strike for better pay. He won the support of the Labour group for offering a £60 minimum wage that turned out to be much more generous than NUPE's eventual national agreement. Extra payments of up to £12.65 a week for the council's lowest-paid employees became known as the 'Camden supplement'. The district auditor later took the Labour councillors to court, alleging that the supplement was 'unreasonable' spending and illegal. The case became a major test of the scope of local authorities' discretion.

Shaw said that Livingstone never expected the Labour group to agree to pay the Camden supplement and that it was simply one more of his tactical demands to discredit the leadership. Livingstone maintains that he was genuinely keen to settle the strike, not least to help council tenants who were on the phone to him complaining that their heating had been cut off. 'It wasn't an unreasonable demand. You would probably have voted for it yourself. You would have been embarrassed that you were employing people in their forties and fifties on £35 a week, given what you were earning. That was, I think, why I won in the end in the group. A lot of its middle-class members, who were earning £10,000, £15,000 or £20,000 a year, were horrified to discover that a lot of our workforce were taking home not much more than they were giving their kids for pocket money.'

The district auditor's case eventually came before the High Court in 1982 when the judges ruled that the Labour councillors had not acted unreasonably. If the case had gone the other way, they could all have been bankrupted. Councillors who vote to spend money unlawfully could be personally surcharged for the full amount. In the case of the Camden supplement, this sum was more than £1 million.

With this threat hanging over the Labour councillors, it became much harder for Livingstone to win majorities within the group by force of argument. When his two-year term as housing chairman was over, he did not get the alternative front-bench post he was looking for. Shaw commented: 'For the last two and a half years anything Ken proposed would almost automatically be turned down because people saw through him. You will find that has happened almost everywhere that he has been.' Livingstone thinks he would have succeeded to the leadership of Camden if he had still been there when the left swept into power after the local elections in May 1982. But (if readers will forgive a phrase which is becoming rather familiar) by then he had moved on to new struggles in different parts of London.

Livingstone had not come to Camden primarily to take over its council. He fully expected to become the Labour MP for Hampstead at the general election that was eventually declared in May 1979. His alliances in the run-up to this campaign provide further evidence of Livingstone's willingness to work with (but not to join) groupings on the fringes of the Labour movement.

In July 1978 he became a founder member of the Socialist Campaign for Labour Victory, an amalgam of several left groups operating in London at the time. It was his participation in this organisation which earned him the reputation as a Trotskyist fellow-traveller, which he did not make any real effort to shake off. So it is important to establish what he and it were about.

The objective of SCLV was set out clearly in an editorial in the first issue (October 1978) of its newspaper, *Socialist Organiser*:

> The SCLV aims for a massive Labour vote, but a vote with a difference. We want to keep the Tories out, but to do so campaigning for socialist policies and against the pro-capitalist 'record' of the Labour Government, which has consistently bitten the hands that voted it into office in 1974 ... The SCLV will draw its life blood from the militants involved in the struggles over the past few years, by women, immigrants, youth and workers fighting the wage curbs. We take inspiration from struggles like the Grunwick workers', the fightback by Asian youth (and white working-class youth in the Anti-Nazi League) against racism and fascism, and the women of Trico who battled for equal pay. Together with these new militants we can reinvigorate the Labour movement, shake it up, and radically rearm and organise it for struggle against capitalism ... Our campaign must make sure that the Tories are combatted, and that the newly-elected Labour Government, from its first days, faces

a vocal socialist left wing, vigorously demanding it cuts its
slavish ties to the bankers and the bosses, and prepared to
struggle against the government every time it sells out.

The language of this editorial gives some clues to SCLV's
parentage. It drew together many of the left groups on the outer
fringes of the Labour Party, with the exception of the Militant
Tendency. Supporters of Workers' Action and the Chartists
played a leading role. Livingstone said he recognised that he and
Ted Knight, who had recently become leader of Lambeth
council, were brought in to give SCLV 'a degree of credibility
with the completely unaligned left' which always outnumbered
members of organised groups within the Labour Party. To that
extent he acknowledges he was being used. But Livingstone
maintains that he was never personally involved in the business of
sectarian politics. His objective and style of operation were to
mobilise alliances on the left to fight specific campaigns on as
broad a front as possible.

Livingstone was disparaging of the post-war British left's
capacity to fragment itself in theological disputes over arcane
points of principle. Once upon a time in the 1940s there was a
relatively clear division between the (pro-Moscow) Communist
Party and the (Trotskyist) Revolutionary Communist Party. The
RCP broke up in the 1950s to form three main strands around
Gerry Healy (Socialist Labour League/Workers Revolutionary
Party), Tony Cliff (International Socialists/Socialist Workers
Party) and Ted Grant (Militant Tendency). These three groupings
have themselves divided over time into further grouplets. As
Livingstone put it:

> From that point on you just had a series of splits, occasionally
> around obscure points of doctrine, like whether or not we
> should consider that Russia is a state capitalist nation or a
> deformed workers' state. Then, overlying that, you have
> massive personality clashes ... Everybody who's been around

for a while on the left has been moving backwards and
forwards across an increasingly larger number of split-off
groups, expelling and condemning each other from those
groups, for 25 years. So there are the most virulent
personality clashes …

I, fortunately, became politically active after most of this
lot had left the [Labour] Party. I just always operated within
the Labour Party and was prepared to work with any left
groupings inside it or outside it on a series of policy issues. So
what tends to happen with me is that for a couple of years I
get on very well with several groupings on the left; then one
of them will fall out with me and condemn me for a couple
of years. Then they come back when they want me to do
something. The relationship goes hot and cold. I just never
get involved in the sectarian infighting between them.

Livingstone's own campaign to win the seat in Hampstead
secured a comparatively good result in a bad Labour year. The
sitting MP, Geoffrey Finsberg, doubled the Conservative majority
to 3,681, but the swing to the Tories in Hampstead was only 2.1
per cent, compared with a national average of 5.2 per cent and an
inner London average of 7.1 per cent. Swings to the Tories in the
neighbouring borough of Hackney (averaging 10.3 per cent) and
Islington (9.3 per cent), and in the other Camden seats of
Holborn and St Pancras South (8.1 per cent) and St Pancras North
(5.4 per cent), suggested that the Hampstead electorate at least
were not put off by Livingstone's left-wing credentials. He got
315 more votes than Labour had scored in 1974. Since Michael
Foot was a Hampstead elector, it can be assumed that the future
Labour leader supported him then (probably for the first and last
time).

3 Phew What a Caucus

Even before his defeat at Hampstead, Livingstone had begun work to prepare for the next battle. By March 1979 his attention had reverted to the GLC. Writing in *Socialist Organiser*, he complained:

> The left ... are giving no thought to the impending GLC election. Already the right have started to organise to revive the discredited old guard who were responsible for the disgusting record of the last Labour GLC between 1973 and 1977 ... Those who have a commitment to a socialist GLC need to start organising now if this motley crew are to be prevented from discrediting the Labour Party in the eyes of the electorate for the second time in a decade.

The article explained changes in the London Labour Party rules which ensured that the manifesto would be prepared by a regional party conference and not by the GLC leadership. It set out the timetable for mandatory reselection of candidates. And it argued:

> The candidates who are selected must be bound by the manifesto, which must give a clear lead in the direction of a fare-free system for public transport and a massive expansion in the housing programme under an expanded direct labour organisation ... There is now a desperate need for a London-wide left caucus of those interested in the GLC and local councils so that we can compare and discuss what is happening in each borough.

Livingstone's interest in the GLC was regarded by most of his comrades at the time as idiosyncratic, not to say a little batty. It was all very well for him to launch attacks on the right-wing leadership (such as his tirade in the *Socialist Organiser* of October 1979 against £17 million cuts made by ILEA). But few people on the left regarded the GLC as worth much attention, let alone the time and trouble of getting elected to it. At that stage Livingstone was advancing orthodox arguments about what it could do and had not yet thought through the policies on job creation and grants that were to take the 1981 administration into pioneering socialist territory.

What he did, however, was to convince a lot of people on the left that the GLC election was the next battle on the agenda. 'I remember going round the Labour Party conference in Brighton in October 1979 and saying to just about everyone who lived in London and was on the left: you really have got to think about standing for the GLC. October 1979 to May 1980 was the critical period to persuade left-wingers to come on the panel of candidates ... I did the work on my own. There wasn't anyone else then. Nobody had paid much attention to the GLC.'

After the conference, Livingstone immediately called a meeting of the London left to discuss how it should organise to take over the council. This drew a furious response from John Keys, the right-wing general secretary of the London Labour Party. He claimed that Livingstone was abusing his position as a member of the regional executive committee (EC). 'It is wrong for members of the EC to in any way undermine the impartial responsibility of the EC by participating in factional meetings which could undermine the integrity of the regional EC,' Keys said in a letter to the committee. Livingstone ignored him and went ahead with the meeting on October 18th, calling it the John Keys Annual Memorial Lecture and using it to begin the process of educating the London left in the procedures for drawing up the manifesto and becoming candidates.

By this stage the regional executive was firmly in the hands of a broad alliance of the hard and soft left; but the left had already pushed through changes in the rules to ensure that control over the manifesto and candidacies was passed to the grassroots level. London was so large that there was little contact between its far-flung constituencies. So to win the GLC for the left, it was necessary to build up political networks to stimulate and co-ordinate local activity. Livingstone organised a series of meetings at rooms he had booked in County Hall to promote discussion on policy areas, such as housing and industry. He also sent out a stream of letters to individuals whose names and addresses he kept on a card index of the London left (probably the most comprehensive outside the Special Branch). These passed on information about selection procedures. 'I sent all the people on the left a list of all the constituencies in order of winnability, with a note about who the present member was, whether they were standing down, what the address of the party secretary was, how to get there – a sort of guide to how to get selected.'

A typical example was a photocopied handwritten note on May 1st 1980: 'Dear Comrade, I enclose information re the GLC seats in London which we can expect to win in next year's elections. Please write immediately to those which you would like to contest with brief statements of biographical details and political views. Send several copies to each CLP [constituency] secretary for ease of circulation to ward branch meetings. Many seats have now started the selection process, so it is essential to write immediately.'

On August 22nd he wrote again. 'Whilst most of the safe Labour seats have selected, most of the marginal seats we need to win from the Tories are still looking for candidates … I get constant phone calls from these constituencies asking if there is "anyone left on the panel worth selecting", so do please write to them with a brief statement of your political views. Yours fraternally, Ken Livingstone.'

This emphasis on the marginals was an important factor in building the eventual victory of the left. It would be misleading to suggest that Livingstone singlehandedly organised the selection process across London. Many of the left candidates who eventually became councillors would deny that he had anything to do with their decision to stand, or with their success in getting selected. But his efforts contrasted with the almost total lack of London-wide planning by the right wing.

Another key development was the founding of a new left periodical called *London Labour Briefing*. In late 1979 the Socialist Campaign for Labour Victory was taken over by a hard-line faction which argued that councils should advance the class struggle by refusing to make any cuts in services or to put up the rates. (This faction subsequently became known by the title of its newspaper, *Socialist Organiser*.) So Livingstone and a number of other activists, including Chartists and independent left-wingers, quit SCLV to set up a new grouping around the campaign to win the GLC for the left. In February 1980 they brought out the first 'Trial Issue' of *London Labour Briefing*, which told readers in an editorial:

> Your initial reaction may be that the left needs another newspaper like it needs another Reg Prentice. However, this is a bulletin with a difference. It is not produced by any one tendency or group, and does not claim to be able to provide full coverage of international events or to give an in-depth theoretical analysis on every issue! We have set ourselves the more modest but vital task of keeping active militants inside the Labour Party and the unions in London in touch with each other and up to date on what is happening in the various battles across the capital.

A lead story written by Livingstone made it clear that the main battle in prospect was the GLC election. Over the next few months *Briefing* played an important role in the left's campaign by providing ammunition against right-wingers (including names of Labour councillors who 'voted with the Tories' on council

LONDON LABOUR BRIEFING

10p   TRIAL ISSUE

TAKING OVER THE G.L.C.

LABOUR MUST WIN IN 1981

by Ken Livingstone
(Hackney North GLC member)

1980 is the year in which we will determine policy and select the candidates for the May 1981 GLC election. For the first time the election will be a major event in the struggle against a Tory government.

By the end of this year the government plan to have passed legislation forcing the sale of council houses and giving Heseltine power to withhold government funds from councils refusing to make cuts.

Undoubtedly the Tories will try to use those new powers and select several London Labour boroughs as the prime targets in their campaign.

The election must be used to rally support for councils refusing to make cuts and to mobilise opposition to the Tories' policies. It will be a major defeat for the Tories if we win a decisive majority on the GLC at the height of Heseltine's attack on Labour councils.

GLC and ILEA finances must be used to help any Labour borough from whom Heseltine withholds government finance.

An immediate decision to close down the GLC Housing Disposals department will stiffen the resolve of borough councils to refuse to sell council houses.

It is this role into which the GLC will be thrust which is responsible for the present interest in GLC election plans — in marked contrast to the past. At previous elections few have been willing to stand due to daytime meetings and the remoteness of the GLC — most activists have directed their attention to the borough councils. This has led to the GLC/ILEA Labour groups being even less representative than the Parliamentary Labour Party. Now there is something close to hysteria amongst these people as for the first time in many years they face a serious challenge to their positions.

Already a third of the Labour group have decided to retire and others are becoming regular attenders at their GMCs for the first time since the last elections.

Three recent decisions by the Greater London Labour Party have disturbed the present Labour group.

1. The London annual meeting has voted in favour of automatic reselection for all GLC members thus ensuring the first selection meeting in living memory in some constituencies.

2. The Regional Executive has decided that the GLC election manifesto shall be determined by the whole party at a full delegate meeting on the 18th of October.

In the past the manifesto was written by a small group (including a full time GLC officer!) and steamrolled through the Regional Executive with threats of resignation if any major changes were made.

This year the Regional Executive will circulate discussion documents to all affiliated organisations and these will be

(cont. on bottom page two)

Editorial:

This is the first trial edition of *London Labour Briefing*. Your initial reaction may be that the left needs another newspaper like it needs another Reg Prentice. However, this is a bulletin with a difference. It is not produced or controlled by any one tendency or group, and does not claim to be able to provide full coverage of international events or to give an in depth theoretical analysis on every issue! We have set ourselves the more modest but vital task of keeping active militants inside the Labour Party and the unions in London in touch with each other and up to date on what is happening in the various battles across the capital.

No doubt you yourself have often been misled or confused by stories about events in neighbouring Boroughs and in other CLPs. If we can lift some of the fog that surrounds us so often then we will be achieving part of our job.

Comrades should also be aware that this year we begin the arduous task of selecting our candidates for the GLC elections in 1981. For far too long the largest local authority in Western Europe has been the 'poor relation' as far as Labour Party organising and activity is concerned. We aim to rectify this by giving full coverage to the many issues involved: housing, transport, education and finance amongst them. We will also cover the various selections and candidates as the need arises.

Perhaps even more important are the Borough elections for the following year. We will systematically cover each borough borough's record, what its Labour councillors have done and the issues locally that affect the Labour movement. We will also follow the new re-selection procedures for parliamentary candidates and sitting MPs, which we strongly support as a means of making our elected representatives more accountable. We will also cover the activities of bodies like the GLRC, GLATCs and the South East Region of the TUC.

If this venture is to succeed we need your help: not in a passive sense of reading and donating to us (though that certainly helps) but as active contributors. If this is to give comprehensive coverage we need input from every Borough in London. If you are willing to be a 'key-person' for your CLP or area, please write to us and attend the various meetings we organise.

We are now at a crucial time for Labour. If a successful fight is to be mounted against the cuts, and if this Tory Government is to be removed, then we must prepare now for the enormous struggles ahead. Organisation and information are the keys to success. Make sure you become an effective component of our overall strength. One contribution towards this will be *your* support for this new publication.

London Labour Briefing, Trial Issue, February 1980

spending cuts) and details of progress on the manifesto and selection. Its early contributors included many who would go on to become GLC councillors in 1981, including Tony Banks, Gareth Daniel, Bryn Davies, Andy Harris, Tony Hart, Lewis Herbert, Paul Moore and George Nicholson. They also included two of the 1983 intake of new Labour MPs, Jeremy Corbyn and Chris Smith. *Briefing* prided itself on an open-door editorial policy. It had 'editorial collective' meetings in Livingstone's room at County Hall which anyone could attend; and it was tolerant enough to carry the occasional article by a right-winger.

The people at the core of the group, however, were Livingstone, Ted Knight (leader of Lambeth council), Corbyn (a NUPE official and member of the Labour regional executive), Chris Knight and Graham Bash (both Chartists). In spite of the open door, only tiny numbers of activists were involved. In the August 1980 issue, Chris Knight reported the launch of a 'major' campaign against Michael Heseltine's proposed Local Government Bill at a *Briefing* conference which was 'the largest rank-and-file gathering of this type for a number of years'. He explained: 'Over 200 delegates, from 30 CLPs and a dozen trades councils (amongst others) attended.' People who have subsequently come to regard Livingstone as a populist politician should remember that his climb to power started as the head of a very small pack.

This article by Chris Knight concluded by making a clear distinction between the *Briefing* group and ideological purists on the left: 'To the extent that we lack the physical power to overthrow the Tories and their system, we are forced to make difficult choices. The task isn't to pass resolutions "demanding" the impossible. It is to fight for real power. This is what those of us around *Briefing* are beginning to do.'

With organisational support from Livingstone and liaison through *Briefing*, the left made big advances in constituency selections of candidates. Some attempts were made to de-select sitting Labour members of the GLC who wanted re-election, but this was only achieved in three cases where special personal or local factors were at play. (One of these was in Bermondsey, where the former GLC leader, Sir Reg Goodwin, was de-selected for reasons of age and local Bermondsey politics that had nothing to do with Livingstone or *Briefing*.) The left's success was mainly in filling vacant winnable constituencies. In these seats the tally was about three to one in favour of the left.

Livingstone himself switched constituencies again from Hackney North to Paddington, a key marginal. He said he only wanted to be on the GLC if Labour was in power, which it only could be if marginals like Paddington were won. On the basis of 1979 general election results, Paddington was Labour's 43rd most winnable seat out of 92 London constituencies and it was only 15 minutes walk from his West Hampstead home. Livingstone won the nomination in a close-fought contest with Jean Merriton, another competent left-winger who stood for Paddington in the 1977 GLC election. He was also in the running for the nearby marginal of Hampstead where Labour eventually lost. If the Paddington selection had not come through first, Livingstone might have taken Hampstead and never have become a councillor in 1981.

During the year before the polls, one of the most familiar sights at County Hall was Livingstone in safari-jacket, scurrying about with his lists of candidates, working out the latest likely tally in the leadership contest which would follow the 1981 election. By polling day he knew that, whatever Labour's possible majority, he was at least two or three votes short of the clear left majority which could have guaranteed his leadership victory. He therefore needed to pull over the votes of half a dozen older councillors in the Labour centre, most of whom were not a little nervous of the young activists from *Briefing*.

The Labour rump which had been left at County Hall after the electoral debacle of 1977 had plodded through another three years under the leadership of Sir Reg Goodwin. Its chief whip, the elfin-featured former Church of England canon Harvey Hinds, had received periodic complaints from senior members of the group that it was time Goodwin was put out to grass. But, as Hinds explained, nothing was done because 'the natural heir and successor was anathema to the elder statesmen'.

The natural heir was Illtyd Harrington, an exuberant Welshman prone to somewhat florid oratory, who had been the darling of the London left in the 1960s. The left ostracised him after 1975 when, as GLC finance chairman, he pushed through Goodwin's package of budgetary cuts.

But Goodwin and the right also disapproved of him because they believed him to be unreliable, probably due more to his extravagant personal mannerisms than his political aptitude or leanings. There was therefore a power vacuum (if that is not too grand a term) at the top of the GLC Labour group. Goodwin did not groom a young right-winger to replace him, preferring to place his confidences with bright young GLC officers rather than with any politicians.

Goodwin's style of departure was typical of his aloofness. 'When I got back from holiday in April 1980, there was a large manilla envelope on my desk,' Hinds recalled. 'Attached to it was a note in Reg's handwriting saying: "Inside you will find a letter which you will doubtless wish to distribute to all members of the Labour group." Inside the manilla envelope were 28 photocopies of a letter of resignation ... It was the first that I, as chief whip, knew about it.'

In the leadership election contest that followed, there were three candidates: Harrington, Livingstone and Andrew McIntosh, a 45-year-old market research executive who was the natural candidate of the Labour right. Livingstone remembers doing a headcount. 'I had four votes. About a dozen were prepared to vote for Illtyd Harrington, but a reluctant majority would have ended up supporting Andrew McIntosh. I spent about two weeks trying to persuade most of the people planning to vote for Illtyd that he could not get a majority, whereas I could.'

Surprisingly Livingstone nearly pulled it off. Due to some incompetent tactical voting by members whose main purpose was to dish either Harrington or McIntosh, Livingstone emerged top in the first ballot, with ten votes. Harrington and McIntosh tied with nine each. In the run-off for second place, Livingstone voted for McIntosh, whom he thought he had a better chance of beating subsequently. (This gave McIntosh 16 votes to Harrington's 12.) In the final ballot, McIntosh beat Livingstone by 14 votes to 13, with two abstentions. Given the left's view of the County Hall Labour group as a bunch of right-wing dinosaurs, this was a remarkably good showing by Livingstone. The measure of his true support was shown in a later ballot for deputy leader when he got only seven votes to Harrington's 21. Yet, with a certain amount of tactical footwork, he came within one vote of winning the leadership.

There is a second astonishing feature of the 1980 leadership contest. Livingstone was responsible for ending Harrington's chances. Yet Harrington and his campaign manager, Hinds, both voted for Livingstone in the final ballot and went on to provide him with the centre support he needed in 1981. This cannot have been for love of *London Labour Briefing*. 'Even McIntosh's victory was preferable to the other main challenger of the right, Illtyd Harrington, whose style of politics we will not comment on as the law of libel can be harsh on small socialist magazines,' it said in its June 1980 issue.

So why did Harrington and Hinds back Livingstone? 'Our assessment of Andrew McIntosh was that he was just a very slightly cleverer version of Reg Goodwin,' said Hinds.

> Reg was a hermit ... He had great expertise in financial matters and my own view is that he was a man of integrity, but a recluse, a sphinx, who couldn't socialise, couldn't talk to people, had to be bludgeoned into actually receiving anyone into his room ... He was brought up in the old LCC tradition of the leader giving maximum attention to chief

officers and minimum attention to elected members' concerns ... When Reg made a speech in the council chamber on whatever subject, particularly finance and the budget, it was always superb, carefully prepared in private, in silence, with able briefing from [officers]. But in the rough and tumble of the Labour group, Reg as a leader was an absolute disaster.

And why did Hinds think McIntosh, a bustling professional, would follow Goodwin's example? 'One of Andrew's weaknesses was that he was too clever by half ... He made the great mistake of talking down to the Labour group and to the regional Labour Party on a number of occasions.' But was not Livingstone's style of activist politics equally distasteful? 'Ken was a leader who knew his mind and knew what he wanted to achieve ... [After Reg] I was yearning for a leader who would lead ... I saw in the likes of Ken and the young people who were just beginning to come through in my local Labour Party the best hope for the future of the Labour Party,' said Hinds.

Harrington had another explanation:

What struck all the older politicians was the speed and efficiency of what we were looking at. We overestimated it [the advance of the left] very much. We thought we were looking at a juggernaut. We were looking at something that was sharper, younger, appeared to be crisper ... They looked unstoppable. They appeared to be fresh, open-minded. These were attractive things to see. We had gone through a long period of appalling local government. It had atrophied ... Things needed to be done in transport, housing, fresh ideas about planning. They all appeared to be alive, marvellously alive.

And so by May 1981, the centre was ready to seek rejuvenation by going for an exhilarating ride on the bandwagon of the left. As

Harrington put it: 'It had flags, whistles, and steam coming out of it at you.'

When Livingstone lost the leadership in 1980, he thought McIntosh would be leader for a decade. 'He started to accommodate to the left. He went along with what was going in the manifesto. He recommended my appointment as planning and transport spokesman. But then, about June, I realised things weren't working for him. The centre who had voted for Illtyd had largely not been won over. He had made no effort to sit down with Illtyd or Harvey and involve them. Actually he just worked with me. They felt isolated and out of it. And they never had liked him terribly much. So I started to work quite closely with them … By mid-July we knew that we had the votes to get rid of Andrew.'

McIntosh later observed that Harrington and Hinds were rather too good at inventing rationalisations for a sell-out to gain senior jobs in the administration. But that may underestimate how close the two men came to Livingstone in the year before the 1981 election. By then both had developed an almost fatherly affection for the prodigal left-winger, his domestic crises (this was the period of his separation from his wife Christine), and his endless supply of little lists of the latest state of play in the constituencies. If not part of his family, they gradually became part of his team.

So, as Labour went into the GLC election, Livingstone had achieved two objectives. Constituency selections had secured nearly enough left-wingers to ensure an overall left majority on the GLC Labour group. And his personal qualities had won over the additional votes necessary from the old-guard centre, provided nothing happened to jeopardise their support. There was a third crucial strand of preparation: the battle over the manifesto.

The process of drawing it up began in June 1979 and involved so much grassroots consultation that only the most energetic party members could stand the pace. The regional executive set up a series of working parties to produce policies for each main area of GLC activity. Party members were able to read their draft reports and attend meetings to discuss them. The output was then submitted to a special conference of the London party in October 1980 for amendment and ratification. This exhaustive and exhausting procedure gave considerable power to the handful of people who were prepared to do the work. Livingstone acknowledges: 'The right wing were very unlucky at this time, in that Reg Goodwin never really put much effort into anything... And there was no group of talented young right-wingers rushing around doing any leg work for him.'

For Livingstone, the big breakthrough was winning a vote on the regional executive to become chairman of the transport working party that would have to tackle the most controversial question of how much London Transport fares should be subsidised. Until then, Livingstone's links with the trades unions had been limited to one-off alliances during disputes in which he was involved as a councillor. He had been hostile to the trade union hierarchy, which tended to vote against everything he proposed on the London regional executive. Work with the TUC and transport unions to prepare the GLC manifesto helped him to build another important part of his political network.

At the outset there was great disagreement about what the GLC public transport policy should be. Most people on the left of the party wanted LT to move over to a policy of free fares to encourage maximum use of the bus and Underground system and to provide maximum benefit to passengers at the expense of ratepayers. The unions, however, were concerned that abolition of fares would mean abolition of ticket collectors' and bus conductors' jobs. They also feared that the LT infrastructure could not cope with a sudden massive increase in passenger demand. Meanwhile the Labour right-wingers were worried about the rate implications of unlimited subsidies to public transport. They agreed that fares were too high, but they wanted to fix an appropriate level of subsidy and then let fares rise with inflation.

Livingstone, who had previously argued for free fares, gradually moved over to a compromise proposal to cut fares by 25 per cent and then freeze them so that the impact of the policy would grow as inflation took its toll on the value of money. He did not, however, feel confident of backing from the left, the unions, or the right. So his working party fudged the issue by presenting options for discussion by the party, representing the three main strands of opinion. Even by the time of the special regional conference in October 1980, it was by no means clear which side would win. Livingstone's speech in favour of the compromise solution was widely regarded as decisive in securing a majority for the compromise.

The eventual manifesto document was never fit for public consumption. It was ridiculously long and in parts repetitive, meaningless or badly written. But it fulfilled Livingstone's basic objectives. It gave cast-iron promises of action on policies that the GLC could implement, leaving no excuses for backsliding. In addition to the cheap fares commitment, the other main pledges were: to form a Greater London Enterprise Board to revive the London economy and create 10,000 new jobs a year by 1984/85; to restore the GLC's strategic housing role, halt the voluntary sale of council houses and freeze council rents at least for the first year of office; to stop the spread of office development in central London, using GLC planning powers to encourage alternative development of housing, open space and light industry; to discourage further road-building; and to terminate 'wasteful expenditure on so-called home defence' (a government initiative to prepare communities to survive a nuclear war). Other less practical policies were expressed as the GLC calling for action rather than being committed to implement anything itself. One example was a Militant-inspired pledge that a Labour GLC would 'demand that the next Labour government will immediately... nationalise the banks and ... annul local authorities' debts, with compensation being paid only on the basis of any proven need of the share- and bond-holders'.

By the time of the election in May 1981, all Livingstone's political networks were in place. Through *London Labour Briefing* he had formed links with many of the left activists in the constituencies. Through the process of drawing up the manifesto, he had established better contacts with the unions. Through his relations at County Hall, he had attracted vital support from the old-guard GLC Labour centre. In this whole elaborate network, Livingstone was the only common link. By election day he had pieced together the alliance which was to deliver him power.

As he concluded: 'In retrospect it really was a question of being the right person in the right place at the right time. If I hadn't been here, Andrew [McIntosh] most probably would have survived, because I doubt if anybody else would have pulled it all together. But it was so easy to pull together. The party was ready for it to happen.'

It was common knowledge during the campaign that Livingstone would be mounting a challenge to McIntosh's leadership as soon as the newly elected group of councillors assembled, enlarged by the expected crop of Labour gains. The GLC Conservative leader, Sir Horace Cutler, said the Labour left was trying to hijack London by campaigning behind the comfortable image of nice Mr McIntosh before ditching him in favour of the sinister Livingstone. 'The Marxist threat to London is no figment of the imagination,' warned the Tory GLC manifesto. 'The old Labour Party has gone. Herbert Morrison would turn in his grave at the sight of today's Labour Party, which is dominated by Marxists and extremists.' Within the 16 pages of the short manifesto, Marx and Marxists were mentioned 17 times. And a week before polling day, in an article in the *Daily Express* headlined 'WHY WE MUST STOP THESE RED WRECKERS', Cutler thundered that the aim of the extremists was to 'establish a Marxist power-base in London from which support can be given to the wider movement to take over the Labour Party: and from which a concerted effort can be made to unseat the government of the day – even a Labour government if it puts nation before party.'

'He told me he learnt about public projection from me …' – Sir Horace Cutler, GLC Tory leader 1977–81 (*Guardian, Peter Johns*)

This was a period of major advances by the left within the Labour Party. Since the general election defeat in May 1979 the party constitution had been changed to provide mandatory reselection of parliamentary candidates (to give constituency parties the power to discard sitting MPs) and establish a new electoral college to choose the party leader (previously the prerogative of MPs). The campaign to win Tony Benn the deputy leadership of the party, which came within 1 per cent of victory at Brighton in September 1981, was also already gathering momentum.

In this context, Livingstone's challenge exerted a fascination on politicians and the media. Just as he saw a left-led Labour GLC as a test-bed of more red-blooded socialist policies for a future Labour government, so he was seen as the pioneer of tactics by which the left could eventually seize power in Westminster, winning a majority under a 'traditional' leader and then ditching him or her once power was secured. Since few people in the press or the Parliamentary Labour Party favoured either the policies or the tactics, Livingstone fitted snugly into the category of 'extremist', a platoon leader of the advance party of Bennite shock troops.

His platoon was not the only one in the field on that local election night in May 1981. With varying degrees of left-wing strength, Labour groups were winning a clean sweep of power throughout the English metropolitan counties. Conservative administrations were defeated in Merseyside, Greater Manchester, West Yorkshire and the West Midlands; and Labour strengthened its grip on South Yorkshire and Tyne and Wear. In the shires, where Labour had been devastated by a Tory landslide in the previous elections of 1977, Labour won control of Northumberland, Cumbria, Lancashire, Humberside, Avon, Nottinghamshire, Staffordshire and Derbyshire. It also deprived the Tories of overall majorities in Bedfordshire, Berkshire, Cheshire, Leicestershire and Northamptonshire.

But the London-based media gave scant attention to any results outside the capital. Senior editors had paid little attention when left-wing administrations seized control of other important local authorities. Sheffield city council under David Blunkett's leadership was already pursuing policies which were just as left-wing as anything Livingstone had to offer. Sheffield council had far more power to make an impact on its area because, unlike the GLC, it had responsibility for a wider range of activities, including housing and social services. Blunkett, who was two years younger than Livingstone, blind, charismatic and with a revivalist style of socialist oratory which none of his contemporaries could match, would have attracted huge national controversy if his centre of operations had not been 150 miles away from London. As it was, the media merely cracked jokes about the People's Republic of Sheffield and more or less let him get on with it.

In contrast, the question of the night in national network television studios was: would Livingstone have enough support to win the leadership of the GLC? He was confident enough in front of the cameras, but privately he knew Labour had not performed as well as expected. He secured a respectable 2,397 majority in marginal Paddington and Andrew McIntosh had a good result in Tottenham. If the swing to Labour shown by their constituencies had occurred across London, Labour would have won 57 or 58 of the 92 GLC seats and Livingstone would have the leadership in his grasp. But the results were patchy. His ally Ted Knight, leader of Lambeth council, was surprisingly beaten in Norwood after a bitter campaign against his council's recent supplementary rate demand. Labour also failed to win Hampstead and a handful of other marginals in which Livingstone supporters had been candidates. 'As the results came through, I became decidedly nervous for the first time since the previous July that we might not have the votes to do it. What it meant was that there was not going to be anything like the number of left-wingers that there should have been. The proportion of the left if we won 60 seats was better than if we won 50. If the centre had wanted to, it could have kept Andrew in power.'

In the 48 hours before polling Livingstone had buttonholed or phoned all Labour candidates who might win and might vote for him in the leadership ballot. He had asked them to attend a left caucus meeting on the day after the poll. (The operation was kept secret for fear of the mileage the Tories would have made of it in the final day of the campaign.) So, as he moved on from the broadcasting stations to catch the tail end of his supporters' party in Paddington, he knew that there was nothing more that could be done that night. By about 3 a.m. he got back to his bed-sitter in Maida Vale. As he pored over the results yet again, he became depressed about the reasons for Ted Knight's defeat in Norwood. Could this same unpopularity attach itself to a left-wing GLC? Was this what would happen when the GLC brought in the supplementary rate implied in its plans for LT? The usually self-confident Livingstone went to sleep full of doubt.

Meanwhile McIntosh was behaving as if his personal victory was assured. He too put in his television appearances before repairing in the early hours to a celebration party at County Hall with the Labour leader Michael Foot, the Parliamentary chief whip Michael Cocks and McIntosh's deputy Illtyd Harrington. The whisky bottles were brought out and, according to Harrington, Foot toasted McIntosh's success with the memorably mistaken prophecy: 'It's going to be fine because you, Andrew, are in charge and you know the machine.' Within 15 hours the man who knew the machine was going to be flattened by it.

McIntosh appears to have been genuinely ignorant of the fate that was in store for him. He counted his supporters and thought he would win by two or three votes. When he arrived at County Hall the next morning, determined to take a businesslike grip on power, he carried with him a letter from Foot endorsing his leadership. This was to be his trump card in winning over waverers in the group. He summoned the chief officers and told them his immediate priorities for action. Then he gave a press conference to tell the world: 'I am going to win. The results of the election show that the people of London wanted the Labour Party to win, but they also wanted a Labour administration of responsible and realistic people. That is what they are going to get.' Due largely to this manifest confidence the *Evening Standard*, London's evening paper, led with the headline 'THE LEFT LOSE OUT' under a strapline 'Red Ted defeated: Moderates "in control"'.

Ken Livingstone faces up to Andrew McIntosh who thought he had the Labour leadership in his pocket, May 8th 1981 (*Guardian, Garry Weaser*)

But McIntosh was not in control. He had wanted to hold the Labour group meeting at 9 a.m. on the day after the poll, to have his leadership confirmed before he decided on the allocation of committee chairmanships and other jobs in the administration over the weekend. The group would have been asked to ratify his choices during the following week. But Livingstone's sympathisers on the London Labour Party regional executive fixed the meeting for 5 p.m., allegedly to allow time for the results of any recounts in close-fought constituencies. That gave him the opportunity to call his caucus meeting at a reasonable time in the afternoon when everyone was ready for action after the revelries of the night before.

'We needed two hours for all the new incoming left people to sit down and argue out what we were going to do about everything. There had been a not greatly debated consensus that I would stand against Andrew,' says Livingstone. 'Beyond that nothing was really firm. What I needed to do was to make sure that we welded together the existing members here who were prepared to vote to remove Andrew with the incoming people. There could easily have been a split between those two groups.'

Livingstone says it is incorrect to call the meeting a left caucus. 'It was basically everybody who was prepared to see a change of Andrew's leadership for mine. So it was people who would be called hard left, soft left and centre and a couple of people on the right who decided they wanted to come and sit in.'

Livingstone's account of the controversial meeting in room 166 at County Hall is as follows:

> We walked into the room and by the time we started a majority of the next Labour group were there. That was a tremendous boost to confidence. People who might have had doubts or reservations suddenly could see that we did have the votes to do it.
>
> I said what I thought had gone wrong in the past and why I thought we should have a change now. Illtyd Harrington said I should stand for the leadership and there was a general murmur of agreement. Then we had a long debate about whether or not we should elect me as leader and then defer everything else until people could go back to their local parties and talk about who were the candidates for particular posts.
>
> We decided that, as it was necessary to start changing the administration quickly, we couldn't wait five or six weeks for that and we would therefore have to go straight into all the other elections. So we sat round the table: I went through all the list of posts and asked if anyone was interested in standing. Where more than one wanted to stand, they each made a little speech and the caucus decided which they wanted to support. There were an awful lot of contested posts. People that I hadn't expected to do things wanted to do them.

The caucus broke up at 4.45 p.m. with a full slate of candidates agreed. It had been attended by two-thirds of the 50 Labour councillors elected the day before. When the full group assembled at 5 p.m., things were still going wrong for McIntosh. He passed up to George Page, the London Labour Party regional secretary, his letter of support from Foot, expecting him to read it out at the start of the meeting. Page stayed silent. Livingstone says:

> The entire regional staff, who no one can say were exactly Militant-dominated, were on my side … They felt in simple party terms that I was the politician who knew how to work the Labour Party and Andrew wasn't.
>
> It seems silly, but one of Andrew's major mistakes was to go to the regional executive with flip charts and give them lectures on what was to be done. He gave them market research presentations. They felt that they were being treated like kids at school. He did it three times. It was the kiss of death.

So the group moved straight to the leadership election with a victory for Livingstone by 30 votes to 20. Only two-thirds of his support could be described as left wing. McIntosh was shattered. He had prepared no list of right-wing candidates for the other important committee chairmanships. So the meeting went on to elect the entire left caucus slate. The whole proceedings took no more than 40 minutes before Livingstone emerged to begin three hours of interviews with the media. The next day the left carried out a parallel coup on the Inner London Education Authority (made up of GLC and borough councillors). Its previous Labour leader, Sir Ashley Bramall, was deposed by Bryn Davies. On Sunday night, as the left were holding a celebratory party at the home of one of the new Labour councillors, Valerie Wise, the news came through that François Mitterrand had been elected president in France. For a while at least it seemed that everything was for the best in the best of all possible leftist worlds.

LONDON LABOUR BRIEFING 20p

No 11 JUNE 1981

SPECIAL VICTORY ISSUE!

LONDON'S OURS!

Ken Livingstone
GLC Leader

After the most vicious GLC election campaign of all time, Labour has won a working majority on a radical socialist programme. The torrent of Macarthy-style red-baiting and gross distortion of the cost of Labour's programme — coupled with extensive media coverage — left no-one in any doubt that this GLC election was the trial run for the next general election campaign. The results need to be seen in this light.

We are not just talking about another mid-term council election showing the normal anti-government swing. Voters in Paddington, where I was the candidate, responded to the campaign on firm class lines. The Social Democractic candidate was crushed, with under 7 per cent of the vote. His only impact was in the safe Tory areas of Hyde Park and Lancaster Gate. In Islington North we won our third highest swing to Labour — clear proof that the SDP took its vote from the Tories.

Rates

The only problem in the campaign was the difficult issue of rates. The emphasis we placed on the need to increase rates was honestly put, but we failed to go on to the attack against the Government on this issue. Our central demand should have been for the restoration of the £300 million Rate Support Grant which Heseltine stole from London. From now on, this demand will be at the centre of our on-going campaign against the Government.

We will go into the constituencies with Tory MPs and lead the demand that they vote in Parliament to restore our Rate Support Grant and Housing programme cuts. Where they refuse, we shall publish their voting records and demand their removal.

We will be working with the NEC's Home Policy Committee to prepare detailed legislation for the next Labour Government. No-one will be left in any doubt that the GLC is now a campaigning organ and a bastion of power for the labour movement within a national context.

Now for the Government

The Regional Executive, London Labour MPs and Local Government Committees will be drawn into the plans for the fight ahead. There is no doubt that the party was damaged in Lambeth and Camden by the supplementary rates which were forced on those councils by the Auditor and Heseltine. We must avoid being trapped in the same way. We must ensure that we plan the way ahead rather than just respond to the Government's attacks as they occur. Part of our task will be to sustain a holding operation until such time as the Tory Government can be brought down and replaced by a left-wing Labour

Continued next page

Labour—Take the Power!

London Labour Briefing, Victory Issue, June 1981

Livingstone's victory gave Fleet Street a field day. 'RED KEN CROWNED KING OF LONDON', said the *Sun*. 'Red Ken ousted moderate Andrew McIntosh, 46, in a private poll by the 50 newly elected councillors. His victory means full-steam-ahead red-blooded Socialism for London,' its reporters explained. The *Daily Mail* news story said:

> A left-wing extremist was installed as leader of the Greater London Council yesterday, less than 24 hours after Labour won control ... And last night the signs were that the Left's victory in London could be repeated up and down the country where Labour has won control of county halls. Mr Livingstone's election came as Mrs Thatcher was warning in a speech at Perth that extremists were busy manipulating Labour's membership to gain power. She said that they had one purpose: 'To impose upon this nation a tyranny which the peoples of Eastern Europe yearn to cast aside'.

The *Daily Express* commented that the Labour group's decision displayed 'their contempt for the voters' by unceremoniously ditching McIntosh in favour of 'the political extremist Ken Livingstone'. It listed some of his left-wing credentials and raised a theme that was to become a running criticism in the press. 'For the last six years and more he has had no proper job. Instead he has acted as a professional local councillor, living on his "expenses" of about £7,000 a year.' (The actual sum was £3,000.)

By Monday the *Evening Standard* was commenting:

> The worst nightmares about the Greater London Council and its new masters on the far left seem to be coming true even faster than we had feared. Mr Ken Livingstone and his fellows have steamrollered their more moderate (and experienced) colleagues out of the way in record time ... The truth which the Left will never acknowledge is that they

are operating on a non-existent mandate. Labour won the election under the moderate Mr McIntosh (and small thanks he got). The Left's best-known candidate, Mr Ted Knight, was rejected out of hand by the voters of Lambeth, against the tide everywhere else. So now it is up to the Government and, in particular to Mr Michael Heseltine [the environment secretary], Mr William Whitelaw [home secretary] and Mr Mark Carlisle [education secretary] to keep some measure of control over London's spending, policing and education.

But it was not only in the right-wing press that Livingstone's coup was criticised. Three days after the group meeting the *Guardian* and the *Mirror* carried lengthy reports of complaints by McIntosh that he had been ousted by means of an illegitimate form of caucus rule. McIntosh told the *Mirror*: 'The danger to the Labour Party is so great that I have decided I must expose what is going on. It's gang warfare – just like the Jets and the Sharks. The left are after personal power.'

McIntosh complained that a handful of left-wingers held a secret meeting in a pub the week before the election at which Livingstone, Ted Knight and others who were not even candidates drew up a list of left-wingers for major committee posts. McIntosh alleged that the left won sufficient support by persuading moderates to back them in return for jobs. 'I don't object to my personal defeat – that's part of politics. But I am objecting violently to what I call the Russian doll strategy, whereby a small secret group of self-selected people organise to impose their will on a larger group. If it becomes the pattern of future elections, the Labour Party is in very serious trouble.'

A *Mirror* editorial argued: 'If a small, unelected group can impose its will on a larger, elected one which, in turn, dominates an even bigger group which runs a city, that is not open government, nor democracy. It is deception.'

The result of all this ballyhoo was further to elevate media interest in the GLC which had already been evident on election night. The GLC in general and Livingstone in particular became newsworthy. No matter that the Livingstone administration set out to implement exactly the same manifesto policies to which McIntosh was also committed. No matter that it had to operate within the narrow band of functions which the GLC was legally permitted to perform. As far as news editors were concerned, 'Red Ken' switched from being a minor bore in the big yawn of local government into a public figure who merited the sort of coverage which MPs crave and seldom get.

But how much justice was there in McIntosh's charge that something unseemly happened on Livingstone's road to leadership victory? It can hardly be argued that Livingstone's victory was a surprise, since the possibility was one of the main thrusts of the Conservative campaign. But Livingstone acknowledges that switching leaders in this way is undesirable if it can be avoided. He says he tried to persuade McIntosh to step down a few months before the election on the grounds that a Livingstone victory was inevitable: 'But Andrew thought I was mad.' Livingstone had also pushed for rule changes to give the London Labour Party conference the job of electing the GLC leader, but this idea was scotched by Labour's National Executive Committee.

McIntosh's complaint was not that there was a leadership election that he happened to lose, but that it was improperly conducted. The theoretical objection to decisions by caucus is that the will of the majority can be flouted. Say 100 people are entitled to choose a leader or parliamentary candidate. The result could be determined by a majority of 51 of them. If these 51 meet separately to make a choice, which they all agree they will be bound by, the eventual outcome can be decided by only 26 people. This smaller group could itself be influenced by the activities of a closed inner caucus or by secret deals between individuals. So, theoretically, a tiny group of people could manipulate the eventual result. This is why caucuses are banned in the selection procedure for Labour parliamentary candidates, as

Livingstone was to learn to his cost in his abortive bid to become candidate for the Brent East constituency at the 1983 general election.

In the case of the GLC leadership election in 1981, the 3 p.m. caucus meeting was not secret. It was open to right-wingers to attend – and at least one overt McIntosh supporter sat through the whole proceedings. The left tried to change the rules in the eventual meeting of the full Labour group to remove the secrecy of the leadership ballot. If they had succeeded, this could have increased the pressure on waverers in the centre to vote as the caucus directed. But the left failed to get the two-thirds majority needed to change the rules. This made it possible for councillors to promise their votes to Livingstone, but vote for McIntosh. Several did.

So McIntosh's objections to the procedures were reduced to two: first, that an inner caucus of the left pre-arranged its slate of major committee chairmanships; and second, that the waverers in the centre were bribed to vote left by the offer of posts in the Livingstone administration. Livingstone's answer was that he was not in a position to deliver jobs to people.

> Lots of them had said to me that they were going to stand for particular things. I made certain not to get involved in that, because it would have been counterproductive. The people who weren't being offered the job would end up voting for someone else ... The real effort had been endlessly talking to people who were going to be elected saying: we cannot come in and sweep everything out of the way and have a completely new machine. We have got to weld together and build the widest possible basis of support there. That meant you had got to have people who had already voted for me at the previous election [in 1980] carried with us in the change.

The two key figures here were Illtyd Harrington who was re-elected deputy leader, and Harvey Hinds, who continued as chief whip. These men of the old-guard centre had it in their influence to make either McIntosh or Livingstone leader in 1981; and the fact that Livingstone backed them in the caucus for senior jobs can probably fairly be said to be more the consequence of their support than its cause. The surprise in all this was not that politicians make arrangements with each other, but that McIntosh did so little to stitch up his own coalition of support. 'I am constitutionally incapable of running two battles at the same time,' he said. 'I was concentrating on winning the election … That took 100 per cent of my time. Afterwards I had no opportunity to change.'

The political epitaph on McIntosh, a resident of the north London district of Highgate, was delivered by the Conservative leader, Sir Horace Cutler, at the first meeting of the new council:

> There lived a man on Highgate Mount.
> He won the votes, but did not count.

In 1983, on Michael Foot's recommendation, McIntosh entered the House of Lords.

4 Salamander Days

Tabloid newspaper editors knew Red Ken made good copy, but they could not at first decide whether to treat him as a threat to civilisation as they knew it or a harmless and rather quirky figure of fun.

The mainstream press had been hostile to the caucus coup which brought him the leadership on May 9th 1981 and suspicious about changes to the council's standing orders which were introduced at the first available opportunity to help Labour get its business through unhindered by its relatively slim majority. There was some alarm about the GLC's early threat (later withdrawn) to suspend £550,000 of grants to the Royal Opera House, Covent Garden, and redistribute the money to community arts centres. There was also suspicion prompted by the decision to reject an invitation for their leader to attend the royal wedding between Prince Charles and Lady Diana Spencer later that summer. Livingstone told the *Observer*: 'I would like to see the abolition of the monarchy, replacing it with an elected president who would be ceremonial ... Some of the characters who are hangers-on and living off public expense are really quite revolting ... What earthly use the country gets out of Princess Anne I really don't know.'

On May 28th *London Labour Briefing* published a victory issue under the headline 'LONDON'S OURS', in which Livingstone pledged to use County Hall as an open campaigning base to bring down the Thatcher government. Two days later the GLC provided accommodation and food for 500 young people who arrived in London from the north on the People's March for Jobs. As the *Morning Star* pointed out on May 27th: 'The marchers will sleep in County Hall on camp beds originally intended for use as part of the council's civil defence programme, which has been abandoned by the new administration.' There followed stories about how the GLC was to spend £400,000 on a council newspaper to be distributed free to all Londoners ('It's propaganda on the rates' – *Daily Mail*, June 6th); and about how responsibility allowances were to be divided up among the administration's central team of full-time councillors.

Most of this early coverage was critical and it was strongly personalised around Livingstone, in spite of his protestations about the more collective style of leadership which Labour had introduced. On May 30th the *Daily Mail* carried a feature by David Norris under the headline 'THE COMMISSAR OF COUNTY HALL'. He said that on the surface Livingstone was as straight-talking as they come, proud of his working-class origins and easy-going man-of-the-people image. 'Underneath the real Mr Livingstone is as elusive as the disappearing natterjack toad – a threatened species which the 35-year-old part-time conservationist is fighting to protect.' Livingstone might sound eminently reasonable in his arguments on subjects such as the need to control the GLC bureaucracy. 'It is only when he goes on to offer his own socialist solution to the problem that the mask of reason and moderation begins to slip and the face of a dogmatic zealot peers through.'

Even the right-wing papers, however, found it hard to sustain this menacing tone when they were deriving so much light entertainment from Livingstone's lifestyle. 'The harsh realities of life confront Kenneth Livingstone soon after he crawls from under his pink-patterned duvet in the simple bed-sitting room, which shakes every time a train passes on the Bakerloo line below,' began Brian Silk in the *Daily Telegraph* ('Bedsitter vision of the Socialists' Mr London', June 15th). 'At 36 he is the leader of the Greater London Council, with responsibility for more people than any local authority in Europe and even some sovereign states. But at the £20-a-week room in Maida Vale he is just one of the tenants who have to share the lavatory. To the neighbours he is the bizarre character who spends his free time searching the local terrain for slugs and woodlice to feed his seven pet lizards.' This account of Livingstone's day ended 'close to midnight when Livingstone comes up the steps at Maida Vale station and stops to buy a packet of chips on the way to his room and his seven cold-blooded friends'.

It was these pets, salamanders acquired when he and his wife Christine took a party of schoolchildren to France in 1976, which were used to reduce Livingstone to the level of a music-hall joke. They popped up from time to time in most of the newspapers and became a popular catchphrase guaranteed to raise a laugh.

So was Livingstone a dangerous Trot or a figure of fun? Most newspapers made up their minds on or about July 21st, when he entertained the mother of one of the IRA hunger strikers from the H-blocks of the Maze prison near Belfast. During the early days of his leadership, Livingstone made a series of statements in favour of the withdrawal of British troops from Northern Ireland and in support of the hunger strikers, who were demanding conditions akin to political status. Nonetheless the visit of Mrs Alice McElwee, whose son Thomas was on the 44th day of his fast, created an explosive impact.

Livingstone told the *Evening Standard* (July 21st 1981) that he wanted to break Britain's bipartisan policy on Northern Ireland and commit the Labour Party to a policy of withdrawal. 'The H-block protest is part of the struggle to bring about a free, united Ireland,' he said. 'They have my support, and they have the support of the majority of the Labour Party rank and file. I have been consistently in favour of withdrawal from Ireland and to get away from the idea that [the government is involved in] some sort of campaign against terrorism. It is in fact the last colonial war.'

The incident was condemned by the Conservative leader, Sir Horace Cutler, as self-seeking publicity by Livingstone that had nothing to do with the GLC. Livingstone replied: 'We have a large Irish community who live in fear of intimidation by the police and the security forces. You can go to any pub in Kilburn and actually see the Special Branch sitting there with their ears flapping, looking for any scrap of evidence they can use' (*Daily Express*, July 22nd). He told a press conference that the bipartisan Tory-Labour approach to Northern Ireland had led to over 2,000 deaths and a campaign of repression the like of which has not existed anywhere else in the world ... The eventual freedom and unity of Ireland for the whole working class is a major blow against international capitalism and the rulers of our state' (*News Line*, July 22nd).

Livingstone explained that Mrs McElwee had been invited by a fellow GLC councillor, Andy Harris, a member of the Labour Committee on Ireland, to give members of the Labour group accurate information about the position of the H-block hunger strikers following the death of Bobby Sands (*Daily Mail*, July 22nd). It was this episode which marked the end of Livingstone's salamander days in the media. Thomas McElwee had received sentences of 141 years after being convicted in 1976 of being a member of an eight-man IRA team which exploded 17 bombs in Ballymena. In conventional political terms, Livingstone's support for his cause (without at that stage condemnation of his act of terrorism) was widely considered to be outrageous. 'In his brief spell on the stage, the insufferable Mr Livingstone has proved himself a menace to stability in public life,' said the first of a series of increasingly vitriolic leaders in the *Sun* on July 23rd.

The day after Mrs McElwee's visit, Livingstone warned a private meeting of London's Labour borough leaders that, if the GLC fulfilled its full manifesto programme, its rates could rise by 120 per cent in the spring. His remark was leaked to the press by one of the borough leaders, most of whom were right-wing opponents of Livingstone within the Labour Party, and all of whom faced borough elections the following May. 'The GLC is in a Walt Disney situation,' John O'Grady, then Labour leader of Southwark, told the *Evening Standard* on July 23rd.

It was this build-up of stories that finally drew the concentrated firepower of Fleet Street. The *Daily Mail* comment column of July 24th catalogued the events of Livingstone's week and concluded: 'Mr Livingstone is a doctrinaire clown. But there is little laughing now at the Rake's Progress on which he is leading the Kingdom's capital city. It is a grotesque portent of things to come; of what could happen to all of us if we let the New Left misrule Britain tomorrow as they are misruling London today.'

The papers that day also reported Mrs Thatcher's denunciation in the Commons of Livingstone's support for the IRA hunger strikers: 'If those reports are true, it is the most disgraceful statement I have ever heard,' she said (*Guardian*, July 24th). In its editorial column the *Evening Standard* observed: 'People, they say, get the politicians they deserve. Yet surely no one – but no one – deserves Mr Ken Livingstone. His rule at the Greater London Council goes straight into the cruel-and-unnatural-punishment class.'

From then on there was an almost daily diet of Livingstonia in the press. The day before the royal wedding he welcomed eight demonstrators from the H-Blocks Armagh Committee who kept up a 48-hour fast and vigil on the steps of County Hall during the national celebrations. 'I can't think of a more appalling contrast between this wedding beanfeast and what is happening in Ireland,' Livingstone said, as the demonstrators prepared to release hundreds of black balloons over London during the wedding procession (*Daily Mail*, July 29th). Below this story it was reported that the London borough of Bromley was planning court action against the GLC supplementary rate, due on October 1st, to pay for its fares cut (see Chapter 5).

It was at this stage that rumblings of disaffection started to surface within the Labour group, alarmed that their manifesto programme was being jeopardised by Livingstone's projection in the media. Minutes of a GLC Labour group meeting on July 27th recorded this item under any other business:

> Public relations: There was a general discussion on the issues of press coverage with particular reference to the 120 per

cent rate increase story and the support given by the Leader
and other members to the H-Block Committee. Reference
was made to the expression of views by the Leader
distracting attention from the work of the Council. The
Leader pointed out that he did not arrange for Mrs McElwee
to visit County Hall and that the rate story had become
public despite the fact that he had only spoken about it at a
private meeting. Other Members referred to the need to
avoid the excesses of the Cutler years ... The point was
made that the Group had a responsibility to the party to
show that the programme on which all are agreed can be put
into practice and be made to work.

This pressure on Livingstone was defused by the break-up of the
council for the summer holidays. There was also some confidence
that the group's newly recruited political press officer, Veronica
Crichton, might in future be able to project more positive aspects
of the Labour administration's performance. Livingstone went off
for a fortnight with his wife Christine to Hongkong, Bangkok
and Canton. (They had by then separated, but were still on
friendly terms.) When he returned, it immediately became
obvious that he was unable or unwilling to tone down his public
utterances.

It is hard to do justice to the sheer volume of anti-Livingstone
press coverage. The tabloids appointed full-time Red Ken
correspondents to provide it. Livingstone received a series of
warnings from his colleagues, culminating in a dressing down
from the Labour whips, including his left-wing allies Valerie Wise
and John McDonnell. But Livingstone could not keep his mouth
shut.

In a phone-in on LBC, a London independent radio station,
on August 23rd, he acknowledged that the Labour group was
talking about 'ways of avoiding this press obsession with me'. But
as Godfrey Barker of the *Daily Telegraph* reported the next day:

There are no signs that he will take the obvious way of keeping quiet. In an hour of vintage Livingstone ... he predicted a coup in Britain, declared that Northern Ireland 'does not exist', said that Mr Owen Carron, the new anti-H-block MP, was welcome at County Hall and that calling the IRA 'criminals and murderers' was nonsense. Then he called for legal controls on the Press, described New York as 'an abominable place to live', announced that tourists were taking over parts of London, said that Labour councils 'went through agonies' trying to reduce the rates and that he personally totally opposed rate increases. Later he relaxed over a glass of sherry and told me he was baffled by Press interest in him.

Barker wrote: 'Labour calm has not been aided by the discovery that Mr Livingstone's speaking list for the rest of the year looks, as he put it, "as if I'm running for president". He is booked to speak at nearly every student union. Speaking and spending three hours nightly answering his postbag eats up a good deal of his 70-hour week.'

On August 30th, David Lipsey reported in the *Sunday Times* that Labour leaders on London borough councils planned to send a round-robin letter demanding the resignation of 'rent-a-quote' Livingstone for fear of damage to Labour's chances in the borough elections the following May. The article pointed out that several GLC Labour right-wingers were potential defectors to the Social Democratic Party (SDP) and that four such defections would be enough to overturn Labour's overall majority.

By this stage Livingstone's projection in the press was widely believed to be contributing to Labour's slump in popular support. It was the period of the meteoric rise of the SDP, a new centre party. Its leader, Roy Jenkins, had narrowly missed victory in the Warrington by-election in July; and the budding SDP-Liberal Alliance came briefly to have the appearance of an unstoppable electoral force. It was also the time of the campaign for Tony

Benn to become deputy leader of the Labour Party under its new electoral college rules. Benn was out of action ill during that summer and Livingstone believes he attracted more critical coverage because he became a surrogate target for attacks on Benn and the left.

Press interest in Livingstone did not, however, let up after Benn's narrow defeat at the Brighton party conference in September. Indeed his worst media showing was still to come.

On October 10th 1981, an IRA gang exploded a nail bomb outside the Irish Guards barracks in Chelsea. Mrs Norah Field, a 61-year-old Pimlico widow, was killed after a 6-inch nail penetrated her heart and 39 other people, including children, were injured. It was the worst IRA terrorist outrage on the British mainland since the mid-1970s. Two days later Livingstone gave a talk to the Cambridge University Tory Reform Group. According to the report in *The Times* (October 13th) he said of the terrorists responsible for the attack: 'They are not criminals or lunatics running about. That is to misunderstand them.' *The Times* explained that Livingstone told a student who pressed him for his views on IRA terrorism:

> Nobody supports what happened last Saturday in London. But what about stopping it happening? As long as we are in Ireland, people will be letting off bombs in London. I can see that we are a colonial power holding down a colony. For the rest of time violence will recur again and again as long as we are in Ireland. People in Northern Ireland see themselves as subject peoples. If they were just criminals or psychopaths they could be crushed. But they have a motive force which they think is good.

The *Sun* used half its front page for a comment headlined 'THIS DAMN FOOL SAYS BOMBERS AREN'T CRIMINALS', which blasted out: 'This morning the *Sun* presents the most odious man in Britain. Take a bow, Mr Ken Livingstone, Socialist leader of the

The *Sun* front page, October 13th 1981

Greater London Council. In just a few months since he appeared on the national scene, he has quickly become a joke. Now no one can laugh at him any longer. The joke has turned sour, sick and obscene. For Mr Livingstone steps forward as the defender and apologist of the criminal, murderous activities of the IRA.' The *Sun* continued with the same quotes provided in *The Times* and commented: 'Among the Socialist members of the GLC there must be many who are as outraged and disgusted by Mr Ken Livingstone as the rest of us. While he continues as their leader he is making the very name "Socialist" stink in people's nostrils. They should kick him out. And right this minute.' Similarly vituperative criticism was carried in other tabloids.

'Dear Mr Livingstone. With the price of nails being what it is, we wondered whether the GLC… ' mac, *Daily Mail*, October 14th 1981 (*Daily Mail*)

Livingstone called a press conference to condemn the coverage as 'ill-founded, utterly out of context and distorted'. He announced that he would be taking action against the *Sun* over its 'most odious man in Britain' editorial. (This gave the *Sun* the opportunity for another unapologetic page-one editorial headlined 'NOW THE DAMN FOOL IS TAKING US TO THE PRESS COUNCIL'.)

Sir Horace Cutler, GLC Conservative leader, successfully requisitioned a special council meeting for October 21st to censure Livingstone for 'misusing his position to further his extreme views on subjects over many of which the council has no jurisdiction'. And a round-robin letter from 20 members of the Labour group was delivered to the chief whip, Harvey Hinds, expressing strong dissatisfaction with Livingstone's recent references to the Irish situation after his pledge during the summer that he would concentrate on London affairs.

Over the week before the censure debate, there was mounting pressure on Livingstone. On October 15th he was attacked in the street and sprayed with red paint from an aerosol can while he was on his way to talk to a meeting of businessmen in the City. The next day he cancelled a speaking engagement at a pro-IRA rally. IRA supporters staged a demonstration outside an office in Kilburn where he was holding a political surgery, in order to try to get him to change his mind (*Daily Mail*, October 17th).

But Livingstone survived. His Labour group rallied behind an amendment to Cutler's censure motion. It asked the council to place on record its deep sense of outrage at terrorist acts of violence in London, which had resulted in bloodshed and the loss of innocent lives. It also regretted that the Opposition and Conservative newspapers had given exaggerated attention to the views of individual Labour members in order to distract attention from the threat to jobs, living standards and services of the people of London posed by Mrs Thatcher's disastrous economic policy. It added that the council committed itself to continue to carry out the programme on which Labour was elected and to defend the people of London from punitive measures by the environment secretary, Michael Heseltine, by a campaign of total opposition to his legislation. This was carried by 45 votes to 39 (*Guardian*, October 22nd).

The *Sun* led its front page on the same day with the story headlined 'RED KEN'S REPRIEVE'. *The Times* reported that the price of this reprieve was explained in a strong speech by Illtyd Harrington, the deputy leader, who said: 'Today the GLC is extricating itself from Northern Ireland. It is beyond any doubt that the leadership of this council is now going to concentrate on the constitutional problems coming from central government. This meeting today marks a watershed. We have taken a decision that we are going to get back on to a sane and sensible line.' In fact the reprieve had no price tag attached and Harrington's prognosis did not prove correct. Livingstone was embroiled in links with Sinn Fein at frequent intervals over the next two years. On each occasion he provoked massive press attention and hostility. As far as this book is concerned, however, it is time to break off from a description of the media's treatment of Livingstone to examine its consequences.

The first and most obvious came the day after the GLC censure debate when Bill Pitt won the Croydon North West by-election for the Liberal-SDP Alliance, taking 40 per cent of the vote, compared with a Liberal share of only 10.5 per cent in the 1979 general election. Labour was beaten into third place. Pitt commented: 'Mr Livingstone was directly responsible for this; and he signifies the drift of the Labour Party towards the kind of policies which people simply cannot accept. He was the unacceptable face of Socialism. During the campaign, the people on the doorsteps were disgusted and outraged about his comments on the IRA. It's appalling that he should have said what he did' (*Evening Standard*, October 23rd). Labour leaders were also blaming the GLC's supplementary rate increase, which landed on voters' doormats during the campaign, and the divisive effects of Tony Benn's deputy leadership bid. In reality, it was hard to separate these specific problems for Labour from the general upward surge of the Alliance at that stage. But the episode cemented hostility to Livingstone within wide sections of the Parliamentary Labour Party.

On October 29th, Anne Sofer won a GLC by-election for the SDP in St Pancras North, a previously impregnable Labour stronghold. She had been elected as a Labour member, but had resigned her seat to join the SDP. Sofer took 43.6 per cent of the vote, compared with 9.9 per cent gained by the Liberals the previous May.

Livingstone acknowledges that during the autumn of 1981 he frequently doubted his capacity to continue as leader.

I realised that there was a likelihood of a strong challenge at the group elections the following May. It was only the lack of an effective challenger that made me assume that at the end of the day I would most probably survive. You could get a majority of people to agree that the publicity was bad and that I might be mishandling it. You had great problems when you had to put together a majority of people in agreement that someone was going to be better than me.

There were repeated rumours about six imminent defections to the SDP, threatening Labour's overall majority. (In the end only Paul Rossi, member for Lewisham East, joined Anne Sofer.) There were doubts about the GLC's financial position: whether the Labour right could be persuaded to accept rate increases large enough to satisfy the left that manifesto commitments were not being sacrificed to expediency. And members of Livingstone's own senior team were making no effort to disguise their view that his rent-a-quote style was to blame for their devastatingly bad showing in the press and the opinion polls. It should not be forgotten that the Cambridge speech in which he was reported to have said that the IRA were 'not just criminals' came only a week after the GLC had cut LT fares by 32 per cent. This policy was meant to be the showpiece of Labour's manifesto on which every effort should have been made to concentrate attention.

As it turned out, Livingstone's crucifixion in the media formed the basis of his subsequent political strength and popularity. He became such a controversial figure that he began to get half-hour interview slots on television programmes whose producers realised that he helped their ratings. These appearances allowed viewers to form their own opinions about him and to contrast them with the reputation that had been handed down to them that he was the 'most odious man in Britain'.

Livingstone had one of the best television styles of the period. His directness, self-deprecation, colourful language, complete unflappability under fire and lack of pomposity appealed to millions of people who were not at that stage supporters of his policies. This projection into television also coincided with a big change in news coverage. The next chapter will explain how by Christmas 1981, the judgments from Lord Denning and the Law Lords against the GLC's cheap fares policy shifted the focus of debate on to the ground where the Labour administration most wanted it to be. Livingstone became a media star, projecting a popular image, defending fairly popular policies.

Some thought that Livingstone was a brilliant self-publicist who courted the initial vilification to get himself into the public eye. He said his early projection in the press was unintended, the result of inexperience. 'I wasn't sufficiently capable as a politician of handling the media at that stage. I didn't realise what I have now come to realise that you have got to try and choose the ground on which what you say is presented to the media. You can't allow the media to set the framework of when issues are launched and raised.'

He claims that a lot of the press attention was either unprovoked or inaccurate. For example, the royal wedding story leaked out in spite of a decision by the Labour group to avoid any fuss by simply asking the Palace not to send an invitation. The story about the 120 per cent rate increase was leaked by hostile Labour borough leaders when he was trying to give them private advice about their budget planning.

He remained angry about the infamous Cambridge speech and claimed he never said 'they are not criminals or lunatics running about'. He did not know until later that there were two journalists present at the Cambridge meeting. One of them, Richard Holliday, was the *Daily Mail*'s full-time 'Red Ken watcher' and his story in the next day's paper was relatively low key and more accurate than the Press Association copy carried by the rest of Fleet Street. 'That was the last speech I made without a tape recorder for about 18 months.'

Livingstone also bitterly resents the press intrusion into the lives of friends and relatives. At the start it was 'hilariously funny' to find a press photographer hiding behind his dustbin in the hope that he would come out in the morning with a companion who might be presumed to have stayed the night with him. But the harassment involved others. One reporter visited his mother in Lincoln professing to ask her views on the new Humber Bridge as an opening gambit to start her talking about her son. Another trapped the father of his ex-wife Christine into making derogatory comments about Livingstone during the divorce proceedings. Christine herself was offered and refused a large sum of money for selling her story. One of Livingstone's female aides at County Hall was disturbed early one Sunday morning by a reporter and photographer who had to be taken up to her bedroom before they were persuaded that Livingstone was not sleeping with her.

Later during the administration, Livingstone and Kate Allen, chair of Camden council's women's committee, started a relationship that was also subjected to intrusive media scrutiny.

But whatever criticism Livingstone may have about individual stories and the behaviour of the press, he cannot deny that he failed to take action to stem the flow. His prime objective at the time was to show that the left could handle power and to ensure that the various factions in the Labour group stayed welded together. So why, after the initial press hysteria became obvious, did he continue to fuel it with off-the-cuff remarks that had no bearing on GLC administration? As Livingstone said in 1983:

> Don't forget there was another major motivation. Yes, the left have to show that they can run the GLC. We have to survive this administration. But we also have to show that we are different from what's happened in the past, that we aren't suddenly going to behave differently in office to the way we did before. Therefore if somebody who's asked me to speak on Ireland half a dozen times in the last ten years comes to me after the election and says, will you say so and so, I'm not going to behave differently. Because once you

start down that route, immediately the whole of the activist wing of the party and beyond them the aware sections of the public are going to say: it's just the same old routine of getting into office, then changing and becoming establishment-minded. We don't have to worry about that now, because I think we have achieved in the public consciousness a perception that we are different from our predecessors. It was very important then. Everyone assumes that you have just got to hold the right with you. You haven't. You have got to hold the right and the left. And the left were the ones who had to absorb all the major setbacks and defeats in the first six to nine months.

That answer does not seem to tell the whole of the story. His early exposure in the press was not so much due to the fact that he held firm to his earlier views when situations came up as to his availability and quotability. His diary for the period was full of interview appointments with journalists, many of them coming back for second helpings, having already rubbished him fulsomely in print.

Reporters who spent their lives squeezing half-quotable sentences out of very cautious and rather pompous public figures found Livingstone's laid-back style and colourful language an absolute gift. He seemed not to have been fitted with the restraining bolt which most politicians have installed somewhere between their minds and their mouths. The reporters also enjoyed Livingstone's sense of fun. He emerged, for instance, from his first confrontation with the transport secretary, Norman Fowler, and told the waiting press: 'He asked to see me again. I think he must want me for my body.' Weightier politicians with weightier bodies do not say this sort of thing. Surely he realised that he was helping the media by providing them with ammunition for their attacks?

Livingstone's explanation was as follows:

I'd spent all the time up until May 1981 trying to get any publicity at all for what I was doing and would get no more than a couple of mentions in the *Standard* in a good year. So all of my instincts were geared to getting any media attention whatsoever. During that period I had to try and re-educate myself to pushing off the media at a lot of points.

Until you go through that near hysteria, I don't think that anything can prepare you for it or that you can be told the best way to handle it. You just have to learn from your mistakes as you go ... It must be pretty much like one of those pop groups that suddenly has a hit. Bang, they go from total obscurity to being number one; and half of them end up dead within five years of overdoses and general indulgence.

Livingstone confessed that he found the early press coverage a bit of a joke and he sometimes took the mickey out of journalists. On one occasion, he got *The Times* to report his views on why it was a socialist priority to eat All-Bran. 'It really was hilarious. People would fall around laughing until they realised that there were people out there actually believing it; and then they started to worry. No one could credit that degree of media interest. Everyone was going round vaguely bemused by it all ... We just went through each week thinking: they will lose interest soon, they will go away, they can't possibly sustain all of this for much longer.'

Instead demands for interviews increased, reaching a peak around the time of the royal wedding.

There were all these film crews from CBS, NBC, every television company in the world. They all seemed to want to do an interview about why I wasn't going to the royal wedding. It got to the point where it was taking too much time. So I said to Karen [Karen Brownridge, his personal assistant], I'm not doing any more interviews ... About a day later she came in almost doubled up in hysterics. She said a woman television researcher had offered to go to bed with me if I'd do an interview about the royal wedding. We just fell about. I never did find out whether the offer was just to get through the secretarial barrier or whether it was really true.

What would Herbert Morrison have said? It was hard to escape the conclusion that Livingstone enjoyed riding the storm of media notoriety and revelled in his ability to withstand the buffeting. He remembers with pride the day (August 21st 1981) when Democratic Unionists (Protestants from Northern Ireland) brought over the Dunlop boys, orphans of an IRA atrocity, to embarrass him at County Hall. 'Nothing can be worse than the screaming media mob that day. I met journalists later who had been in the scrum pulling me backwards and forwards. They said they couldn't believe it, that it was terrifying. That doesn't terrify me or frighten me. If you can go through that, there is nothing they can actually do to you, I think. You just lead a much cleaner life than you might otherwise do.'

This capacity to soak up media punishment became one of the keys to Livingstone's survival. But at the time his love-hate relationship with the press was devastating for the morale of his Labour group. Their continued backing for him in crunch votes owed more to their distaste for the press vendetta than to any feelings of personal loyalty and warmth. Livingstone's exposure entirely obscured the policies they were trying to implement and it offended against the principles of collective leadership that they wanted to adopt. As the Livingstone administration completed its first six months in office, it was foundering in a sea of press cuttings.

5 Vandals in Ermine

Problems faced by the GLC's Labour majority could not all be attributed to its leader's unbuttoned lip. Even if Livingstone had been a camera-shy recluse, his administration would still have faced apparently insoluble financial problems. As it was, many doubted it could survive its first year.

Like other local authorities, the GLC was being subjected to heavy pressure from the government to cut spending. In theory, Tory ministers were committed to local autonomy and philosophically opposed to restricting councils' long-standing freedom to levy rates to finance whatever level of spending they deemed appropriate. In practice, the government was determined to do everything necessary to reduce public spending, a key part of its monetarist agenda. Since defence, social security and the NHS were protected by pledges in the Conservative 1979 election manifesto, ministers decided to squeeze services such as housing and education that were mainly provided through local government.

The Cabinet minister responsible for organising this in England was Michael Heseltine, secretary of state for the environment and darling of the blue-rinse brigade at the Tory party conference. He did not want to antagonise these supporters from the shires by taking direct control of local budgets, but he thought he could achieve the intended economies by reorganising the distribution of central government grants to local authorities. In 1979/80 the English councils were planning to spend £14 billion (nearly a quarter of public spending) and the government was funding 61 per cent through grants. So the opportunities for leverage seemed to be substantial.

By the time Livingstone's administration was elected in May 1981, Heseltine had already put through legislation to reform the grant system. The machinery he introduced was so complex that few councillors ever fully understood it, but the upshot was that local authorities in most areas would lose grant as they increased spending above a level that ministers deemed appropriate to provide a standard level of service. In June 1981, Heseltine further tightened the screw when he ordered that all councils, low-spenders as well as high-spenders, would be penalised if they did not deliver a big real-terms cut.

In the GLC's case the sums were particularly devastating. The main plank of Labour's manifesto had been to cut London Transport fares by 25 per cent in October 1981 and freeze them thereafter. Andrew McIntosh had carefully calculated the costs before he led Labour into the May elections: after making good an LT deficit bequeathed by Cutler's Tory administration, the policy would add £100 million to GLC spending in 1981/82. His plan was to recoup that by levying a supplementary rate of 5p in the pound that would have cost the average household £1.31 a week from October 1981.

Heseltine's new grant system destroyed that relatively simple arithmetic. Loss of grant for overspending government norms, combined with penalties for failure to make the required cuts, would almost double the cost to ratepayers.

Far from backtracking, the Livingstone administration decided to enhance the fare-reduction package. When the LT chairman, Sir Peter Masefield, presented his proposals for implementing the pledge, many members of the Labour group were appalled to find that their constituents could end up paying more for public transport. Under a simplified zonal system, Masefield wanted big reductions for commuters on the Underground travelling between the centre and the outer suburbs, but he proposed small fare increases for many bus passengers and people travelling on short Underground journeys in inner London. This might have made sense to a transport economist, but to the politicians it looked like a kick in the teeth to the voters in Labour's inner-city heartlands. The Labour group decided to top up the manifesto commitment to produce a zonal system with no losers. That raised the average fare reduction from 25 per cent to 32 per cent and increased the cost of the package to £117.3 million.

Under Heseltine's funding formula, that level of extra spending would deprive the GLC of £111 million of the £122 million grant for which Cutler's administration had budgeted. The total burden on ratepayers became £228.3 million and the supplementary rate necessary to pay for it increased to 11.9p in the pound. (Ratepayers in inner London were also presented with a 3.2p in the pound supplementary education rate from the ILEA.)

There was never any suggestion in the Labour group that the GLC should cave in to Heseltine's demands and abandon the cheap-fares policy. McIntosh's only criticism of Livingstone was that he 'hadn't got the guts' to resist the pressure of inner London members to turn the 25 per cent package into 32 per cent. But that was a relatively minor element in the total financial package.

The reality was that the public-transport initiative, which came to be known as Fares Fair, was regarded throughout the Labour Party as a moderate and mainstream policy. It was modelled on a fare freeze that had worked well in South Yorkshire since 1975. Labour groups that came to power in other metropolitan counties in May 1981 all had some form of commitment to cheaper fares following a concordat, arranged with the help of the shadow transport secretary, Albert Booth, at Labour's local government conference in Blackpool in February 1981. The man who helped to fix that deal was Peter Mandelson, Herbert Morrison's grandson, who was Booth's political adviser before making his way into broadcasting at London Weekend Television as a staging post before taking over as the party's head of communications and arch-moderniser. Fares Fair could not seriously be portrayed as an eccentric extravagance of London's hard left.

Even after Heseltine's grant penalties, the cost of the

supplementary rate was outweighed by the benefits for most Londoners. Even after the cheap-fares policy was introduced, the GLC rate formed less than a fifth of the average Londoner's 1981/82 rate bill. The exercise produced some transfer of benefit in favour of people who used public transport, but that was what it was meant to do. The policy made sense because it encouraged people to leave their cars at home and relieve London's congestion. It worked in the conditions prevailing in 1981 because LT was not running at full capacity and could carry the extra passengers attracted by cheaper fares without an immediate need for further capital investment. The real cost of the exercise fell on London's businesses, which paid 61 per cent of the GLC rate. But even they benefited when cheap fares reduced their employees' need for pay increases and relieved congestion for transporting their goods. They ended up subsidising the public transport system less than their counterparts in Paris under its right-wing Gaullist mayor, Jacques Chirac, later president of France.

Such arguments did not wash with Heseltine who usually travelled in a chauffeured Jaguar. From his perspective, the GLC and metropolitan counties were wrecking his chances of delivering the public-spending target. In response to his request for economies, 257 of the 413 English authorities offered to make cuts worth £196 million in their spending for 1981/82. But a handful of councils sent in revised budgets increasing their spending by £211 million. Heseltine was made to look foolish and he had no doubts about where to pin the blame. The GLC, West Midlands and Merseyside had together increased their original budgets by £167 million to pay for cheaper fares. Heseltine became convinced that his efforts to curb council spending were being thwarted by a tiny number of 'extremist' Labour councils. He determined that their 'overspending' had to be curbed by more direct means. The GLC was top of his hit list.

In November 1981 he published a new Local Government Finance Bill. It said councils would still be expected to issue their main rate demand in the spring, but they would only be allowed to finance up to a level of spending acceptable to the government. Any authority wanting to spend more would be made to ask for a supplementary rate in June. Businesses were to be at least partially protected from this supplementary. So the burden of extra spending would be cast disproportionately on to domestic ratepayers. Moreover, councils would not be allowed to levy the supplementary unless they won support for it in a referendum of their local electors. If the voters said no, the councils would be forced to ask the government to bail them out with a loan. The strings attached to such loans would be tantamount to spending control from Whitehall.

The strategy was cunning. It allowed Heseltine to argue that he was giving power to the people, but in reality he was dealing all the winning cards to the government. Ministers would decide the spending level at which the referendum trap would be sprung. Their propaganda machine would be set in motion to persuade people that any extra spending was profligate. It was almost inconceivable that the electors would vote to pay supplementary rates that would be loaded against households in order to protect businesses.

Although the legislation did not spell out the details of the scheme, there was no doubt that Heseltine intended the GLC and ILEA to fall into the trap. To avoid the referendum, it looked as if the GLC would have to raise fares and rents, scrap its industry programme and abandon every item of budgetary growth promised to the electorate in May. Alternatively, the councillors could try to keep their promises and pay for them by trebling or quadrupling the domestic rate, but there seemed no chance that such a steep increase would be approved in a referendum. As the Heseltine plan emerged in a series of leaks and statements between July and November, the Labour group began to realise that it would have to choose between surrender, resignation, or tactics of confrontation and defiance.

It was the critical nature of this impending clash that made

Livingstone's colleagues so angry about his media profile at the time. His statements on Ireland and other issues distracted attention from the worst crisis Labour local government had ever faced.

Livingstone's view about how the council should respond was spelt out in a front-page leading article in *Labour Herald*, a socialist weekly paper that he set up with Ted Knight (leader of Lambeth council) and Matthew Warburton in September 1981. Its aim was 'to act as a forum for the preparation of a fightback in local government'. On October 16th they wrote:

> Legislation proposed by the Environment Secretary, Michael Heseltine, to take control of local government finance, places Labour controlled councils in a new and intolerable situation. The manifestos which won Labour control of all the metropolitan counties and many county councils in May were drawn up on the basis that the community as a whole, including industry and commerce, should contribute to the cost of providing services. The basis of this is to be invalidated by a single Act of Parliament. There is no way in which Labour councils can balance the books under the proposed new system without either making impossible cuts or domestic rate increases. *Labour councils must refuse to vote for cuts in services or rent and fare increases. But they must also refuse to vote for rate increases under the Tories' new system.*

This strategy would have breached councils' obligation to balance their books. It had been proposed before by hard-left supporters of Socialist Organiser, but never implemented because it was clearly unlawful. *Labour Herald* explained:

> There will be comrades who will argue that we should resign from councils, let the Tories make the cuts and boycott the resulting by-elections or contest them on the basis that we will refuse to take our seats. Such a course would be

> completely wrong. It would leave the workers in each
> council exposed to massive attacks because they cannot run
> away from their jobs. Ordinary families in the community
> would never understand why the Labour council failed to
> defend them and left them to resist the cuts alone. Labour
> councils must stay and fight ... We should merge our
> campaigns for the restoration of government grant with our
> opposition to the new legislation by imposing a full rates
> freeze in next year's budget and voting down any proposal
> from the Tories to cut ...

The scene was therefore set for confrontation. It remained extremely unlikely that Livingstone would win sufficient support from his Labour group to carry an illegally unbalanced budget at the rate-making meeting in February 1982. But, whether he did or not, it seemed impossible for Labour to stay in office implementing its manifesto promises. The GLC Labour group was to be put on the rack and stretched to breaking-point.

Other problems were also crowding in on the administration. During its first six months in office, the Labour group suffered a series of punishing reverses on important manifesto pledges. A promise that ILEA would cut the price of school meals from 35p to 25p was overturned following legal advice that councillors could be surcharged and disqualified from public office if they sanctioned such 'unreasonable' expenditure. Although a majority of the Labour group voted to go ahead anyway, they could not carry enough members with them to win the vote in the full ILEA council.

Legal and political difficulties also thwarted manifesto plans to stop the transfer of GLC-owned housing to the London boroughs and revive the council's house-building programme. Perhaps even more disturbing were the setbacks to Labour's industry and employment policy, the most innovative part of its manifesto. This programme envisaged setting up a Greater London Enterprise Board which would use funds provided by the council, its workers' pension fund and the financial markets to invest in the industrial regeneration of London. According to Livingstone: 'We discovered that without our permission or knowledge, the officers had rushed off to get a legal opinion from someone who was bound to be damning. Mike Ward [the industry committee chair] then had to spend months getting other legal advice to override that opinion.'

Livingstone blamed many of these early reverses on obstruction by the GLC bureaucracy.

> What the officers realised was that, given our narrow majority, any legal opinion saying we were at risk of surcharge meant they could block what we wanted to do. They rushed off to get the school meals opinion without our being involved. They rushed off to get the GLEB opinion without members' knowledge, We discovered that there had been a tradition in the building that whenever there was a Labour administration, the officers went to known Conservative barristers for opinions. And when there was a Tory administration they went to known Labour barristers – just to be safe. No large corporation in this country ever goes to a barrister and asks for an academic exercise about his view of the law. They go and say: we want to do this, find us a justification.

GLC officers denied these allegations, arguing that local authorities, unlike companies, often need to take a legal opinion to demonstrate that they care about the law. Livingstone's administration responded by issuing instructions that no officer could seek a legal opinion without the permission of the ruling policy committee or, if necessary, the leader himself. The GLC's panel of barrister advisers was also 'balanced up' with people of 'a more radical turn of mind'. That produced a flow of much more favourable opinions.

The one area of the manifesto where such legal gamesmanship

seemed unnecessary was the cheap-fares policy. At no stage did anyone even contemplate that Fares Fair might be illegal. Neither the GLC's politicians, nor its officers, doubted that the council had the statutory discretion to implement Fares Fair. Nor did anyone imagine that the courts would find it unreasonable for the GLC to implement a major policy commitment that had been put before the electorate. These presumptions were shattered in one of the most sensational court defeats that a local authority has ever experienced.

On November 10th, Lord Denning and two fellow Appeal Court judges declared that the GLC's cheap fares were illegal. Two days later, in an unconnected but equally extraordinary development, Heseltine was forced to withdraw his Local Government Finance Bill. In one of the few successful revolts of the Thatcher years, Tory back-benchers rejected his plan for referendums as an alien concept that might spread to national politics and could undermine British notions of democracy.

These events transformed the politics of the GLC. Livingstone had been heading into a political and financial cul-de-sac from which there appeared to be no escape. He would surely not have been able to maintain the support of right-wingers in his group for defying Heseltine, using the unlawful tactics he set out in *Labour Herald*. He could not have satisfied the left if he had given in to Heseltine's demands for cuts. There was disappointment on both wings of the party about lack of progress on implementing several of the main planks in the manifesto. And there was resentment that Livingstone's handling of the media was contributing to these problems. Harvey Hinds, the chief whip, had doubts whether the administration would survive.

Then everything changed. In retrospect it is clear that Livingstone was saved by the mistakes of the judges and his Conservative enemies. But at the time it seemed as if he was being sucked into an ever-deepening crisis, as the GLC had to work out its response to a head-on challenge to its democratic mandate.

The legal challenge that destroyed the GLC's transport policy was set in motion one Sunday lunchtime at the Bird in Hand public house in Gravel Road, Bromley, a prosperous commuter area on the city's south-eastern fringe. Dennis Barkway, Tory leader of Bromley borough council, was having his regular weekend drink with three political chums.

As in so many pubs across London that day, the conversation did not take long to get round to the latest exploits of Red Ken. Wasn't his supplementary rate demand disgraceful? One more nail in the coffin of London's industry and commerce. It was unfair to people in Bromley who lived miles from the nearest Underground station. They'd have to pay more rates without getting the full cheap-fares benefit. What about the stockbrokers commuting in from Kent and Surrey? No extra rates for them, but they'd get the cheap fares when they reached central London. And the tourists! Why should foreigners on holiday be subsidised by the citizens of Bromley?

This was in July 1981 when the press campaign against Livingstone was at its peak. Barkway later suggested that he and his fellow councillors might have done nothing more than grumble about the supplementary rate if they had not been so outraged by Livingstone's comments on Ireland, gays and the Royal Family. As it was, they began to ask themselves whether the GLC's cheap-fares policy was legal.

Surely, they mused, councillors had a legal obligation to act reasonably. Anything more unreasonable than this supplementary rate demand was hard, they thought, to imagine. And so Barkway, charged up by nothing more than his usual pint of lemonade, resolved to act. He consulted the Bromley council solicitor, Richard Pugh, who agreed there might be the basis for a legal challenge. An opinion from counsel confirmed that the GLC might have acted unreasonably and with unlawful haste.

That might easily have been the end of the matter. Court action was going to be expensive and Bromley was never keen to spend the ratepayers' money. But Barkway persisted and persuaded his Tory group to press ahead on the assumption that other Tory boroughs would join in later with financial backing. They never did. Barkway said he received one letter from Peter Bowness, Tory leader of Croydon and chairman of the London Boroughs Association, warning that the action hadn't got a snowball's chance in hell.

Most experts assumed the Bromley action would fail because they knew what the Labour government intended when it passed the Transport (London) Act in 1969, giving the GLC power to make grants to the London Transport Executive 'for any purpose'. During the second reading in the House of Commons, Richard (later Lord) Marsh, then transport minister, said: 'The Council might wish, for example, the Executive to run a series of services at a loss for social or planning reasons. It might wish to keep fares down at a time when costs are rising and there is no scope for economies. It is free to do so. But it has to bear the cost' (*Hansard*, December 17th 1968, cols. 1247–8).

The Bromley action was thrown out by the Divisional Court on October 28th and swiftly went to appeal before the Master of the Rolls, Lord Denning, sitting with Lord Justice Oliver and Lord Justice Watkins. On November 10th they unanimously declared that the fares cut and the supplementary rate were unlawful. The most vigorously damning judgment came from Oliver, who focused on a clause in the act that said the LT Executive had a duty to balance its books 'as far as practicable'. He interpreted that to mean the Executive had an overriding obligation to run its affairs on ordinary business lines and the Fares Fair experiment had been a clear breach of the businesslike principle. Oliver's devastating conclusion was that the GLC did not have the power to run LT at a deficit in the interests of Londoners.

This was hard enough for the GLC Labour group to swallow. But Denning and Watkins produced concurring judgments larded with comments of such political insensitivity that any question of their legal merit was obscured in the ensuing public debate.

Denning said that the majority on the GLC had decided to honour their election manifesto 'come what may', even after they had been told that it would injure ratepayers far more seriously than they had originally realised (before Heseltine's grant penalties were invoked). A manifesto issued by a political party in order to get votes was not to be regarded as a gospel. It was not a covenant, Denning said. 'Many electors did not vote for the manifesto, they voted for the party. When a party was returned to power, it should consider what it was best to do, and what was practical and fair.'

Watkins said that the council's decision arose out of a hasty, unlawful and arbitrary use of power. 'Gladstone has said that power was the true test of a man or a class or a people. Just after the election the Leader of the GLC had sought out Sir Peter Masefield [chairman of LT] and said that the GLC intended forthwith to put their fares policy into effect. He was talking in a position of strength to a chairman who seemed to have no authority. It was a bad case of an abuse of power, which totally disregarded the interests of the ratepayers.'

Their observations caused apoplexy on the left and were the foundation of much of the ensuing popular support for the GLC. The whole struggle of the Labour left had been to shape the internal mechanisms of the party to ensure that its representatives and leaders carried out manifesto policies. Here was 82-year-old Lord Denning suggesting that the first thing an elected council should do on assuming office was to put its manifesto on one side and consider 'what it was best to do'. Here was Lord Justice Watkins disapproving of Livingstone's 'abuse of power' in giving directions to a GLC appointee to prepare options for the council. If there was a single policy understood by the electorate in May 1981, it was Labour's commitment to cut fares. What right had unelected judges to flout the will of the people by declaring that policy invalid?

Denning and Watkins did have respectable legal grounds for the judgment they gave. Councillors (unlike MPs) are bound to go through certain approved motions in reaching their decisions. They must demonstrate the reasonableness of their actions partly by showing that they have accumulated and studied relevant data before they do anything. But the GLC's lawyers believed that the council had made its decisions correctly. They were confident that the judgment would be overturned on appeal to the House of Lords.

Livingstone recalls: 'We were told that we might just lose on a technicality to save Denning's face, but we'd be able to do it all properly and the fares would stay down. Therefore we were absolutely stunned to find that we lost on all the basic points of law. That's why we weren't geared up for the media campaign. We were completely unprepared.'

Five Law Lords unanimously ruled on December 17th that the GLC's cheap-fares policy and the supplementary rate which funded it were unlawful. Four of them – Lord Wilberforce, Lord Keith, Lord Scarman and Lord Brandon – accepted most of Oliver's strict statutory interpretation. As Scarman put it: 'It is plain that the 25 per cent overall [fares] reduction was adopted not because any higher fare level was impracticable, but as an object of social and transport policy. It was not a reluctant yielding to economic necessity, but a policy of preference. In doing so the GLC abandoned business principles. That was a breach of duty owed to the ratepayers and wrong in law.'

Lord Diplock disagreed. He accepted that the GLC could deliberately choose to subsidise LT in pursuit of its public-transport policies, but he said Fares Fair was unlawful because it imposed an undue financial burden on London's ratepayers. He implied that the GLC might have got away with a 25 per cent fares cut, but the enhancement of the package to 32 per cent was unlawful because it triggered extra grant penalties from Mr Heseltine. 'It was thus a breach of the fiduciary duty owed by the GLC to the ratepayers.' This opened up the suspicion among Labour groups throughout the country that the judiciary had given Heseltine's targets something closely akin to the force of law. Heseltine was in no hurry to disillusion them.

Livingstone's opinion was that the judges' decisions were politically motivated.

> All through the cases I'd been told it would be better for me not to go near the court, because my presence would upset the judges. The judges were just generally antagonistic to us. I now think that whatever case we'd ended up on in the Court of Appeal and the House of Lords, we would have lost. If we hadn't been done on the fares, I most probably would have been done on the Camden surcharge [see pp. 54–5]. I think it was the reaction against the judges on fares that most probably saved the Camden councillors because the judges at that stage had started to pull back.
>
> At the time we were advised that we had a very good chance of winning in the House of Lords. When the names of the judges to hear the case were published, we were told that was good, because they were all the liberal judges. In retrospect we would have been better off with deeply conservative people in the legal sense of a strict constructionalist approach to the law. We had the misfortune, I think, to get five judges, four of whom liked to dabble in the classic American supreme court sense, to interpret the law in a political way.

Misfortune or not, the GLC Labour group was faced just eight days before Christmas with the complete collapse of its central policy plank. The transport chairman, Dave Wetzel, condemned the Law Lords as 'vandals in ermine'. They had, he said, done more damage to public and private transport than any vandal does when he smashes a light on a bus or snaps an aerial on a car.

Livingstone summoned a press conference to challenge the government. Unless ministers rushed through emergency legislation, the result of the judgment would be a 200 per cent increase in fares, cuts in services, the complete abandonment of

Livingstone's face shows the strain after the Law Lords' ruling on December 17th 1981 (*Guardian, Garry Weaser*)

some bus routes, closure of Underground stations and branch lines, and the loss of about a quarter of LT's 60,000 jobs, he said.

In truth no one knew exactly what the judgment meant. The Law Lords said Fares Fair was illegal, but they gave no guidance about what level of fares subsidy would be lawful. Masefield's advisers at LT suggested that a 150 per cent fare increase might be enough to keep within the law. The Transport Secretary, David Howell, said 60 per cent would be adequate, enough to restore the status quo of the original Cutler budget for 1981/82 by reversing the October fares cut and allowing for one year's inflation.

It was generally assumed at the time that both Livingstone and Howell were plucking figures out of the air to suit their political convenience. Howell's interest was to demonstrate that the whole mess was the fault of Livingstone and the loony left; he did not find palatable the idea that nice old Sir Horace might have been happily breaking the law for years with his more modest dollops of subsidy. Livingstone's interest was to demonstrate that the Law Lords' decision would produce mayhem in the streets of London as people took to their cars to avoid absurdly high bus and tube fares. He wanted to force the government to solve the problem with legislation to restore the GLC to the position everyone had believed pertained before Denning's judgment.

But Livingstone was not making the numbers up. They were being provided by council officials who were trying to find an administrative solution that would avoid another legal challenge. By December 23rd the officers had prepared an even more gloomy interpretation of the judgments. They said that even a trebling of fares would be insufficient for the GLC to maximise its revenues, as the judges said it must. The council would also have to abandon concessionary off-peak fares for pensioners. On the same day Larry Smith, Transport and General Workers Union national executive officer, warned of plans for a combined Underground and bus strike in protest at the Law Lords' ruling. If it lasted more than a day London would seize up 'like a glue pot', he said.

For the GLC Labour group, one fortunate by-product of the judgment was the first sustained bout of supportive media coverage about the wisdom of the cheap-fares policy. But after the Christmas holiday the divisions opened. On the right there were councillors who were terrified that they could be personally surcharged for the £125 million deficit created by Fares Fair, bankrupted and disqualified from office. On the left there was growing despondency about remaining in control of a council which was thwarted in all its key objectives. Should not the Labour group resign en bloc, or go into majority opposition? If the council was legally obliged to carry out Tory policies, let Tory councillors do their own dirty work.

This was similar to the argument Livingstone had been using during the autumn in the face of Heseltine's proposed new law to control local-government spending through referendums. But now he put forward an entirely different strategy. Labour should stay in office, but refuse to put up the fares. It should defy the law and force the government to intervene.

Even those of us who were close observers at County Hall at that time were never sure whether Livingstone seriously intended this illegal tactic to succeed. Many suspected that it was designed to preserve his left-wing credentials without sacrificing office. According to this point of view, it was obvious that the full GLC council would never pass a resolution recommending open defiance of the law. So, the cynics argued, Livingstone was playing a calculated political game. He wanted to appear defiant, but he also wanted to be beaten so that he could stay as leader of the GLC implementing the fare increases with the excuse that the manifesto had been betrayed not by him, but by the votes of the Labour right.

But Livingstone's own explanation of events was plausible and, if nothing else, was illuminating because it showed how he wanted to be remembered.

> My first problem was to make sure the left didn't come to the conclusion that there was no point in carrying on. We were perceived (wrongly as it happens) as the first left administration anywhere. The last thing we could do was to fail. At the end of the day, if we were smashed and totally defeated, that was an acceptable end to the exercise. But to give up, or to take ourselves out of control when there was still something we could do, was not. It would immediately have painted the whole of the left for the foreseeable future as people who might win power but then might actually be unable to deliver, who might give up or disintegrate. And that was a stain which would be absolutely indelibly sloshed all over us by the right wing.

Livingstone says he was supported in this by the attitude of the unions. 'They were determined that we should stay in office. We convened a meeting of all the transport unions. And the advice of all of them was: you must be joking even thinking of resigning; we expect you to stay and fight because if you go out of office, there's going to be Tories running the show.'

But, if resignation was unacceptable, so was implementing the Law Lords' ruling.

> My worry was that if we went ahead and voted for the fare increases and cuts in services, we would let the government off the hook. Once we started to comply, they didn't need to do anything. I could see us getting in a position where we devastated the public transport system in London. The government would have just sat back and crowed; and we would have ended up destroying ourselves as well as the public transport system.
>
> My guess was that if the council refused to comply with the Law Lords' judgment, the government had to move. Either it had to take over and run the system itself, in which case it couldn't go along with devastating cuts, given that there were 49 Tory MPs in the London area. Or it would have had to back down and let us have the legislation we needed to run it as we wanted.

So, as the GLC launched its public campaign in defence of Fares Fair (using £300,000 of ratepayers' money), Livingstone started to work on members of his group to persuade them that the line was defiance, not resignation.

Of course that was not a sustainable long-term strategy. The GLC could not have passed a budget to pay for continuing Fares Fair. If it had tried, its rate demands would have had no legal status and it would have rapidly become bankrupt. Livingstone maintains, however, that the strategy was viable in the short term.

> The only time you can effectively defy government is when you are being asked to do something and refuse to do it. We would have reached a crunch within days. Remember the

Fares unfair: Valerie Wise, Ken Livingstone, Andy Harris and Tony Banks campaign against the London Transport charges (*Guardian, Garry Weaser*)

coverage at the time – cameras, telly, everyone going berserk. Just imagine the largest council in the country, refusing to comply with the law as laid down by Denning. It would have meant an immediate constitutional crisis. It would have been the biggest act of defiance against central government by a local authority ever. We were talking about a third of a million pounds a day in illegal spending. It would have been a major issue in Parliament. It would have meant the government had to do something quick.

For a while it looked as if Livingstone might just pull off this strategy. By January 11th 1982, GLC and LT lawyers had agreed what measures would be needed to comply with the Law Lords judgment. They included an immediate doubling of fares on March 21st, to be followed by further increases of 50–100 per cent at some unspecified time in the future. Pensioners' bus passes were to be retained pending legislation promised by the government to ensure their legality. But there were to be 15 per cent service cuts and other savings. The Labour group decided by 23 to 22 to accept Livingstone's recommendation to vote against this package at a meeting of the full council on January 12th. But councillors would be allowed to follow their consciences on a free vote.

Meanwhile in the Tory camp, Sir Horace Cutler was preparing a strategy to expose Labour's divisions. He would move an amendment for a 60 per cent fare increase, as proposed by the transport secretary David Howell. That would be defeated by Labour. Then the Tories could abstain on the main motion, leaving Labour split down the middle.

All went according to plan until the ground was cut from under Cutler's feet by legal advice from the GLC director-general, Sir James Swaffield. Any substantial departure from the officers' recommendation 'could mean that the council was in breach of its statutory duty and in contempt of court'. The Tories would themselves risk being surcharged for any additional costs that might arise. Panic spread along the Tory benches. Messages were passed in from wives and husbands in the members' restaurant beseeching spouses not to put their farms and Bentleys at risk for a silly political principle. After a few more procedural manoeuvres, the Tories caved in – just enough. Three of them went into the division lobby alongside 21 Labour and three Liberal-SDP Alliance members to provide a 27:24 victory for legality. The rule of law prevailed.

This Tory disarray sustained the morale of the Labour group and Livingstone's credibility as leader at a point of potential humiliation. But some of those closest to him were convinced that he was bluffing when he urged the group to defy the law. The deputy leader, Illtyd Harrington, who flew back from America on Concorde to attend the vital group meeting, said:

That was the point when the moderates held the ground. There is no doubt in my mind that, if we had voted not to give a direction to LT, then we would have had a commissioner sent in and a major part of our executive function would have gone from us ... Some of us had to make decisions to obey the law to sustain the administration ... I think Ken was opportunistic because he knew that the law would have to be obeyed, but he knew other people would see to it that it was done. He was in a hell of a position: the darling of the left. He had no option but to vote with them. I understand that.

Idealist or opportunist? There were two possible outcomes on January 12th: confrontation or compliance. Livingstone says he could have coped with confrontation. What he showed subsequently was that he lived with compliance. In a sense he never made the choice for himself. By its collective vote the GLC determined that Livingstone and his administration would head for legitimacy. Like thousands of politicians before him, Livingstone decided that, since he could not do all that he wanted, he would do the most that he could. Under pressure, he moved to a compromise that would keep the show on the road.

It took the left a little while to follow suit. There was another serious split in the Labour group a fortnight later when the council was due to vote through the detail of the fare increases. This time Livingstone voted with the right to accept the LT proposals, arguing that further resistance would be an empty gesture. The package was defeated by an unholy alliance of left-wingers and Tories, but LT went ahead and raised the fares anyway.

John McDonnell, the most vocal of the left-wingers, was appalled by Livingstone's behaviour. 'To go into court, lose and then have our own side voting in favour of the ruling, plus Livingstone as well in the second vote, was catastrophic, quite honestly. It destroyed the credentials of the leadership for the hard left within the Labour group for a long period of time,' he said.

On January 29th some of the left councillors, including McDonnell, Dave Wetzel and Valerie Wise, started the Can't Pay Won't Pay campaign. They urged passengers to refuse to pay extra after the fares went up and to give the conductor or ticket collector a 'promise-to-pay' slip with their names and addresses. This would explain that their action was a protest against the increases enforced by the Law Lords' ruling and that there was no intent to defraud. Can't Pay Won't Pay never became a mass campaign. Wetzel, among others, ended up in Lavender Hill magistrates' court where he was found guilty of fare dodging. During the proceedings the magistrate criticised him for making chimpanzee-like gestures.

Meanwhile Livingstone was insisting that all Labour's efforts should be channelled into the council's official Keep Fares Fair campaign to change the law. Sympathetic planners at Labour-controlled Camden council told him that, if the fares went up and services were cut, they could take court action against the GLC for failing to provide an efficient transport system. (This argument became the basis of the subsequent strategy for getting round the Law Lords' judgment and cutting fares again in 1983.)

Livingstone's official campaign achieved great success in winning the argument for cheap fares. In the public debate he ran rings round the faltering transport secretary, Howell, who at times showed signs of political stage fright. But at no point did the GLC look likely to convince the government to back down and legalise Fares Fair. It won the support of many Tory commuters who had enjoyed paying less for their season tickets. But it did not mobilise the people who were probably worst affected by the Law Lords' judgment: the poor, the unemployed and the house-bound women, for whom cheap fares had been a passport to greater freedom.

The continued defiance of the left did not last long. On February 8th the group passed a budget plan for the new financial year which implied acceptance of the fare increases and other manifesto defeats. And at council meetings on February 15th and 16th, Labour members unanimously voted it through.

Over the next two months McDonnell, who had been the most effective of Livingstone's critics on the left, began to emerge as one of his closer political allies. In May, with Livingstone's backing, he was promoted by the group to the key job of chairing the finance committee in which he gained a reputation for tough scrutiny of his colleagues' expenditure bids, pleased to expand spending, but determined to avoid wasteful over-budgeting. At the same elections Valerie Wise was appointed to chair a new women's committee, a pioneering venture later copied elsewhere, which produced an important resource centre for the women's movement. Wetzel stayed in the transport chair and began to get down to the work of producing the 'balanced plan' of more modest fare reductions which the GLC eventually got through the courts in January 1983. Mike Ward stayed at industry to push through the painstaking detail of the job-creation strategy that he had prepared for the Labour manifesto. John Carr, as chairman of the staff committee, proceeded to reform the equal opportunities policy, using contract compliance to spread best practice among the council's suppliers. Tony McBrearty, who had supported McIntosh in preference to Livingstone in 1981, took over from Gladys Dimson as chair of housing and started to redefine the GLC's strategic housing role within the constraints of the earlier defeats. Sir Ashley Bramall, the former Labour leader of ILEA, whom Livingstone had once criticised so bitterly, was chosen by the group to be the next GLC chairman. So started what may be called the second Livingstone administration. The Labour group got down to the art of the possible.

The change was not lost on critics from the left. *London Labour Briefing*, which was then coming under the control of the Socialist Organiser faction of the Labour left, had attacked Livingstone's refusal to support Can't Pay Won't Pay. In its April issue, there were four articles of fierce criticism against the 'compromising' policies of the GLC Labour group.

Keith Veness, a Chartist member of Islington Central constituency Labour party and one of Livingstone's long-standing political friends, wrote:

> As a result of the Denning and House of Lords judgments, the GLC is now being forced to tear up the main plank of our manifesto ... A slow, gnawing process of disillusion is being started that will result in a gradual wasting of our support. There is not now sufficient reason to stay in office [at the GLC], despite the plans in employment, education and housing. These are little more than palliatives and will neither generate the enthusiasm we need nor make up for the failure to confront our enemies in the government and the Law Courts. Majority opposition is now the only honourable course for the comrades at County Hall to follow. A decision to do anything else is the road to disaster. This is the acid test to distinguish socialists from socialist administrators. It cannot and must not be ducked.

In an open letter, John Bloxam and John O'Mahoney of Socialist Organiser said: 'You talk about doing better next time, in a different fight later. But if the GLC left will not fight for its main manifesto plank, what will it fight for?' This is exactly the sort of argument that Livingstone himself would have deployed against previous generations of Labour leaders. Had he sold out?

Certainly Livingstone's political alibi was better than Goodwin's in 1975. He kept the faith until he was defeated in the council. But both Livingstone and Goodwin were overcome by surprise circumstances that were never envisaged in their manifestos. For Livingstone it was the Law Lords. For Goodwin it was hyperinflation at 26 per cent. Both chose in the end to buckle down, stay in power and make the best of it.

'Being defeated is not a betrayal,' Livingstone says. 'Carrying on fighting and using the building to carry on that fight is what the Labour movement expects its representatives to do. What they can't ever forgive is when they give up without a fight.'

The GLC went on to deliver a great deal within the narrow areas left to it by the law. For now it may be worthwhile drawing together the strands of the story so far. Livingstone's failure to button up in the face of the early media campaign against him made him into a nationally known politician, but also caused a serious strain on the loyalty of his Labour group. Heseltine's efforts to curb council spending changed the arithmetic of implementing the manifesto to such an extent that it began to seem politically impossible to achieve. The Labour group was plausibly heading for disintegration.

Then, due to a maverick legal challenge by the Bromley councillors, the cheap-fares policy was outlawed. Efforts to defy the judgment and campaign against it gave Livingstone the best possible issue to win support for his policies and rehabilitate his popular image. The judgment also scaled down the cost of Labour's programme to manageable proportions. It moderated the left-wing councillors' aspirations and eventually created a surprising unity in the Labour group. Yet Livingstone continued to be attacked by the media for being a raving lefty, largely due to minor items of expenditure on grants to gays, feminists and blacks. People just failed to notice that on or about January 12th, 1982, Livingstone's GLC went legit.

6 Brent Crossed

Three weeks after the Law Lords' judgment, when the GLC Labour group's morale was at its lowest ebb, a giant sign was erected on top of County Hall showing the number of unemployed in London: a shocking total of 326,238. It was placed on a parapet, at an angle which made it clearly visible from the Houses of Parliament across the river, to provide a constant reminder of Labour outrage at the economic policies of the Thatcher government.

This sign was updated every month to reflect the latest official jobless total and it became the most public manifestation of the GLC's campaigning role in the wider forum of national politics. The ruling Labour group used the council's resources of cash, expertise and visibility to mount a running guerrilla war against the government. It exhausted countless hours of civil servants' and ministers' time by rooting out anomalies in legislation and statutory instruments that could be exploited for propaganda purposes.

For example, the GLC public services and fire brigade committee, an apparently humdrum municipal appendage, tied the Home Office up in knots over regulations governing local authorities' responsibilities to plan for civil defence in case of nuclear war. Legal opinions were commissioned which enabled the committee's chairman, Simon Turney, to prove that the GLC could evade government orders to make civil-defence preparations. This provided ammunition for about 150 other local authorities which declared themselves nuclear-free zones as a gesture of protest at government policies on defence and civil nuclear energy. It obliged the Home Secretary to bring new regulations before Parliament in an attempt to enforce compliance with the government's will.

These propaganda raids into the national political arena were backed up in many cases by expensive advertising campaigns. Over the first three years of the Livingstone administration they cost Londoners about 17p each, a tiny part of GLC outgoings, but huge in comparison with previous local government practice. The result was that the council took on the appearance of a vigorous fighting machine. For Livingstone and the left, the use of the GLC as a platform for political expression was some compensation for defeats at the hands of government and the law that denied them the opportunity to expand services as promised. Their unemployment sign could not actually reduce unemployment, but it could demonstrate a capacity to keep up the fight.

It might have been thought that Labour MPs would have welcomed this feisty anti-Conservative campaign, but most of them were irritated by it. Livingstone made no secret of the fact that he regarded the GLC as the 'alternative Opposition' and thought it was doing a better job than the official one in Parliament. Individual Labour MPs, including many on the left, found it infuriating that Livingstone could summon a press conference and get his points across in the media, when their own speeches in the Commons went ignored by the political correspondents. His publicity was bad for their egos.

A more serious problem for Labour was that Livingstone was using the GLC platform to attack the performance of his own party leader, Michael Foot. For example, when Foot criticised Tony Benn for breaking ranks with the parliamentary leadership in a Commons debate on energy policy, Livingstone's paper, *Labour Herald*, responded: 'The message from the Party to its parliamentary representatives must be ignore Foot and back Benn' (November 20th 1981). The paper argued against the expulsion of the Militant Tendency 'or the outlawing of any other Trotskyist group from the Labour Party' (March 26th 1982). It

Fleet Street's three favourite bogeymen gather at the *Labour Herald* rally, Labour Party Conference, Blackpool October 1982 (*Camera Press*)

launched a virulent attack on Foot's stance over the 1982 Falklands war after he supported the government decision to send a naval task force: 'The only credible claim to sovereignty of the Malvinas is that of Argentina. It is the Argentine nation to which the claim attaches, not the corrupt junta which is currently in control of it' (May 7th 1982). In an editorial on the same day, headlined 'THREE YEARS OF NOT FIGHTING THATCHER', the paper condemned the party leadership's failure to provide a credible alternative in the face of the government's 'concerted attack on British workers, particularly blacks, trade unionists and women'.

Such statements of opinion, repeated by Livingstone at political rallies around the country, did not endear him to the party leadership. Michael Foot had been a rebel himself for most of his political career and he was not likely to be over-sensitive about being attacked in a political weekly with a circulation of only about 5,000. He was bound to recognise, however, that derogatory statements by the Labour leader of the GLC fuelled discord within the party in a damagingly newsworthy way. And Foot was unable to ignore the political impact of Livingstone's frequent forays into the debate on Northern Ireland, showing a degree of identification with the Sinn Fein cause that bordered on outright political support.

Although Sinn Fein was a political party that fought elections in Northern Ireland, its leaders did not disown the violent tactics of the Provisional IRA. This made it unacceptable, not only to the British government, but also to a wide range of Republican sentiment. For example, Charles Haughey, then Ireland's prime minister, said on November 1st 1982: 'Speaking on behalf of the overwhelming majority of the Irish people, North and South, I should immediately and categorically condemn the decision of the Sinn Fein Ard Fheis at the weekend to require their election candidates to be, in their words, "unambivalent in support of the armed struggle". This represents a serious and ominous development in our national life. No political organisation can adopt such a policy and be regarded as legitimate or democratic.'

Livingstone's involvement with Sinn Fein became particularly controversial towards the end of 1982, when 26 members of the GLC Labour group invited Gerry Adams and Danny Morrison, newly elected Sinn Fein members of the Northern Ireland Assembly, to come to London for private talks at County Hall. The visit was scheduled for December 14th and the group's political press officer was deliberately kept in the dark for fear that she would blow her top. The initiative was clearly going to upset her efforts to rehabilitate the GLC's image in the eyes of Fleet Street and the electorate.

Steve Bundred, vice-chairman of the police committee and prime instigator of the invitation, circulated a news release that caused an initial flurry of hostile press coverage on Monday December 6th. That evening Michael Foot let it be known that he had sent a letter to Livingstone repudiating the visit. Although he did not ask for the invitation to be withdrawn, he suggested Livingstone and his colleagues should tell their guests that the

Labour Party was absolutely opposed to 'the barbarous methods of the Provos and other terrorist groups'.

Later that night, in one of the worst ever atrocities in Northern Ireland, a bomb exploded at the Droppin Well pub disco in Ballykelly, County Derry, killing 16 and injuring 66. A device containing 10 pounds of explosive had blown out the wall of the single-storey hall where about 150 people, half of them British soldiers, were drinking and dancing. This brought the reinforced concrete roof, weighing many tons, crashing down on to the crowded dance floor.

In the Commons the following day, Mrs Thatcher said it would be intolerable if the GLC invitation was not withdrawn. The SDP leader, Roy Jenkins, told Foot: 'Following the carnage at Ballykelly, it would be an outrage if the visit went ahead.'

But Livingstone did not back down. He put his name to a statement confirming the visit and suggested that the bombing was an attempt by the Irish National Liberation Army to discredit the IRA's political wing. In its report on Wednesday December 8th, the *Sun* began: 'GLC leader Red Ken Livingstone became the most hated man in Britain last night after he insisted: The IRA's spokesmen are still welcome in London.'

Throughout that Tuesday and Wednesday the County Hall corridors where the councillors had their offices were thronged by journalists, stirring up the story and putting tremendous pressure on the 26 signatories to the invitation to change their minds. Several who were disturbed at the turn events had taken were reluctant to be bullied into cancelling the visit by what they regarded as media harassment. Others became convinced that, however right it might have been to invite Sinn Fein, it was impossible to have a rational discussion with them in the charged political atmosphere after Ballykelly.

During Wednesday, Foot had a private discussion with Livingstone at which he urged him to withdraw the invitation. Livingstone said he would report the leader's views to a meeting the following afternoon of the 26 signatories. That meeting, which plausibly would have forced Livingstone into an embarrassing retreat, never took place. On the Wednesday evening, the home secretary signed exclusion orders under the Prevention of Terrorism Act banning Adams and Morrison from entering mainland Britain. The act entitled the Home Secretary to exclude anyone who 'is or has been ... involved in the commission, preparation or instigation of acts of terrorism'. So, once again, Livingstone was allowed to escape from a difficult political corner by having the decision taken out of his hands. Sinn Fein was able to argue that the Home Secretary's decision:

> proves what we have been saying all along, that the British government fears the message which Republicans wish to deliver, and were prepared at their peril to deliver, to concerned politicians in London. We want to see an end to the war in our country and we believe that peace can only be achieved when the British withdraw, allow the Irish people the right to self-determination and allow the Irish people to resolve their differences. It is now ludicrous for the British government to claim that the Six Counties are part of the United Kingdom and then go and exclude its so-called citizens from entering one part of Britain – London.

This propaganda victory for Sinn Fein was consolidated when Livingstone wrote an article in *The Times* on December 11th attacking the exclusion order. 'If there is any evidence that the Sinn Fein representatives are involved in terrorism, then they should be arrested and charged. On the other hand, if they are free to walk the streets of Belfast, then they should be free to do so in London. The real explanation of the ban is that it is a response to the hysteria whipped up by the press.' Livingstone stated that he deplored all acts of violence without qualification and concluded: 'The lesson to be drawn from the history of Ireland is that force cannot be used to impose a solution. Therefore at some point a dialogue must begin. Those who have

Ken Livingstone and Gerry Adams give a press conference at County Hall,
July 26th 1983 (*Guardian, E. Hamilton West*)

condemned our initiative must say what they propose as an
alternative. Or are they prepared to see another thirteen years of
horror?'

At a GLC council meeting on December 14th (the day the
Sinn Fein talks would have been held), Livingstone was defeated
in a censure motion moved by the Conservatives over the issue of
the invitation. Nine of his fellow Labour councillors abstained.
This was one of three occasions at various stages of his local-
government career when members of his own party allowed
opposition censure motions to succeed. Each time he carried on
regardless.

The affair totally obscured the Labour group's attempt to win
support for a new round of London Transport fare cuts which it
was preparing to take through the courts. It also distracted
attention from efforts to embarrass the Tories by setting up an
inquiry into councillors' links with housing associations. But, in
spite of criticism from other GLC Labour councillors, Livingstone
continued to push the Irish issue. On February 26th 1983 he went

to Northern Ireland for a weekend visit as the guest of Sinn Fein. Before he flew back the next day he told a press conference that Provisional Sinn Fein 'is not the caricature that it is made out to be'. It was, he said, developing socialist policies and a desire for peace.

At the general election in June 1983, Gerry Adams was elected MP for Belfast West, but refused to take his seat in the Westminster Parliament. Livingstone and Jeremy Corbyn, the newly elected Labour MP for Islington North, invited him to London on July 26th. Adams said he saw the visit as part of a long-term attempt to open up a dialogue with the British people and their representatives and to break down the 'wall of disinformation' erected by the British government around Northern Ireland. He was given an unprecedented opportunity to put his views over to the public in extended television interviews.

A month later Livingstone said on Irish state radio that what Britain had done to Ireland over 800 years was worse than what Hitler had done to the Jews in the Second World War. His views were condemned by contenders in the election to succeed Michael Foot as national party leader. 'Extraordinarily eccentric', said Neil Kinnock; 'absurd and offensive', said Roy Hattersley; 'inflicting shame on the whole Labour Party', said Peter Shore; and 'most unfortunate Ken Livingstone put it the way that he did', said Eric Heffer.

On each of these occasions, Livingstone's association with Sinn Fein fuelled major controversy in the media. His stance also contributed to a breakdown of relations between the GLC and London's monopoly evening newspaper, the *Evening Standard*. The GLC withdrew all its advertising from the *Evening Standard* to try to force it to print an apology for a cartoon by Jak that Livingstone held to be offensively anti-Irish. The Press Council subsequently condemned the GLC's action as 'a blatant attempt by a local authority to use the power of its purse to influence the contents of a newspaper and coerce the editor'. Livingstone called the Press Council 'an appalling Tory body' and kept up the

The controversial Jak cartoon, *Evening Standard*, October 29th 1982 (*Express Newspapers Limited*)

advertising ban. By doing so, he ensured continuing hostility from a paper that might otherwise have been more inclined to support the GLC in its later fights with the government.

Livingstone could not deny that he allowed his commitment to British withdrawal from Northern Ireland to get in the way of his domestic responsibilities as leader of the GLC. Nor did he wish to do so. He explained his passionate commitment to Irish unity in 1983, during which he said that he 'boiled with outrage' when he read histories of Britain's colonial exploitation of the Irish. As he put it then:

> It is a most appalling record. It ranks with the way some of the Middle Eastern races have been liquidated by the Turkish Empire or the Russians. It rates worse than the way

in which the Kurds have been butchered by virtually everyone around them from time to time. It is the most appalling chapter. It spans 800 years, but it's as bad in those 800 years as what Hitler did to the Jews in six. It's only because it's spread over 800 years that we don't see it in such horrifying terms.

The population of Ireland was still less than it was before the potato famine that forced millions to starve or emigrate. And the British were still guilty of racism towards the Irish. 'You hear people say we have to be there to prevent them killing themselves. There is the absolute moral arrogance that somehow we are more able to control that situation than the Irish themselves – ignoring our major role in the butchery over the years.'

During the 1983 interviews Livingstone acknowledged that there was a conflict between his position on Ireland and his role at the GLC.

> I'm asked to choose all the time. It undoubtedly would be easier to say we'll just concentrate on GLC issues. But that involves me ignoring what is happening in Ireland. I can't do that. I don't actually want to do that. I don't want to save local government by doing nothing for Ireland. I think it's an obscene calculation to make because people are dying over there. There wouldn't be 1 per cent of doubt in my mind about sacrificing the whole of British local government if it meant we got out of Ireland. The two principles cannot be equated: the organisation of local services within the state cannot be weighed against the right of the Irish to be free.

Livingstone's view in 1983 was that his public stance helped free the Irish community in London from the fear of discussing British withdrawal from Northern Ireland.

Two years of activity have allowed hundreds of thousands of
men and women in this country to say honestly what they
believe about the history of Ireland. We didn't plan how we
would raise the issue. But, by standing firm and not giving in
and doing what the media demanded I do each time – which
was just to make a solitary condemnation of the IRA and
ignore the troops that shoot the face of a child with a plastic
bullet – we have moved the entire area of the public debate
through about 90 degrees.

For readers taking stock of these views more than 15 years later, it
may be difficult to understand why Livingstone's advocacy of a
political settlement caused such outrage. After peace initiatives by
John Major and Tony Blair in the 1990s, a political consensus
built up in Britain that the problems of Northern Ireland were
best solved by negotiation. But at the time Livingstone's views
challenged the conventional wisdom that Sinn Fein should be
isolated to demonstrate that the IRA's campaigns of violence
could never achieve political success. (His approach also differed
from the Major/Blair initiatives in that he said Britain should
withdraw from Northern Ireland and he did not accept the need
to persuade the Unionist community before doing so.)

As Livingstone now sees it:

Thatcher's strategy was to isolate and criminalise the IRA, to
deny they had any political motive. She portrayed them as
gangsters and psychopaths who were just going round killing
people. The line was that one day we would defeat them. So
any dialogue that presented them as humans with a political
agenda was frowned on. It was important to break that up
and force people to come to terms with what was motivating
the IRA. That was why we deliberately sought to wreck
Thatcher's strategy of isolation. By going there, we made
sure they were on the news being interviewed. So
Thatcher's reaction eventually was to ban the interviews. It

> was one of her worst moments. The people I met
> unofficially from the British army and those I talked to from
> the Republican movement knew there could not be a
> military victory on either side.

The subsequent ceasefire settlement required the IRA to make concessions. 'When I first met Adams in 1983, their position was to offer an immediate ceasefire if the British promised to withdraw in two years. By 1987 that had become five years. But the IRA had to drop a specific timetable for British withdrawal and come to rely on getting a normal economy with modern jobs. Give it five years within the framework of the EU and the border [between North and South] will almost dissolve away.'

From the perspective of 1983, Livingstone's interventions on Ireland and other national issues were regarded by the party leadership as impertinent posturing by a mere councillor, irritating because of his continuing ability to command media attention. They believed that he was a major loser of votes for Labour – that every time he opened his mouth he disaffected another few thousand of the white Anglo-Saxon heterosexual working class which formed the bedrock of the party's electoral strength. A composite view from Livingstone's opponents in the Shadow Cabinet and NEC was that he and his colleagues at County Hall were a group of 'political pre-adolescents' who turned London into an 'adventure playground' for a 'variety of zany left-wing causes' that alienated 'ordinary' people. They preferred 'ineffectual sloganising' to getting on with the job of improving local services. Livingstone bent his 'undoubted talents' to fighting internal party wars 'in complete forgetfulness of the impact on the wider electorate'.

When the party conference in October 1982 produced a shift to the right on the NEC, Livingstone was exposed to determined efforts to block his political advancement. For the right-wing majority and its leading organiser, John Golding, the task of keeping Livingstone out of Parliament became one of the top priorities for rehabilitating Labour's image in the eyes of the electorate. The scene was set for the battle of Brent East, a classic struggle between left-wing constituency activists and the power of the national party machine.

Within weeks of gaining the leadership of the GLC, Livingstone was receiving overtures from Labour activists in several London constituencies that they would like him to be their parliamentary candidate at the next general election. He says he rejected an exploratory invitation from Islington South and later a firm approach from Newham North-West because he felt an 'affinity' for the constituency of Brent East where friends and supporters were urging him to stand.

Brent East was a predominantly working-class area, including a high proportion of ethnic Irish voters, in a part of north-west London around Kilburn, Neasden, Willesden and Cricklewood. Relations between officers of the constituency party and its MP, Reg Freeson, had become increasingly strained during 1981. In letters to the party secretary, Ron Anderson, on March 10th, July 7th and August 10th, Freeson complained about the local party's failure to invite him to speak at its public meetings. He subsequently argued that he was given few opportunities to make the MP's customary parliamentary reports to meetings of the constituency's General Management Committee. He said he was denied access to party members' names and addresses, preventing him from sending them parliamentary reports or other political messages. And he protested that it was made impossible for him to meet new party members. Freeson, who had been brought up in the West Norwood Jewish Orphanage, was by no means a right-winger. He was a founder member of CND, a consistent opponent of Britain's membership of the EEC and a supporter of the reunification of Ireland. So although he was getting on increasingly prickly terms with the officers of the Brent East party, it was quite possible that he could have won support for his reselection from the independent left-wingers in the local party who far outnumbered activists associated with particular hard-left tendencies.

Livingstone says that both the old-guard council leadership on the right and the Chartist and Socialist Organiser factions on the hard left pursued 'very over-the-top tactics' during the rows over selection of candidates for the local elections in 1982. He blamed the old council leader, John Lebor, for starting the aggravation, but he acknowledged that the hard left's behaviour alienated a substantial body of opinion on the softer left. Livingstone was being pushed by the Chartists for Brent East Parliamentary nomination, although he was strongly opposed by Socialist Organiser. So Freeson had a chance of isolating him and winning a reselection majority with the support of the main body of independent left-wingers.

Freeson failed to make the most of this opportunity. Several of the leading members of the independent left in the constituency approached him during the summer of 1982 and urged him to lead a fight back against the hard left. Freeson made it clear to them that he did not have the stomach for it. If he could be reselected as candidate, all well and good, but he did not want to become involved in factional infighting. Freeson gave the soft left the impression that for both personal and political reasons he was ready to turn his back on the whole sorry business.

According to Livingstone's account:

> After their last meeting with Freeson, the soft-left people invited me to go and see them ... I made it quite clear that I was not prepared to join them in a purge of the hard left, but equally I was not prepared to join the hard left in a purge of them. The two groups had got to work together. We didn't come to any conclusion. We were just all quite frank for an evening. Then people went away on their holidays. By the time they came back in September, the soft left, without taking any formal decision about it, had basically come to the conclusion that most of them would vote for me. And that

gave me the majority ... I think I was ideally placed as candidate to work with both those groups and weld them together. And it started to work, because as soon as the soft left decided to support me, the hard left started being much more pleasant to them.

In wooing the centre (that is the Brent East centre; from the perspective of Westminster and the Labour Party HQ all Livingstone's supporters were deemed pretty extreme), Livingstone did not extricate himself from the battle on the hard left. On August 29th 1982 a letter was circulated by Pete Firmin, a constituency branch secretary, to more than 60 members on the left of the Brent East party. This letter formed the basis of Freeson's subsequent allegation that he was being opposed by a form of caucusing that was outlawed under the Labour Party constitution. It said:

> Dear Comrade, I have been asked to convene a meeting of Brent East Labour Left on September 12th to decide on a left candidate for the parliamentary selection procedure. This follows a preliminary meeting held on Sunday July 4th attended by 16 people (from 7 Brent East Branches) at which it was agreed to invite 'prospective' candidates whose names were put forward to a further meeting (it was also agreed that this should be on September 12th). After discussion, particularly about whether a local person should be encouraged to stand, the only names put forward were those of Ken Livingstone (GLC Leader) and Gerry Byrne (of Putney CLP). Both of these have been invited and have agreed to attend on September 12th. At the first meeting it was agreed that it is essential that we have a united left candidate if we are to stand a chance of defeating R. Freeson, and it was thus agreed by all present that they would back (i.e. seek nomination for, argue for, and, where applicable, vote for) whoever wins a majority at the 12th September

meeting, as this is the only way for the Left to make the necessary impact on the selection. This second meeting is thus open to all members of the Brent East CLP who accept the need for a Left replacement of Freeson as prospective parliamentary candidate, and agree to back the united Left candidate.

The meeting took place at the Trades and Labour Hall in Willesden. According to Livingstone, it was a ploy by Socialist Organiser to win support for its candidate, Ms Gerry Byrne. 'The whole of the meeting was a debate about whether or not there should be a woman candidate. No one discussed the word mandating. It wasn't even used. The whole debate was about whether or not I should be a woman. It was quite a good-humoured debate about the inadequacy of my not being a woman.'

Inadequate or not, a vote was taken in which Livingstone beat Byrne by 37 votes to 16. On September 17th the story was carried in the local paper, the *Brent Chronicle*, under the headline 'RED KEN V REG: SECRET BID TO DUMP BRENT MP'. It predicted renewed civil war in the Brent East party in selection procedures which it expected to begin in October.

That reselection process, however, never happened. In an unrelated development on September 22nd, Labour's NEC approved the recommendation of the committee of inquiry under Eric Heffer, Neil Kinnock and David Hughes, set up a few months before to investigate alleged malpractices in the selection of some candidates for the council elections. They reported that it was 'impossible to test the truth of the allegations made'. And they concluded: 'We believe that in the interests of fair play all round and that of the officers in particular there is a need for close supervision of the running of the Brent Local Government Committee and the Brent South and East Constituency Labour Parties for at least six months.' Joyce Gould, the assistant national agent and chief women's officer, was given this unenviable supervisory job. The reselection process was put on ice pending her report. So although it was widely assumed in the press that Livingstone had the nomination sewn up, Freeson and opponents of Livingstone on the NEC began to realise that they had the chance to freeze him out.

Freeson, who had been almost ready to chuck in his hand during the summer, was outraged by the left caucus meeting of September 12th. As he sat in the Labour Party conference in Blackpool later that month, without yet knowing how to topple Livingstone, he became determined to make a fight of it.

On October 27th he wrote to the party's general secretary, Jim Mortimer, listing 38 complaints about what had gone on in Brent East. He said that, until these matters had been investigated, 'effective supervision will not be possible'. Freeson argued that the Brent East Labour left 'pre-selection' meeting on September 12th seriously prejudiced his position. And he concluded: 'I think that the information available shows clearly that there has been serious unconstitutional conduct over the Parliamentary candidature and that anything arising from it should be considered invalid.' In Freeson's eyes the September 12th meeting had been a caucus which mandated those present to vote for Livingstone at any official selection meeting which might follow. According to Livingstone, there could be no question of mandating because the final selection would have been by secret ballot. His argument was that he merely attended a meeting, organised by political opponents from Socialist Organiser, which was no more sinister (and much less disciplined) than meetings run by trades unions in many constituencies to choose a candidate to back at selection meetings.

Freeson thought that was rubbish. In his view, Livingstone had not just turned up to an event run by opponents. He had been closely involved in planning a meeting that was run as if it were a formal selection procedure, with candidates, speeches and manifestos. People, some of whom did not even live in the constituency, had been invited to it by name.

This row was never settled. On October 25th the national agent, David Hughes, wrote to Pete Firmin expressing concern about the phrases 'agree to back the United Left candidate' and 'discuss various aspects of the fight to replace Freeson'. He thought they suggested there might be an attempt to mandate delegates. But the NEC decided to defer investigation of Freeson's complaint until after Gould's six-month inquiry was completed.

On March 7, 1983, Freeson wrote again to Mortimer. This time he pointed out that clause 14(7) of the party constitution stipulated that, in the case of a sitting Labour MP, the reselection process must start within three years of the last general election. Since three years and ten months had elapsed, he asked for guidance from the NEC. Freeson's argument was that the Brent East general management committee had failed to carry out a reselection in time and that it was by then too late to start one.

At its meeting on March 23rd the NEC decided to seek legal advice on the matter from Lord Milner of Leeds. The Brent East party responded by asking for a counsel's opinion from Lord Gifford. Gifford struck first, advising the Brent party on April 4th that they had a legal responsibility to begin a reselection as soon as possible. Milner responded with a view that the NEC was entitled to take the matter into its own hands and dispense with the normal reselection procedure.

Meanwhile Gould had completed her six-month period of supervision of the Brent parties. In her report to the NEC she noted the facts of the pre-selection meeting of the Brent East Labour left without passing judgment on them. She concluded that the Brent parties 'were now operating with the rules and constitution of the party'. This removed one obstacle to reselection going ahead. On April 20th and 24th the Brent East party secretary wrote to Mortimer requesting the NEC's cooperation in agreeing a reselection timetable. On April 27th the NEC decided not to allow reselection to proceed. The next day the Brent East GMC agreed by 71 votes to 4 to go ahead anyway on the basis of the Gifford legal opinion. The affair seemed to be heading inexorably towards a battle in the courts between the constituency party and the NEC.

On May 9th, however, Margaret Thatcher went to the Palace to request the dissolution of Parliament for the general election. David Hughes, the national agent, wrote to the Brent East secretary, citing a special rule which ensured the automatic reselection of sitting MPs if the normal selection procedures had not been completed before Parliament was dissolved. 'Therefore Mr Reg Freeson is the Labour Party candidate for the Brent East constituency in the General Election to be held on 9 June 1983', he said. On May 11th the NEC decided by a majority of 19 votes to 9 to endorse this interpretation. Only Tony Benn, Frank Allaun, Judith Hart, Eric Heffer, Jo Richardson, Audrey Wise, Dennis Skinner, Tom Sawyer and Lawrence Coates voted for reselection to go ahead.

For a few days the Brent East party refused to back down. It threatened court action and went ahead with arrangements for a selection conference on May 18th. When the day arrived, however, the local party reluctantly accepted the NEC decision. According to a letter sent by its secretary to the national agent: 'A vote was then taken by a show of hands as to who we would have liked to have selected had we been allowed. This resulted in 53 votes for Ken Livingstone and 2 votes for Reg Freeson, with 3 abstentions.'

On June 9th Freeson won his seventh parliamentary election in the constituency. Although his majority was cut to 4,834, it was not a bad result for Labour. After allowing for small boundary changes, the notional swing to the Conservatives was less than 1 per cent, compared with an inner London average of 2.3 per cent and an outer London average of 4.6 per cent.

So Livingstone's ambition to become an MP was thwarted for another parliamentary term. Nobody emerged with much credit from the affair. At no stage did the NEC decide the rights and wrongs of it, preferring instead to play for time until the election was called. Livingstone's view was that he lost out purely because the NEC elections in 1982 produced a right-wing executive under the sway of John Golding, known to the left at the time as the 'witch-hunter general'. 'The Golding majority on the NEC was trying to ensure that in the aftermath of the election there was the minimum hard-left presence in the Parliamentary Labour Party so that Kinnock or Hattersley would be able to emerge as the eventual choice of the party in the succession [to Foot]. I think they were thinking that far ahead.'

In truth, opposition to Livingstone was probably more personal. Rightly or wrongly he was perceived by much of the NEC to be Labour's biggest potential loser of votes in the country. He had to be kept out as a sign that Labour was not the party of the so-called loony left. Livingstone's problem was that he was too well known. He became the victim of his own image-building.

7 Abolition

Livingstone's failure to be selected to fight in the 1983 general election seriously dented his popular image as an unstoppable political force. People who had once looked on him as a potential leader of the Labour Party, or at least the eventual inheritor of the mantle of Tony Benn, started to wonder if his career had already passed its peak. Was he, like the hulahoop, a craze that was bound sooner or later to go out of fashion? The problem was not only that he had to sit out another Parliament, but also that he was becoming increasingly isolated and accident-prone.

At the GLC his style of leadership had changed after the first frenetic year of the Labour administration. His front-bench colleagues got on with looking after their own portfolios with minimum interference from him. It became a much more collective team affair and, although there was still a good deal of private anguish about the way Livingstone hogged the headlines, relationships became more calm and supportive.

In the spring of 1983, however, a battle developed over the leadership of the Inner London Education Authority that soured the atmosphere. Until its abolition in 1990, ILEA was the largest education authority in Britain, with 300,000 pupils, 21,000 teachers and a budget of around £800 million (about the same as the GLC's). Its members were GLC councillors from inner London constituencies and representatives from the inner London boroughs. Although the authority was technically a subcommittee of the GLC, it tended to be a semi-independent fiefdom; and GLC members chose whether to concentrate on GLC or ILEA business. Livingstone played little part.

From May 1981 the leader of ILEA had been Bryn Davies, a

Livingstone ally on the Labour left. But in April 1983 Davies was challenged for the leadership by his deputy, Frances Morrell, another left-winger and former political adviser to Tony Benn. At one stage it seemed as if Davies would step down, but Livingstone launched into a vigorous fight in his defence. The campaign for Morrell as leader and Ruth Gee as deputy leader adopted a feminist ticket. Their supporters argued that their election would be an important step in breaking down the male domination of leading institutions. The point carried with it heavy sarcastic overtones against Livingstone on the grounds that he talked a lot about supporting feminism, but had an almost all-male front-bench team at the GLC.

Livingstone responded in a bitter and ill-advised letter to *Tribune*:

> Socialist feminists have pointed the Labour Party in several new directions in terms of how we should work with collective leadership, consultation, shared and supportive methods of working, and a move away from the authoritarian and aggressive operating styles which are so often used within the party. It is because no attempt has been made to consult the party outside County Hall, the organised left within it, or to raise any demands for policy or organisational changes that this leadership campaign has degenerated into the traditional back-stabbing, arm-twisting and intimidatory methods which I have often seen before in this building.

Other members of the GLC Labour group responded in the same issue of *Tribune* that these allegations were untrue.

Whatever the merits of the argument and the rival candidates' abilities, Livingstone's intervention was widely regarded as over the top. He had no personal standing in ILEA, yet he seemed to be cracking the whip to make sure his own man got the job. Morrell went on to beat Davies by 19 votes to 13. So Livingstone was seen to have tried to exercise his authority and failed. His leadership of the GLC was not at risk, but his stature within County Hall was diminished. For years afterwards, colleagues from ILEA tended to be a lot more critical of his capabilities than those whose main focus was the GLC.

A more serious threat was that Livingstone's brand of politics began to look out of place in the atmosphere of studied harmony that descended on the Labour Party after its general election defeat in June 1983. His style had been to straddle hard- and soft-left groupings without joining any of them. But when Neil Kinnock emerged as the new leader of the party, this straddling act became much harder to perform. The soft left took up positions inside the ring fence erected around Kinnock, while much of the hard left outside Parliament resumed their traditional hobby of attacking the leadership. Livingstone found himself in a no-man's-land. The word most often used about him by the young party apparatchiks was that he was 'marginalised', meaning that he had become peripheral to issues of power in the party.

There was a third setback for Livingstone during this period. He was wrong-footed over a somewhat half-hearted attempt to stand for the Labour Party's National Executive Committee. He told his local party members in Paddington that he would like to be their delegate to the 1983 Labour Party conference in Brighton if, and only if, he became a candidate for the NEC. They took the decision out of his hands by choosing – while he was absent at a GLC council meeting – to send someone else. Without being a delegate, he could not be a candidate. Although he said subsequently that he would not have stood anyway for the NEC that year, the episode was unfortunate.

At that conference David Blunkett, leader of Sheffield council, was voted on to the NEC, extending his local-government power base into the wider party network. Blunkett, not Livingstone, became the left-wing council activist at the top of the party tree.

Over the next few months Livingstone participated as a presenter on a London Weekend Television late-night chat show

Livingstone embraced by show business in the shape of Janet Street-Porter,
London Weekend's 'After Midnight' show, October 1983 (*LWT*)

with Janet Street-Porter. Older members of the party
establishment began asking why he did not quit politics and go
full-time into show business where he so obviously belonged. But
Livingstone's political career was not over. Instead he was

preparing for his biggest campaign so far – the fight to save the GLC from extinction.

Mrs Thatcher's government had approached the 1983 general election with a record of failure in its dealings with local authorities. For the time being, her long-term ambition to abolish domestic rates had been thwarted (although it was to be revived later when she introduced the ill-judged poll tax proposal in her 1987 manifesto). At that stage her ministers kept telling her that there was no acceptable alternative form of local taxation. The most obvious option, a local income tax, was rejected for fear of giving the likes of Ken Livingstone a buoyant new source of revenue.

A more pressing problem was the failure of the policy to force down English local authorities' spending. In spite of the system of grant penalties for overspenders (described in Chapter 5), many Labour councils resolved to withstand the pain of huge rate increases rather than cut services.

In the rush to prepare the Conservatives' 1983 manifesto Margaret Thatcher and her party chairman Cecil Parkinson seized on the only two ideas that were ready to hand to 'do something' about the rates. The first was abolition of the GLC and the six metropolitan counties of Greater Manchester, Merseyside, South Yorkshire, Tyne and Wear, West Midlands and West Yorkshire. This proposal had been recommended in outline by a Cabinet committee under William Whitelaw, but had not yet been properly analysed to find out if it could work. The second was an idea from Leon Brittan, then chief secretary to the Treasury, to make it illegal for 'extravagant' councils to fix 'excessive' rates. This notion, known as 'rate-capping', had been repeatedly rejected by the Cabinet as at best unworkable and at worst a serious encroachment of the traditional Tory support for local freedom against state centralisation.

In her haste, the prime minister threw both schemes into the manifesto. Given the absence of many other firm legislative

Neil Kinnock visits County Hall for the first time since becoming Leader of the Labour Party, November 30th 1983. Left to right: Bill Bush (head of GLC Labour group secretariat), Tony Banks (GLC Arts Chairman and MP for Newham North-West), Illtyd Harrington, Harvey Hinds (GLC Chairman), Kinnock, Jack Cunningham (Shadow Environment Secretary), Livingstone, Nita Clarke (GLC Labour group press officer), John Carr (GLC Staff Committee Chairman) (*GLC*)

commitments, they became key items for opposition by the Labour Party in Parliament. Both threatened the GLC. So, far from being marginalised, Livingstone was brought back into centre stage. Much as the bulk of the Shadow Cabinet might have wished to ignore him, they felt bound to join with him in the campaign to kill the bills. By Christmas 1983 a degree of understanding had built up between Livingstone and the new shadow environment secretary, Jack Cunningham. Neil Kinnock had been lunched at County Hall and everyone was being nice to each other.

It was a fragile unity. From Labour councils outside London came the sound of constant grumbling that Livingstone was personally to blame for goading the government into the commitments to abolition and rate-capping. But Livingstone had a campaign on stream that could use his populist talents to the full. Before developing the story of this new struggle, it is worth standing back to pick up the strands of what had been happening in the meantime at the GLC.

The key decision of the Livingstone administration had been taken by the Labour group on February 8th 1982. Their problem at the time was to clear up the appalling financial mess left by the Law Lords' judgment seven weeks before. The Lords had not only ruled that Labour's cheap-fares policy was unlawful, but also that the supplementary rate demand which funded it was null and void. Anyone who had paid it was entitled to a refund or a credit. Although the GLC rapidly passed a vote to raise the fares, it was not going to be possible for London Transport to complete adjustments to ticket machines and introduce the increases before March 21st 1982. So by the time the fares went up, Londoners would have enjoyed cheaper travel for six months without contributing anything towards it by way of extra rates. LT would be left with a thumping deficit of £125 million, which had to be financed by someone.

Ministers refused to provide funds to rescue the GLC from what they regarded as a mess of its own making. But the transport secretary, David Howell, was anxious that he might take the blame if the GLC decided to recoup the missing £125 million either through a further round of fare increases or by adding it to rate bills in April 1982. He decided therefore to make the GLC councillors an offer he thought they could not refuse. He secured a ruling from the Attorney-General that no additional fare increases were necessary and he promised legislation to allow LT to borrow the £125 million on condition that the GLC paid off the debt in instalments over five years. He imagined that the council would jump at the chance to keep its next rate increase as low as possible.

But Howell's idea was regarded as outrageous by the GLC's comptroller of finance, Maurice Stonefrost. It breached a cardinal principle of British local government that councils should never borrow to cover current expenditure. So for Stonefrost there was a clear issue of financial conscience. He argued that the deficit should be paid off immediately by raising the full £125 million in the 1982 rate demand. He also pointed out that the instalments option suggested by the government could double the eventual cost to the GLC because both the repayments and the interest would count as overspending and be punished annually by grant penalties. He feared that the government's real objective was not to help the GLC out of a fix, but to lock it into indebtedness just at the point when it was beginning to reap benefits from a long-term policy of reducing its reliance on borrowing for investment purposes.

This argument was music to Livingstone's ears. He realised immediately (and acknowledged to journalists at the time) that a decision to pay off the deficit in one go would transform the politics of implementing the rest of the Labour manifesto over the final three years of his administration. It would mean that a £125 million item would be added to the rate bill for 1982/83, which would not recur in future years. So by 1983/84 there would be £125 million available for spending on other programmes without the need for a further rate increase. The GLC budget would be raised in one leap on to a plateau which could not otherwise have been reached without a long, painful and unpopular climb.

Livingstone took a budget proposal to the Labour group to double the rate demand set by Cutler's Tory administration a year before. The increase was partly to pay off the £125 million deficit, partly to cover the anticipated reduction in government grant and partly to provide a contingency in case the grant was taken away entirely. Using Stonefrost's arguments about financial rectitude rather than his own ideas about establishing a new high rates plateau, Livingstone won the group's support. But a price had to be paid. Only about £40 million could be allocated for new initiatives from the manifesto in Labour's second year in office, the crucial period when any administration should be gearing up to fulfil its promises. Londoners were to be faced with doubled GLC rates and doubled LT fares without any significant increase in services to show for it. This combination of misery might have been disastrous for Labour popularity in London, but in the aftermath of the Law Lords ruling it was hard for the voters to know where to pin the blame. By the time of the borough elections in May 1982, the rate and fare increases were overshadowed by the national political crisis of the Falklands war.

Over the following year, careful effort was made to revive the cheaper-fares strategy, by constructing a new less ambitious package which could get through the courts. This produced a so-called 'balanced plan' which cut fares again by 25 per cent to bring them (on average) back to almost exactly the same level in cash terms as when Labour took office. The GLC's case was that it had a duty not only to make LT break even 'as far as practicable' (the point which had troubled the Law Lords), but also to provide a more economic and more efficient transport system for London. To avoid accusations of haste or devotion to political dogma, the balanced plan was prepared with meticulous attention to detail and a ponderous mock display of open-mindedness. It incorporated a simplification of fare structures through a new zoning system, a new Travelcard season ticket and greater integration of LT with British Rail.

LT's executives were delighted with the plan, which would increase their passenger traffic and streamline their operations; but they feared that it might nonetheless contravene the Law Lords' harsh interpretation of the law. So they brought a friendly action in the High Court against the GLC's instruction to cut the fares. The LT case carefully avoided the Law Lords' ruling that the GLC had a duty not to overcharge ratepayers in the interests of passengers. It concentrated entirely on public-transport law.

On January 27th 1983, Lord Justice Kerr, Mr Justice Glidewell and Mr Justice Nolan ruled unanimously in favour of the GLC. Kerr said the council's balanced plan was a 'totally different exercise from the arbitrary decision in 1981 to introduce Fares Fair'. It was not done on the basis of 'a statement in an election manifesto', but as a carefully researched strategy for transport in London as a whole. Kerr acknowledged the Law Lords' ruling that LT should break even 'as far as practicable', but he said: 'No one now contends that the "break-even" option is either practicable or the correct answer in law. This could only be achieved by cutting down the present service and effectively destroying the transport system for Greater London, as we know it.' The GLC had to strike a balance between the obligation to break even and the duty to provide an efficient and economic transport system.

In 1981 this argument had failed to convince the judges that Fares Fair was legal. But by January 1983, with a more modest fare-cut proposal backed by a more methodical presentation of public-transport economics, the GLC won its case.

Kerr made no attempt to assess whether the council was maintaining a fair balance between ratepayers and passengers. 'Whether the balance has been struck at the best point, and even at a permissible point, is not a matter which this court can evaluate, or which it is any part of our function to assess in any way,' he said.

The government opposed the GLC's plan for further fare cuts as an unwarranted increase in public spending and burden on London's ratepayers. And, waiting in the wings, the Conservative leadership at Westminster city council was planning another court action against the GLC as soon as it passed its 1983 budget, to challenge the 'reasonableness' of extra spending on transport subsidies. But by that time the political winds were blowing in the GLC's favour, as Livingstone reaped the reward for pushing up the GLC rate so high in 1982. By paying off the whole £125 million Fares Fair deficit in the 1982 budget, the GLC Labour group had £125 million to play with in the following year. This margin of financial slack was sufficient to provide for the 'balanced plan' fare reductions (£81 million), a sevenfold expansion in the programme of the women's committee (£7 million) and extra support for the Greater London Enterprise Board to create jobs through grants, loans and acquisitions (£30 million).

The result was that even after inflation and the loss of the last vestiges of government rate support grant, the GLC rate in 1983 went up by 14 per cent – a comparatively modest amount in those inflationary times. This was enough to finance a 28 per cent growth in planned spending on subsidies and services at a time when every other council in the land was being squeezed by the government to make cuts. So Livingstone's GLC drove a coach and horses through Heseltine's controls.

The apparent modesty of the 14 per cent rate increase should have made no difference to the validity of a challenge by Westminster council to the reasonableness of a new round of fare cuts. But, whatever the legal merits of their case, the Westminster councillors realised that the GLC had cut the political ground from under them. Livingstone was now offering cheaper fares and (at least by the standards of the time) low rate increases. It would do the Tories no good to mix it with him in the courts. The 1983 budget went through without legal challenge and with barely a murmur of popular protest. And by February 1984 Livingstone was able to offer a 7.5 per cent rate cut for the coming financial year, without any important sacrifices of achievable policy objectives.

So the Livingstone administration escaped the trap in which almost every other Labour authority was caught. Elsewhere councillors had to choose between unacceptable cuts in services and intolerable rate increases. They remained prisoners of the rate support grant system. If they failed to make the cuts required by government, they would be penalised by the loss of grant and their ratepayers would have to pick up the bill. These penalties were made tougher year by year in order to make it impossible for councils receiving grants to escape the government's financial squeeze. By budgeting to lose all its rate support grant early on, the GLC escaped from the system. Indeed its main financial problem was the exact opposite of the one faced by other councils. Persistently the GLC committees failed to spend the allocations for which they had budgeted. Hard as they tried, they just could not shift the money fast enough.

In a private report to the policy committee (Labour's collective leadership group), Livingstone complained in December 1983: 'There is a general problem of underspending on agreed programmes in 1983/84, as there was in 1982/83. This is most serious in those newly established programmes which have quite rightly attracted major funding but which are seeking to implement complex policies from a standing start ... We must introduce procedures which will make such underspending against budget less likely to occur.' He listed a series of ideas for using up the unspent money which, in the first half of the 1983/84 financial year, amounted to 5 per cent of the revenue budget and 23 per cent of the capital budget. It must be concluded that for the GLC the problem was not lack of cash but lack of speed and organisation in making the practical arrangements for growth. The gulf between high rate levels and low actual achievement levels was a serious failing, but one for which no political price had to be paid.

In political terms the big area of difficulty was not the total amount of money spent, but the way in which a small fraction of it was distributed by way of grants to voluntary organisations. The one issue which the Tory opposition succeeded in getting across to the electorate was that the Livingstone administration was giving unprecedented financial support to women's groups, ethnic minority groups, gays and other campaigners against the white, male, heterosexual order in society. Week by week stories appeared in the press ridiculing or condemning grants to bodies with exotic-sounding titles. The all-time favourite was Babies Against the Bomb (the name chosen for a disarmament campaign organised by a group of mothers who brought their infants along to meetings).

Conservative criticism of GLC grants capitalised on popular prejudices against gays, lesbians and blacks. Since these prejudices appeared to be particularly strong among the white working class, this brought the GLC into disrepute in many bedrock Labour areas. The disaffection of Labour voters became a major reason for criticism of the GLC within the Labour Party, especially outside London in areas where 'traditional' socialist values had not had to come to terms with the demands of the women's movement and the increased aspirations of disadvantaged minorities.

The argument within the party was not that it was wrong for the GLC to fund these groups, but that it was politically imprudent. Policies which could not carry the working class with them should, it was argued, be shelved until ordinary people were ready for them. Although Livingstone himself had little to do with most of the controversial GLC grants decisions, this was an argument he was prepared to meet head on. 'The Labour Party is no doubt going to win votes by supporting for example the reintroduction of hanging and deporting all black people. That isn't really what we're there to do,' he said in 1983.

> I think politics is not just looking at what is the most popular position to take and then taking it. Granted some people come into politics because they want to line their pockets; others because they want a nice comfortable job. I came into politics because I wish to change society. And that means changing the hearts and minds of people. You start from an unpopular position and you plug away consistently. If you're right, eventually you win. I've no doubt at all that by the end of this century, if we continue to fight for it, we will be living in a Britain where there will be complete tolerance towards sexual preference ... If the leadership of the party, as one of their standard positions, argue for women's rights, gay rights and a proper equal opportunities policy for blacks, we'll eventually change attitudes nationally.

In this context, the GLC's grants policy was not a blunder. Like the Irish issue, it was a clear expression of Livingstone's political approach.

The Conservatives made capital out of attacking controversial grants, but they also feared the effectiveness of the programme as a whole. By Christmas 1983 the GLC had funded more than 1,000 voluntary organisations and its annual grants budget was running at nearly £40 million a year. The Tories began to worry that Labour had invented a piece of political machinery capable of delivering large blocks of votes at election time.

The view was explained in a speech by Richard Brew, who briefly succeeded Sir Horace Cutler as GLC Tory leader in 1982:

> In the May 1981 elections the turnout in the decisive marginals was about 50 per cent. That means that the socialists were returned in such seats on a vote of below 25 per cent of the electorate. Livingstone is not interested in the support of 'Londoners' – that is too difficult. He only needs 25 per cent of Londoners – and this is how he is going about it. Leaving aside the ideologically committed, he is seeking out the feminists and the gay activists. He is topping up these with the ethnic groups and the Irish. He is mobilising the anti-police brigade and he is seeking out the pressure groups – CND, Babies Against the Bomb and so on. In other words he is going for the nutters. As everyone knows, what nutters want is a plentiful supply of nuts. And these Livingstone is providing through the GLC's grants policy ... In this whole question of grants, do not fall into the trap of mocking the socialists over some of the questionable organisations they are funding. It is not at all a case of Livingstone having lost his sense of the ridiculous, as some people say, but rather it is hard-headed manipulation ... It is vital that we Conservatives do not make the mistake of laughing too loudly at what we may feel are 'own goals' being scored by the socialists. They know exactly what they are doing and where they want to go – 25 per cent of the vote.

Brew suggested that GLC grants would by 1984 be providing a living for about 2,000 'left-wing activists' outside County Hall. The votes necessary to boost Labour support to 25 per cent of the electorate were being bought with grants and they would be garnered with the help of the activists. 'With Livingstone's grants policy, the socialists are developing a system of winning power with methods not seen in this country since the eighteenth century,' he said.

Apart from Brew's offensive description of ethnic minorities and others as nutters, there was a grain of truth in what he said. The GLC Labour group may have lost votes through their more controversial grants, but members were amazed by the grassroots support they also seemed to be winning as a result of the programme as a whole. Where Brew was wrong was in attributing this to a well-laid Labour plan. The policy was one that the group stumbled on almost by accident. Their 1981 manifesto had made scant mention of grants. This was partly due to a general trades union view that unpaid volunteers take away workers' jobs, but more because little thought had been given to the subject by the politicians.

Bill Bush, a GLC official who headed the Labour secretariat, was mainly responsible for inserting support for a grants programme at various points in the manifesto while he was doing the staff work on its preparation. His argument was that working with community-based groups was an efficient way of finding out what people want and then delivering it to them. Small amounts of money could be made to go a long way using large amounts of voluntary energy. And funds could be moved out quickly without the need to set up a cumbersome bureaucracy. But no one in 1981 knew how big the grants programme would become.

Soon after the election, a grants panel was set up under John McDonnell (later chairman of finance) to handle applications coming in from voluntary groups. It started by meeting the needs of organisations which were sophisticated enough to present a coherent case; but later it developed systems for seeking out bodies which needed help and assisting them to make applications. Meetings were arranged with various client groups or organisations. When the women's groups met, their outrage at the fact that their grants were being run by a man provided the genesis of the GLC's women's committee. Eventually each committee became responsible for grants in its own field. The programme mushroomed.

McDonnell says the Labour group started out on the grants policy with the somewhat altruistic motive of helping groups like local law centres and community associations which had lost funding from their boroughs: 'Within three months each constituency member was realising that the political returns were absolutely enormous.' Councillors came back from performing official opening ceremonies of grant-funded premises or presenting cheques, convinced that grants were the best thing since politicians invented kissing babies. McDonnell did not accept Brew's 25 per cent theory: 'I don't think grants influence a constituency on a large basis; but they did establish our credentials within certain communities.'

During the GLC years there was never any thorough analysis of where the borderline lay between looking after the interests of Londoners and using public money for political advantage. Councillors could not be criticised for winning votes by implementing popular policies, but they could be tainted with sleaze if they used the council's rate income as a substitute for party funds.

There were three areas in which the Labour GLC was in danger of crossing over this borderline. Grants were given to bodies whose main purpose was to oppose the Conservative government on issues such as nuclear disarmament and the health service cuts. A large advertising budget was given over to campaigns specifically directed against government policies. People were recruited on to the GLC payroll whose political motivation made them almost indistinguishable from the Labour councillors they were supposed (impartially) to serve. The amount of public money involved was tiny as a percentage of GLC income, representing only a small fraction of a penny rate. So the problem had more to do with political morality than so-called overspending.

The Labour GLC's advertising budgets included: £300,000 spent on fighting the Law Lords' judgment against Fares Fair; £200,000 fighting government decisions to withdraw rate support grants from London; £150,000 on fighting the bill to take responsibility for LT away from the GLC; £200,000 on Peace Year; £80,000 on the GLC's declaration of itself as a nuclear-free zone; and £100,000 on a mailshot to Londoners giving medical evidence about the effects of a nuclear holocaust.

Individually these campaigns were justified, after careful scrutiny by the GLC's legal branch, as legitimate expenditure in the interests of Londoners. But collectively they clearly amounted to political propaganda funded from the rates. During the 1983 election campaign it was sometimes necessary to read the small print to distinguish poster advertisements financed by the Labour Party from others financed by the GLC.

Livingstone argued that any attempt to draw a distinction between political and non-political advertising was bogus. 'Everything is political,' he said. 'Your sex life is political. What you eat is political. Everything about us is political because everything about us stems from the division of power and wealth in society. There is no such thing as a non-political part of life.' So while he accepted that it would have been improper to channel GLC funds into the Labour Party, he saw no other limits to campaigning activity of a political nature. As he put it in 1983: 'Fifteen years ago councils had no need to do it ... The government went on the offensive with the Housing Finance Act in 1972. Since then councils have been under attack from central governments, both Labour and Tory. Gradually they geared themselves up to reply ... The Tories don't have to do it that much because they already have the media on their side. If you're trying to survive as we are in a hostile media environment ...

you've got to have some way of explaining to the people who vote for you what you are doing and why.'

This argument took the GLC into uncharted and dangerous political territory. The Labour group's attitude to the standards of personal behaviour to be expected of a councillor was strict, almost puritanical. The suggestion that a penny of ratepayers' money might have corruptly entered a councillor's pocket would have caused deep and genuine outrage. But their standards of corporate behaviour were lax. It seemed fair game to channel money into a favoured political cause so long as some justification could be found to placate the lawyers. They did not ask if it was right, only whether they could get away with it.

The employment of activists in official positions in the GLC bureaucracy was inevitably the issue that most disturbed top GLC officials, although no one challenged the propriety of any individual's appointment. Perhaps the most controversial posting was the choice of Reg Race, former Labour MP for Wood Green, to a well-paid job as head of the programme office in the GLC director-general's department. The fact that Race appeared to be the best qualified of the applicants and went on to do a good job slicing the fat off the bureaucracy did not quieten top officials' fears that the Livingstone administration had lost sight of the conventional borderline between politicians and their civil servants.

Similarly in the grants field there were fears that councillors could not separate their role as policy-makers in the public interest from their political positions as activists with links among grant recipients. As one member of Livingstone's policy committee anonymously put it:

> There was a time when you had to watch out for the Masonic or Roman Catholic link between councillors and the people who got their favours. Now with our grants policy you need to watch out for common membership of a ward Labour party. Our people don't seem to remember the

Poulson scandal and they don't seem to have read the code of practice that was drawn up after it to guard against corruption. As far as I know there are no scandals over grants, but the fact that you can ask the question is evidence that there is a problem.

Ministers were privately delighted with the GLC's grants and advertising policy; it gave them ammunition to attack a council which missed no opportunity to cause them aggravation. Their main concern, however, was with the wider economic issue of local authority 'overspending'. The system to discipline local expenditure, which had been established by Michael Heseltine in 1981, relied on withdrawal of grants from authorities which spent over government targets. But by 1983 the GLC had no more grant to lose. Its £867 million budget for that year was 53 per cent above its target and 82 per cent above the government's estimation of what it would need to spend to provide a standard level of service. No other council defied the government's rules by such a wide percentage margin; and none had such a large cash budget. The GLC contributed £301 million of the total £770 million 'overspend' by all English authorities. When an ILEA 'overspend' of £97 million was added to the GLC total, ministers could argue that the Labour councillors in London's County Hall were responsible for more than half their local government problem. And they had no powers to do anything about it.

These official government figures were somewhat misleading. The GLC's spending 'excess' was as much due to the way ministers juggled the rules for fixing targets as to the council's socialist priorities. In October 1983 Maurice Stonefrost calculated that for the council to achieve its target in the following financial year, it would need to do the following. Increase LT fares by 45 per cent; abolish concessionary fares for pensioners; increase council rents by an extra £5 a week; freeze all staff recruitment; cease all grants under the programmes for women, ethnic minorities, police and voluntary and community groups; halt revenue spending on the industry and employment programme; make all administrative, professional and technical staff redundant; and cancel agreements with London boroughs to maintain roads, bridges and traffic signals. Whitehall officials knew Stonefrost was right when he said that the GLC could not possibly meet its target without stratospheric increases in LT fares (which the government claimed it did not want to see).

Such niceties were lost on Thatcher and Parkinson as they wrote the 1983 Conservative manifesto. The political fact of life was that the despised Ken Livingstone was cocking a snook at the government and getting away with it. He had to be stopped. Their manifesto aimed to put an end to the style of municipal socialism which they thought he personified.

After the election, the Cabinet rushed forward legislation designed to eliminate defiance by up to a score of Labour authorities, including the GLC. Tom King (who succeeded Michael Heseltine as environment secretary in January 1983) opposed the plan and was switched to another department. In December 1983 the new environment secretary, Patrick Jenkin, published a Rates Bill to make it illegal for councils to finance levels of spending well in excess of government norms. Although he did not name the authorities on his hit list, the GLC and ILEA were clearly uppermost in his mind.

His plan had serious implications for local democracy. It meant that the government's decision about how much each council ought to spend could become more important than the wishes of the local electorate. Granted, the scheme would only chop back spending well over the government's norms; and for administrative reasons the Department of the Environment could not use it against more than a handful of authorities at any one time. But it was a big stride down the road of state centralisation. The bill also sought a reserve power which would allow the government to control the rate increases of all authorities, should the need arise.

Rate-capping, which was regarded by Conservative council

leaders from the shires as a serious breach of traditional Tory principles, would have been quite sufficient to give Whitehall control of the big 'overspenders'. Ministers would have been able to force the GLC and other 'profligate' councils year by year to change their policies and economise. But they were also committed to move on two other fronts. Legislation was introduced to take responsibility for LT away from the GLC and vest it in a quango appointed by the transport secretary. Since ministers said fares need not rise faster than inflation, it was unclear how this initiative would do much to cut public spending. Subsidies would be removed from the GLC's ledger, but they would still be charged to London ratepayers.

Now if the GLC's rates were to be capped and it was to lose control of LT, it was hard to see how it could any longer do much damage from the government's point of view. But the Conservatives had given a firm pledge in the manifesto that the GLC and the six metropolitan counties would be abolished on the grounds that they were a 'wasteful and unnecessary tier of government'. It is true that the government had done its best to make the GLC unnecessary by whittling away its strategic housing and planning powers, but it was less obvious how ministers thought abolition of the GLC would save money. None of the GLC's remaining functions was to be abolished. Most of them were to be parcelled out to the London boroughs. A new joint board of borough nominees was to be set up to run the fire service. A new quango called the London Planning Commission was to be set up to advise the government on the capital's strategic planning issues. Another would take over administration of the GLC's £2 billion debt. The government itself was to assume responsibility for 70 miles of trunk roads. The job of flood protection was to go to the Thames Water Authority.

The government claimed this would lead to administrative savings, although it refused to quantify them. In fact only 7.5 per cent of the GLC's employees were in administrative and managerial jobs; they represented less than 2 per cent of total GLC costs. So, even if all these jobs could disappear (which they could not), Londoners would not have noticed the saving. Arguably, more administrators would be required to cope with the GLC functions when they had been dispersed.

That was not to say that the GLC budget could not be cut; but savings worth the name could only come from changes in policy: cutting transport subsidies, raising rents, abolishing grants, abandoning the industry and employment programme, and reducing standards of fire cover and other services. Ministers found it embarrassing to argue that they were changing the structure of London's government because they did not like the policies of the existing GLC regime. If it was policy changes they wanted, they should have waited until the next GLC elections in May 1985 and advised the electors to boot Livingstone out. Even if that did not do the trick, they could have used the intended rate-capping power to force Labour to scale down its policy objectives.

The argument against abolition, which for many Londoners seemed to be the clincher, was that England's capital, alone among the great cities of the western world, would be left without an elected voice. The GLC Tories, by then under the more dynamic leadership of Alan Greengross, played this line for all it was worth.

Greengross and his colleagues, confident that they would have won an election in 1985, were appalled at the idea of abolition; but, as is the way in the Conservative Party, they said that the manifesto commitment was right as a first step towards fundamental reform. Fine, abolish the GLC, said Greengross, but when London's local government was restructured 'a democratically-elected body must surely be established to provide an effective and financially disciplined voice and direction for the specific tasks that must be done for London as a whole.'

The government's abolition White Paper, *Streamlining the Cities*, was published on October 7, 1983. It envisaged legislation in the 1984–85 session of Parliament to abolish the GLC in May

1986. A shorter 'paving bill' was to be put through Parliament in the spring and summer of 1984 to abort the GLC elections due in 1985. For its final year the GLC was to be run by nominees of the London boroughs, among whom there was likely to be a Tory majority.

The timetable for Livingstone was clear. If the government had its way, Labour would lose control of County Hall in May 1985 when the existing councillors' four-year term of office expired. There were 18 months left to mobilise the resources of the GLC to fight for its life. Before the 18 months were over, the reselection process for Labour Party Parliamentary candidates would have begun. He was ready for the campaign of his life and, in terms of his own political career, he was back on course.

8 Say No to No Say

The GLC's fight against its abolition was the most sophisticated campaign ever run by a local authority in Britain. It was also the most expensive. Between October 1983 and March 1985, the council spent £14 million on an advertising and public relations blitz which managed to change the image of the GLC from an impersonal bureaucracy into the cherished bastion of Londoners' democratic rights.

A memorable series of giant posters was displayed across London's hoardings. Under the slogan 'Say No to No Say', they hammered home the message that the government was behaving undemocratically by cancelling the GLC elections and handing power to faceless central-government civil servants. 'If you have any complaints when the GLC goes, you'll be talking to Whitehall', said one poster, picturing a brick wall wearing a bowler hat and pinstripe suit. 'Imagine what London would be like run by Whitehall', said another ingenious adaptation of the idea, in which the entire poster hoarding was bound up in a lattice of red tape. By awakening public antipathy towards the Whitehall bureaucracy, the campaign contrived to make people believe that the GLC was local, accessible, friendly and democratic. This remarkable achievement won the advertising industry's accolade for best poster campaign of the year for the GLC's agency, Boase Massimi Pollitt.

On top of the declared campaign budget, another £11 million was spent on other GLC advertising which nominally had nothing to do with the abolition issue, but which in practice was deliberately used to boost the GLC profile. One example was public-service television advertising warning against fire hazards, which reminded Londoners that the GLC ran the fire brigade.

The size of this advertising budget was unprecedented for a local authority. But the scale of the campaign did not just rely on the amount of money spent. The GLC organisation performed a bureaucratic tour de force. Its whole apparatus was turned into an engine of propaganda. Each of its labyrinthine departments was scoured for evidence of its own usefulness. Suppliers, employees and the people they served were mobilised into action on the GLC's behalf. Special-interest groups ranging from the elite arts lobby to hand-to-mouth voluntary groups were enlisted. The GLC's name was branded on everything the council ran, from traffic lights to fire stations and from waste disposal barges on the Thames to the rubbish dumps where the suburban middle classes disposed the clippings from their laurel hedges.

At the heart of the operation the Labour group politicians hatched a continuing stream of policy initiatives designed to wrong-foot the government, often goading ministers into ill-judged responses which were challenged in the courts. And at the top, Livingstone, the master showman, made himself available for every broadcast interview, every press conference and every photo opportunity stunt which could conceivably tempt the increasingly sympathetic media. Fuelled with data from the GLC machine, he poured out the usable quotes which got the council's case over to Londoners.

And the people responded. As the campaign got into gear in the early months of 1984, there was a dramatic swing of opinion in the GLC's favour. A MORI poll conducted for the council in January showed that 50 per cent of Londoners disapproved of the government's decision to abolish the GLC. By September a Harris poll conducted for Thames TV News was showing that the disapproval rating had increased to 74 per cent.

It would be wrong to accept advertising industry sales talk that this was simply the result of a well-financed campaign by a professional agency. This was not just a question of people being taken in by a few slick slogans. The truth was that the government

Ken Livingstone points a new banner at the MPs over the river, November 6th 1984 (*Guardian, E. Hamilton West*)

never had a good enough case for abolition. It never won the intellectual argument and the huge numbers of hostile responses to its consultation exercises were never satisfactorily answered. Of course the GLC's own claims that London would virtually collapse if the council disappeared were also seriously exaggerated. But the onus of proof was on the government to justify a major administrative upheaval – inevitably expensive, as all bureaucratic change is. It paid the price for Mrs Thatcher's hasty insertion in her manifesto of an ill-considered pledge.

Another important factor was the personality of Patrick Jenkin, her environment secretary. Jenkin was a clever lawyer with an immense capacity for hard work and an ability to absorb enormous quantities of fine-grain detail, but he was one of the least political of politicians. He would have made a good permanent secretary at the top of any Whitehall department. Yet his tendency to appear smug and his lack of public-relations skills made him a wholly inadequate adversary for Livingstone. Jenkin was remembered for advising the nation to brush its teeth in the dark to save electricity during the power cuts of the 1973 miners' strike, advice which looked even more foolish when the papers subsequently carried bedtime pictures of his own house bathed in light from every available bulb.

The combination of the government's weak argument, a minister in the wrong job at the wrong time, and the professionalism of the GLC campaign created the volatile political chemistry of the abolition struggle. The stage was set for a tremendous fight between a powerful but increasingly demoralised government and a GLC which was bursting with enthusiasm, cheek and creative ideas.

That is certainly how the battle will be remembered. But it did not look that way when Livingstone's own demoralised leadership group started planning their defences about six weeks after Mrs Thatcher's 1983 election victory. Their position seemed hopeless. The council's public relations chief, Tony Wilson, had commissioned some precautionary opinion research in February 1983 in case the Tories put abolition in their election manifesto and got a big enough majority to implement it. It showed there was continuing hostility among Londoners to the notion of Red Ken and his 'IRA/lesbian' approach to life in general and the governance of the GLC in particular. The pollsters also found a dismally low level of public awareness about what the GLC did.

The task was therefore to mobilise a partly hostile, substantially apathetic public to produce such a level of support for the council that a government with a Commons majority of 144 (the largest since 1945) would feel obliged to back down from a cast-iron manifesto commitment. It had to do this at a time when the Labour Party was shattered after Michael Foot's disastrous general election showing. It says something for the resilience of Livingstone and his team that they even bothered to try.

Tony Wilson identified for them a series of target audiences that a campaign would have to address. There were the MPs and peers, the opinion-formers in the media, the vested interest groups ranging from the arts lobby to council tenants and staff, the labour and trades union movement, and finally, at the base of the pyramid, the general public. Wilson argued that the public was the vital ingredient because it was only if they could be persuaded that the politicians would have to take notice. He asked for £2.7 million as an initial budget for the first three months of the campaign.

It was by no means clear how Livingstone and his Labour group would respond. They prided themselves on their socialist instincts. Was it not the case that Tory governments should be fought by marches, demonstrations, strikes and the defiance of martyrs who would rather break the law and go to jail than obey the agents of capitalism? Could it seriously be supposed that the class enemy would be defeated through the medium of an advertising agency financed by a levy on the rateable values of workers' homes?

In the event there was little argument. Wilson recalls that Livingstone chaired the crucial meeting in his usual laid-back style without, at first, revealing his own view. It was the left-winger Paul Boateng who came up with the telling point. Labour must learn the lessons of its general election defeat, he said. If the Tories could win votes using the Saatchi and Saatchi advertising agency, Labour must do it too. If that cost £2.7 million, so be it. The direction was established. From then on there was never any argument within the Labour group about the amount of money that was being spent. The admen got what they needed and reached saturation point in their coverage.

In the autumn of 1983 Livingstone and his entourage set off on a GLC road show around all the party conferences. His fringe meetings at the Liberal and SDP assemblies produced reactions bordering on adulation from younger delegates and were instrumental in moving the Alliance parties towards outright opposition to the government's abolition plans.

As Christmas approached, the GLC leadership was split

between those who wanted the campaign to concentrate on the council's capacity to deliver jobs and services and those who believed there should be a simpler, less cluttered message about Londoners' right to vote to run their own affairs. Livingstone backed the democracy theme.

In their enthusiasm for the fight, the Labour group dropped many of their socialist hang-ups. None of them could forget that in their early months in office they decided that Livingstone should reject his invitation to Prince Charles's wedding. Yet now, when an opportunity presented itself to get the Queen to open the GLC's new Thames Barrier, the group jumped at the chance to get favourable publicity for the council. When the big day came in May 1984, the ceremony was the occasion for a media extravaganza with live outside broadcast television catching the magic moments as the Queen boated down the river with Livingstone's mum Ethel, and her dutiful son Ken bowed to shake the royal hand. Was this the man who had called in 1981 for the abolition of the monarchy and expressed himself revolted at royal hangers-on like Princess Anne? As one council adviser put it: 'Once the Labour group had bitten the bullet of agreeing to the royal visit, there was nothing we couldn't do with them.'

Well, not quite nothing. The council's original choice of advertising agency to handle the anti-abolition campaign was Norman Craig and Kummel. When it was discovered that it had been taken over by a firm with offices in South Africa, the contract was cancelled. The GLC, which had named 1984 as Anti-Racist Year, then inadvertently asked two other agencies with South African links to tender for the work. The contract was finally placed with Boase Massimi Pollitt, an agency unencumbered with South African connections which started work in January 1984.

Given the government's massive Commons majority, the agency's strategy was to persuade ministers that the political costs of unpopularity that would result from pursuing their policy would outweigh the benefits of getting the legislation through. It set about trying to change the ground of debate to territory on which, opinion research suggested, the GLC could win over the public. BMP focused on the critical weakness of the government's plans: not the idea of abolition, but the timetable for its implementation.

A Cabinet subcommittee, code-named MISC 95, had been wrestling with this timetable problem since the summer of 1983. It concluded that there was no way the council could be eliminated before the next GLC elections, due in May 1985. The earliest that Department of the Environment officials thought the job could be done was April 1st 1986. Moreover, the sheer complexity of the legislation (which was also to abolish the six English metropolitan counties) meant that it would not be ready to bring before Parliament before the Queen's speech of November 1984; and it could not be enacted until after the May 1985 elections.

Patrick Jenkin was astute enough to realise that, if the elections went ahead, Labour would turn them into a referendum on the abolition issue. What is more, the Conservative government was likely by May 1985 to be going through a mid-term slump in popular support. So probably the Tories would lose the GLC vote just as the abolition bill was going through parliament. Ministers would be seen to be going against the will of the people. Jenkin decided that the only answer was some preliminary legislation to scrap the elections.

A fascinating insight into government thinking on this subject was given in an exchange of confidential memoranda between Jenkin and the prime minister, which fell into GLC hands and was leaked to the *Guardian*. (I have no knowledge of the exotic route along which the documents travelled before GLC politicians handed them over to the *Guardian* and their authenticity was established. Livingstone later claimed in his book, *If Voting Changed Anything, They'd Abolish It* (HarperCollins, 1987), that the papers fell out of a minister or civil servant's briefcase at a brothel specialising in sado-masochism and bondage. But this story always sounded too good to be true.)

The first of the Jenkin minutes, dated July 27th 1983, followed two meetings of the MISC 95 committee, the Ministerial Group on the Abolition of the GLC and Metropolitan County Councils. It noted that the Cabinet agreed on May 10th 1983 (reference CC '83' 17th Conclusions, Minute 3) that the government should introduce the main abolition legislation early in the 1984–85 session of Parliament, with the aim of completing the transfer of GLC and metropolitan county functions by April 1st 1986. The minute makes it clear that at this stage Jenkin was planning legislation to allow the Labour administrations at the GLC and metropolitan county councils (MCCs) an extra year of office until abolition could be effected in 1986. He wrote:

> A bill to defer the GLC and MCC elections due to take place in 1985, and to counter obstruction if necessary, is included in the legislative programme for the current session. MISC 95 agrees that we should avoid any statement in the immediate future about our determination to combat obstructive behaviour, since that might itself provoke obstruction. We would need to be ready to act quickly, however, if such behaviour began to occur.

His reference to obstruction showed that the government was already concerned at this early stage about the GLC's potential to make trouble if councillors were allowed to stay in office for the extra year. During the summer, however, Jenkin came under increasing pressure from Tory back-benchers to change his mind. They thought it ludicrous to begin the process of 'getting rid of Red Ken' by passing legislation to prolong his period of power. By the time of his second minute to Mrs Thatcher, on September 20th, Jenkin had accepted their argument:

> Elections to the GLC and MCCs are due in May 1985. The [Ministerial] Group are agreed that they cannot be allowed

to go ahead: other objections apart, abolition would be a major issue in the elections, so that there would be a major public debate going on after the House of Commons had voted for a second reading of the abolition bill.

There are two options for replacing the elections.

(i) *Deferral*.

It would be in accordance with precedents of past reorganisations to defer the elections for a year; existing councillors would continue in office. The deferred elections would then be overtaken by abolition of the GLC and MCCs on April 1, 1986.

(ii) *Substitution*.

Councillors appointed by the London boroughs and the metropolitan districts would take over the role of the GLC and MCC councillors almost immediately after the date on which elections would otherwise have taken place ...

The views of the Group on the options were divided. Some members argued that there were constitutional and political objections to substitution: in particular, that we should be accused of creating a new procedure in order to engineer a change in political control in the GLC area and possibly (depending on the results of elections between now and May 1985 and on the basis of selection of the substitute councillors) some of the MCC areas.

A small majority of the Group, however, considered that both our own supporters and the wider public would find it incomprehensible that we should, in effect, extend the terms of office of the GLC and the MCCs. Moreover, to do so would provide those bodies with scope for obstruction at a time when this would be most damaging to our policies. They therefore favoured substitution...

In political terms this is probably one of the most sensitive decisions we have to take. My own recommendation is in favour of substitution. I propose we should announce this in the white paper.

Mrs Thatcher disagreed. A minute from one of her private secretaries, Michael Scholar, to Jenkin's private secretary, John Ballard, replied that the prime minister preferred deferral of the May 1985 elections to substitution.

The leak of documents ran out at that stage and it was never fully understood why she decided in the end to accept Jenkin's advice. With the benefit of hindsight, it was a terrible mistake. If the Iron Lady had stuck to her gut instincts, she would have avoided what was probably the worst humiliation of her administration. But, when the White Paper was published on October 7th, it announced that the GLC was to be run for the last 11 months of its life by the nominees of the London boroughs. Power would pass from Labour to the Tories.

That was the expected scenario as the BMP agency began work for the GLC. Its polling research:

> identified that 'democracy' had the potency to popularise the debate in a non-party-political manner and to outweigh existing prejudices against the controversial Labour-controlled council. Presenting abolition as a constitutional issue about the rights of every Londoner to control the running of the city promised to convert Conservative voters to opposition to the proposed reforms, which was vital if the government was to be dissuaded from its proposed reform. The advertising was thus to perform the bold task of changing the grounds of the debate and of establishing new grounds on which opponents of the government's policy could win.

BMP said the campaign was intended to function as a catalyst, setting in motion a series of influences which would surround the government and convince it that to continue to pursue its reform was increasingly unwise. Tory activists would become alarmed, Tory MPs and peers would express their concern, and this would put pressure on the government.

That is exactly what happened as the 'Say No to No Say' posters went up around London. One portrayed a dustbin in the style of a ballot box with a slit in its padlocked lid. 'Next year all Londoners' votes will go the same way', it warned. Another, aimed directly at MPs and peers, pictured the Houses of Parliament with the slogan: 'What kind of place is it that takes away your right to vote and leaves you with no say?'

One early campaign success was the government's decision to grant direct elections to the Inner London Education Authority. Ministers' original plan had been to put ILEA under the control of nominees from the relevant boroughs. The public argument about London democracy persuaded them to allow the voters to choose by establishing separate four-yearly polls for the new single-purpose education authority. They absolutely refused, however, to show any sympathy to demands from Alan Greengross, leader of the Tory group on the GLC, for a directly elected slim-line successor to the GLC to run services which could not be devolved to the boroughs. Mrs Thatcher quashed all argument on the possibility by labelling the idea 'son of Frankenstein'.

As far as the public was concerned, the debate at this stage was dominated by the government's intention to scrap the GLC elections. Preparatory legislation was published on March 30th 1984, snappily entitled the Local Government (Interim Provisions) Bill, but known by everyone involved as the Paving Bill because it paved the way for abolition. When it came for its second reading in the Commons on April 11th, as the opinion polls were starting to turn in the GLC's favour, 19 Tory backbenchers voted against the government. The former Tory prime minister, Edward Heath, told the Commons that the bill 'immediately lays the Conservative Party open to the charge of the greatest gerrymandering in the last 150 years of British history'. He said the Tories could be accused of 'just funking elections'. Both Heath and another former Tory Cabinet minister, Francis Pym, focused on the democracy angle and the unacceptability of switching power in London from Labour to Conservative without giving the people a chance to vote. Pym said: 'The imposed change of party control in these circumstances will cause the government and this party no end of trouble. It isn't worth it, the price is too high.'

Given Heath's legendary bitterness towards Mrs Thatcher and the general disaffection of Pym and other Tory wets, the party whips did not at that stage regard the revolt as threatening. In spite of continuing Tory sniping, the bill got its third reading on May 23rd after a sitting lasting more than 32 hours, the longest since the Second World War. But, as Jenkin celebrated, the GLC was preparing to humiliate him in the House of Lords.

In addition to the BMP advertising campaign, which aimed to influence the parliamentarians through public opinion, there was a quite separate GLC lobbying operation targeted directly at MPs and peers. It was run by Roland Freeman, a former Tory GLC member who switched to the SDP and stood as a parliamentary candidate for the Liberal–SDP Alliance in the 1983 general election. Freeman also concentrated his message on the unacceptability of the government's plan to scrap the GLC elections and hand power over to Tory nominees. But he had another constitutional argument of particular relevance to the peers.

The Paving Bill was built on the hypothesis that it would be followed a year later by the Abolition Bill proper. The government could not, however, write one piece of legislation on the assumption that Parliament would later pass another bill, which at that stage did not even exist. The reason was obvious. If, once the GLC elections had been scrapped, the main Abolition Bill failed to get through, then the council would be put indefinitely into the hands of nominees.

But Jenkin could not afford to wait until the Abolition Bill was passed before triggering the powers to scrap the elections. The GLC poll was due in May 1985 and the bill could not be enacted until mid-summer. The Paving Bill therefore said that cancellation of the elections would not be triggered until the main Abolition Bill passed its second reading in the Commons.

This was something of an insult to the peers because it assumed that, when it came their turn to consider the main Abolition Bill, they would endorse the view of the MPs. In other words they were being asked to pre-empt their own procedures. The message was hammered home to the peers whom Freeman wined and dined and entertained in batches at receptions at County Hall. It was echoed in a parallel campaign for the metropolitan counties, run by the lobbyists GJW.

The irony of the GLC socialists relying on the House of Lords for defence against the will of the elected chamber was not lost on their critics. But there was never a pause for serious self-doubt as the combined advertising and lobbying campaign headed towards its denouement.

On the evening of the second reading debate on June 11th 1984, the House of Lords had its biggest attendance since the 1971 vote on British entry into the Common Market. The Tory chief whip, Lord (Bertie) Denham, had issued one of his rare three-line whips to maximise his turnout among the usually absent hereditary peers. The opposition parties had buried their differences to agree an amendment designed to draw wide support from the cross-benches (the politically unattached peers) and from Tory rebels.

It was generally assumed that the government could rely on the Tories' big inbuilt majority to get its way, but, as the debate continued, it became clear that the constitutional arguments had hit home. Peer after peer complained, not about the principle of abolition, but about the dangerous constitutional precedents which were being set. At the end there was a 20-vote victory for the government when the amendment attacking the Bill was defeated by 237 votes to 217. But, from ministers' points of view, the narrowness of the result was a terrible blow to morale. Worse was to come.

When the bill started its committee stage on June 28th, a

wrecking amendment was tabled by Labour, Liberal, SDP and rebel Tory peers. It was designed to prevent the elections being cancelled until the main Abolition Bill became law. As has already been explained, this was impossible for the government to accept, since the Abolition Bill could not be enacted until after the elections were due.

But Denham had already shot his bolt. Given the genteel etiquette of the upper chamber, where most Tory peers voted as a favour rather than an obligation, he felt that a further three-line whip would be counter-productive. So he sent out a (less compelling) two-liner. It was the first day of the Lord's test; Henley Regatta and Wimbledon tennis were also under way. The Tory backwoods peers, unconvinced by the government's arguments and no doubt tempted by these rival seasonal attractions, voted with their feet. The government's defeat was sensational. The wrecking amendment was carried by 191 votes to 143, a majority of 48. It was the most humiliating reverse of the Thatcher administrations. As many as 40 Tories sat on their hands during the vote in a public show of abstention and distaste. Jenkin's plan was in tatters. He was forced to announce that the existing GLC and metropolitan county councils would be given an extra year of office until the end of March 1986.

The *Daily Express* commented two days later: 'Who could have believed it? Red Ken Livingstone is now appearing as champion of the British Constitution – courtesy of the Peerage – and a friend of democracy. That is what the Tories have managed to contrive by their fumbling, bumbling, botched handling of the bill to abolish the GLC and the other metropolitan counties.' The paper called for Jenkin to be replaced by someone who could 'mix it' more effectively with Red Ken. In fact Jenkin, a talented man who was willing and able to do everything for his prime minister except change his personality, survived for another unhappy year before being sacked in the reshuffle of September 1985. To lend him support, Mrs Thatcher gave him a new deputy. In September 1984 she appointed as local government minister

Kenneth Baker, a bright and highly political politician who would never let a bad case stand in the way of making an appealing argument – skills that he was later to deploy as party chairman. As a Conservative, Baker was rather too wet for Mrs Thatcher's taste, but as a performer 'Blue Ken' was a better adversary for his Red namesake.

Of course the government's defeat in the House of Lords was hailed as a personal triumph for Livingstone. And in a sense it was. Without him as the charismatic figurehead, the public could well have been bored to death by the campaign. Without him as the unchallenged chairman of the key campaign-strategy committee, the operation could have foundered in policy and personality clashes. Perhaps even more important, without him as the bogeyman figure, the essence of socialist awfulness in the minds of Tory back-benchers, it is doubtful that the government would have made the mistake of trying to scrap the GLC elections in the way it did, the key ingredient in turning the campaign into a battle for democracy. The idea of giving Red Ken an extra year in power was so outrageous for the Tory rank and file that Mrs Thatcher went along with what she believed was an error.

Yet again Livingstone triumphed because of his enemies' mistakes. If his cheeky high-profile style was to take the blame for goading the Conservatives into abolishing the GLC in the first place, then it also had to take the credit for causing his opponents to make the critical misjudgment.

But this was not a one-man show. Livingstone delegated most of the campaign work to colleagues, allowing him to get on with the broad-brush popular appeal. Political control of the GLC operation was divided into three groups covering public relations/advertising, parliamentary activity and trades union/GLC staff campaigning. The public relations side was run by John McDonnell, whose appetite for hard work and grasp of detail was credited by GLC officials for much of the success. McDonnell, who succeeded Illtyd Harrington as deputy leader of the council in May 1984, was also finance chairman and during this period he was taking a grip on most of the important political levers of the GLC machine. A monumental bust-up between Livingstone and McDonnell lay ahead in the spring of 1985, but at this stage the two men enjoyed a relationship of considerable political trust. McDonnell was not a wholehearted fan of Livingstone's politics, but they shared a common purpose and Livingstone relied on his lieutenant heavily.

Political control of the parliamentary operation was run by Tony Banks, who remained a GLC councillor after becoming Labour MP for Newham North-West at the 1983 general election. Mobilisation of the trades unions was supervised by Mike Ward, who continued as chairman of the industry committee as it pressed on with its experiment in socialist economic planning through its Greater London Enterprise Board arm. The work of the three groups was harmonised at a weekly campaign co-ordinating committee chaired by Livingstone every Monday. This settled disagreements such as the running tension between the advertising group, which wanted to achieve maximum popular impact, and the parliamentary group, which feared that excessive display would alienate MPs and peers.

The BMP advertising campaign outraged many Tory back-bench loyalists, but careful monitoring showed that it never became counter-productive with the target audiences. Its success was later to have an important impact on the Labour Party, which adopted the GLC's public-relations techniques in the run-up to the 1987 general election.

The council was forbidden by the Independent Broadcasting Authority from using Livingstone's voice on its public-service commercials; and it was obliged to change its slogan from 'Working for London' to 'Working in London' on radio and television ads. But the campaign team cheekily avoided the controls by erecting its publicity material at sporting fixtures. A test match at the Oval was interrupted when BBC television complained that it could not continue coverage until GLC 'Working for London' slogans had been masked. But nothing stopped the televising of the England–Romania football international at which the GLC slogans were prominently displayed behind the goals. The match was being played in Bucharest.

This piratical panache was a feature of the campaign. It permeated the whole GLC operation and it is likely that the expensive advertising campaign would not have had nearly so much success if it had not been backed up by clever news-making stunts conceived by Livingstone's personal staff, notably his ebullient press officer, Nita Clarke.

The Paving Bill struggle caused – or at least coincided with – a massive increase in Livingstone's personal popularity. In March 1983 a MORI poll had shown that 58 per cent of Londoners were dissatisfied with him and 26 per cent satisfied. By March 1984 the number dissatisfied had fallen to 42 per cent and the number satisfied had risen to 43 per cent. This later poll coincided with the first flush of the BMP advertising campaign and a lull in anti-Red Ken coverage in the popular press.

The agency felt sufficiently confident about the Livingstone image to use his picture in full-page newspaper advertisements on the day of the Paving Bill's second reading debate in the Commons, coupled with the message: 'If you want me out, you should have the right to vote me out.' But the flow of more sympathetic media coverage did not come until May and was triggered by extensive coverage of the Queen's opening of the Thames Barrier.

An analysis by BMP of Livingstone's media exposure in selected newspapers shows that he had the equivalent of three full tabloid pages of hostile press coverage in January, compared to one page's worth of neutral coverage and two pages of supportive coverage. The figures were identical for February and March. In April there were the equivalent of three pages of supportive material, two neutral and one hostile. Then in May the tally jumped to 12 pages supportive, none neutral and two hostile.

Equipped with the new asset of general personal popularity,

Livingstone set about the next stage in the struggle with the government by resigning his council seat to fight a by-election on the abolition issue. Three days before the government's defeat on the Paving Bill in the House of Lords, Livingstone announced on June 25th in a radio debate with Patrick Jenkin that he and three other Labour GLC members for marginal constituencies would resign to fight by-elections in September 1984. Jenkin immediately condemned the move as a stunt and suggested that the Tories would not put up candidates. Livingstone condemned him for 'the biggest act of political cowardice since the war'.

By-elections were held in Livingstone's seat of Paddington, in John McDonnell's seat in Hayes and Harlington, and in the constituencies of two other Labour members, Lewis Herbert in Lewisham West and Ken Little in Edmonton. Although Livingstone's popularity seemed likely to secure his own re-election, the others were taking an enormous risk. Without Tory candidates, there could have been a massive switch to the Liberal-SDP Alliance, which also opposed GLC abolition. All the seats were marginals, won by Labour in 1981, but with Tory MPs returned at the 1983 general election. If Labour had lost even one, its stunt would have backfired.

The by-elections were the occasion for the rehabilitation of the GLC with the Labour leader, Neil Kinnock. On the day the four resigned, Livingstone read out a message from Kinnock announcing the 'full and committed support of the whole Labour Party'. Only a year before, Kinnock's aides had gone out of their way to prevent an encounter between the two men at the Labour conference in case a stray photographer might produce a picture which would tarnish the Kinnock image. Now Kinnock made himself available for photo opportunities with Livingstone and one of his salamanders alongside Paddington schoolchildren. Labour MPs who a year or two before would not have touched Livingstone with a barge-pole also jostled to get in on the act.

The by-election results were an anti-climax. Labour won large majorities in all four, but with such a low turnout that claims of

In cold blood: Neil Kinnock, Livingstone and salamander campaigning in the anti-abolition by-elections, September 12th 1984 (*Guardian, Frank Martin*)

massive popular opposition to GLC abolition were un-substantiated. Livingstone blamed torrential rain on polling day and the Tory boycott, but the upshot was that he and his colleagues had proved little more than their political courage. Only Livingstone himself increased his 1981 vote, securing 78 per cent of the poll to resume his seat and his leadership.

The extra 11 months in office conceded to him by the government opened up a whole new range of opportunities for obstruction. Not only could the council continue campaigning against its demise, it could also set about managing its affairs to secure 'life after death' by funding other London boroughs and voluntary groups to carry forward GLC objectives. To choke off some of this activity, Jenkin introduced new clauses into the Paving Bill at report stage in the House of Lords to impose ministerial control on contracts over £100,000. The GLC redoubled its complaint about central government interference by pointing out that Ministers were now vetting even the council's contract for baked beans (which it bought in bulk for London schools and other municipal establishments). In the fortnight before the new rules became law, GLC committees went on an unprecedented spending spree, approving contracts worth £40 million to beat the new controls. A 20-month game of cat and mouse was under way.

The Local Government Bill to abolish the GLC and metropolitan counties was published on November 22nd 1984. Its sheer bulk – 98 clauses and 17 supplementary schedules – was a sign of the complexity of the task of dismantling the councils. Ministers claimed the result would be to shed 7,100 jobs and save ratepayers about £100 million a year, half in London and half in the metropolitan areas. The GLC in contrast produced detailed costings designed to demonstrate that abolition would cost at least £225 million extra over five years. The discrepancy was never properly resolved. From this point on the abolition debate became more confused and less satisfactory from the GLC's point of view. Whereas the campaign against the Paving Bill was able to concentrate on clear issues of democracy and constitutional propriety, the arguments now became diffused into technicalities of waste management, planning controls and the like.

But the GLC and its advertising agency were still able to play the democracy card by arguing that two-thirds of the council's budget was to pass into the less accountable hands of central government, quangos and joint boards of borough representatives. And they could raise the nagging question why London, alone among western capital cities, would be left without an elected voice.

This was the point Edward Heath seized on when the bill came for its second reading in the Commons on December 3rd and 4th. Describing the case for abolition as unproven, he complained that there had been no proper study of the issue. 'The government talked about the case being justified because abolition was in the manifesto. It was put in just nine days after the election was called, against the wishes of the party policy committee, and without the agreement of London MPs,' he complained. Heath asked Jenkin to 'think ahead to the stage at which he will be required to provide an overall [elected] authority for the greatest capital in the world'.

Although Heath and a dozen other Tories abstained on the second reading, the main Commons revolt was to come when the committee stage opened on the floor of the House. On December 14th, at the end of a two-day debate, an amendment proposed by dissident Tory back-bencher Patrick Cormack was defeated by a slender majority of only 23. It was the government's worst showing since the 1983 election. Cormack had proposed that the GLC should be replaced by a directly-elected authority covering the same area, and that its functions and powers should be determined by Parliament following an inquiry by a Commons select committee. More than 100 Tory MPs failed to support the party line. It is probable that any other post-war government would have bowed to such continuing pressure of internal dissent. Not Mrs Thatcher's.

The internal Tory debate was fuelled by detailed proposals from Alan Greengross, leader of the GLC Tory group, who produced a pamphlet at the request of dissident Tory MPs explaining how a slim-line elected London-wide council could work without developing into a high-spending GLC Mark Two. When the bill went upstairs to complete its committee stage in a smaller standing committee, the government's majority was cut from 11 to 3 on an amendment to create just such a body. The argument was gaining force among Conservative back-benchers and it began to look possible that the House of Lords would feel able to exercise its constitutional muscle. There was a convention that the peers would not vote down a proposal that had been in a government's election manifesto, but the dissident Tory MPs were providing them with a loophole. Given the internal disagreement among Tories in the Commons, the peers could argue that there was nothing in the manifesto to say that, once the GLC had been abolished, another London-wide council could not be set up. No one could predict the outcome with any confidence.

It was at this stage, when the bill was still going through its Commons committee stage, that the GLC Labour group descended into the bitterest period of internal strife in its history. Livingstone and his deputy McDonnell ended up accusing each other of treachery, and rifts were established that looked for a while like a permanent split between Livingstone and the hard left. The subject of the dispute had nothing to do with the abolition campaign, but the vehemence with which it was pursued sapped the morale at the GLC in the run-up to the big abolition battle in the Lords. We turn to the crisis over rate-capping.

It was explained in the previous chapter how the government passed legislation to gain control over the budgets of what it called the most 'profligate' local authorities. In July 1984 Patrick Jenkin told the GLC, the ILEA and 16 other councils that they were to be rate-capped in the following financial year. The authorities banded together in a pact of defiance, arguing that, if they did not make a stand in the first year of the new policy, they would eventually become the mere pawns of central government. There was a continuing debate within the Labour movement about the most effective resistance tactic, but by January 1985 opinion coalesced around what was called the 'no rate option', that is, refusing to fix a rate until the government had been persuaded to make concessions.

The idea was forcefully expressed by John McDonnell at a meeting of the Association of London Authorities on January 15th. The councils should agree to synchronise their budget meetings on March 7th when they should pass resolutions refusing to make a legal budget or rate on the grounds that they could not meet the needs of their communities. They should make arrangements for payments to continue to their workers during a period of confrontation, establishing that any money

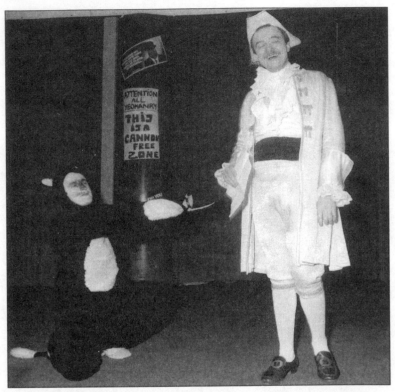

Cat (John McDonnell) and Dick Whittington (Ken Livingstone) do a turn again at GLC panto, December 19th 1984 (*Guardian*)

available should be spent on wages and services instead of interest payments to the banks. By defaulting on debt, the councils would put pressure on the money markets and, through them, the government. Faced with a financial crisis and the possibility that administration in these hard-pressed urban areas might eventually collapse, ministers would be persuaded to negotiate seriously. The councils should then demand the return of the £9 billion in rate support grant which had been 'stolen' from them since 1981. With this money in their coffers, the councils could afford to maintain services and cut the rates.

It is fair to say that not all – probably not even a majority – of the leaders of rate-capped Labour councils fully believed in this scenario. Some hoped that the mere threat of causing a crisis would be enough to make Jenkin negotiate an acceptable settlement. Some appeared to have no idea what would happen, but were fearful of being accused of betrayal if they failed to take a hard line. But, whatever their motives, they agreed, to head towards illegality by refusing to set a rate.

At the GLC, Livingstone left most of the detailed work on rate-capping to McDonnell, but there was no doubt that he supported the principle of defiance. As early as February 1984, he told Labour's local government conference in Nottingham that in some cases law-breaking was acceptable. 'I do want to see a Parliament that is supreme,' he said. That would be necessary for a future Labour government to control the economy. 'But what are we to do if Parliament acts to take away freedom? I don't necessarily believe we should give a blank cheque to the present majority in Parliament.' Livingstone argued that the councils should refuse to make cuts and should support their staff in disobeying government commands. Ministers would have to accept the chaos and confusion that would be caused by their measures. 'If that puts us outside the law, then it is the laws that are wrong,' Livingstone said.

In January 1985 he told a London Labour Party conference that Labour councillors and trade unionists should occupy their town halls to ensure that services continued during the struggle. 'We will effectively operate within the state in defiance of the state. That will provide the most dramatic challenge, apart from the challenge of the miners' strike, that this government has faced since 1979,' he said. Common action by the London councils was essential. Ministers should be faced with 'the prospect of a city in revolt'. There was a chance to inflict 'the most savage defeat' on the government.

It should be remembered that this rhetoric was being delivered while the GLC's cuddly respectable image was being purveyed in the campaign against abolition. Although it was thoroughly reported in some places, it went almost entirely ignored in the popular press. Having rehabilitated Livingstone, editors seemed uninterested in attacking him again for 'extremism'. By accident rather than by design Livingstone got away with the trick of playing it hard with the left on rate-capping and soft with everyone else on abolition.

The explosion occurred in March 1985. Until then the rebel Labour councils – including the 16 rate-capped authorities under Labour control and several others such as Liverpool and Manchester which were hard-pressed by cuts in their grants – had preserved a remarkable degree of unity. They had been shepherded by David Blunkett, leader of Sheffield, into a position designed to bring maximum pressure on the government while still leaving the door open to negotiation. By the end of February, however, it had become clear that Jenkin was too weak politically to dare to concede anything. He had been hammered by the GLC over abolition and criticised in his own party for appearing to have made concessions to Militant councillors from Liverpool during the previous summer. His objective was now to re-establish his credibility in the Conservative Party by calling the rebels' bluff and forcing them into a humiliating climb-down. His advisers assured him that the councillors' nerve would crack and that the government could easily survive any temporary disruption to local services.

The statutory timetable was crucial. Upper-tier authorities, such as the GLC, ILEA, Merseyside and South Yorkshire, had a legal obligation to set a rate by March 10th. The law was written that way so that their demands could be passed down to the lower-tier borough and district councils for incorporation into their own rating decisions before the start of the financial year in April. Failure to meet this March 10th deadline would lead to the upper-tier councillors being surcharged, disqualified from public office and possibly bankrupted. In contrast, the lower-tier councillors had no statutory rate-making date. Although common practice suggested it should be done by April 1st, there were precedents for some delay. Only if the timetable drifted substantially could these councillors be accused of unreasonable behaviour by causing their authorities to lose money (for example, by borrowing to cover for uncollected rates).

The rebel group of councils obviously predicted this possible cause of division in their ranks. They agreed that all of them should hold budget meetings on March 7th at which, in a synchronised act of defiance, they would pass motions saying it was impossible for them to make a rate.

Blunkett realised that the upper-tier authorities were taking a risk which the lower-tier councils did not yet face. So he gave them a chance in late February to get off the hook and climb down gracefully. South Yorkshire and Merseyside took him up on the offer and agreed to set a rate, while promising not to implement any cuts (a potentially illegal form of deficit budgeting). The GLC and ILEA, however, refused and pressed on towards immediate confrontation.

The crisis began on Thursday February 28th, a week before budget day. According to Livingstone, it was then that he learned for the first time the true state of the GLC's finances. Since the previous autumn the council had been claiming that its rate-cap limit of 36.5p in the pound would force it to make cuts worth £135 million on its base budget of £852 million (the cost of continuing services at existing levels). On this assumption the Labour group politicians whipped up support from council workers and the public, especially voluntary groups which were encouraged to fear that their grants would be cut. Early projections of council budgets are always more gloomy than the eventual results and it could be said that such figures were used with cynical and manipulative abandon by the GLC (and other affected councils). Although many observers knew they were exaggerating the problem, it was hard to gauge by how much.

During January and February, GLC officials led by Maurice Stonefrost (by then promoted to be director-general) set about preparing a package to close the apparent £135 million gap. Using all the creative accountancy techniques at their disposal, including squeezing balances and writing off LT debt, they managed to reduce the need for real service cuts to £30 million – in GLC terms a drop in the ocean, equivalent to only 3.5 per cent of spending. Livingstone says that he got the first wind of the true budget arithmetic on the Thursday evening before budget week. Reg Race, the left-wing former MP, who was then working as a senior GLC official, came to him with a reformulation of the Stonefrost package which contrived to produce £24 million of growth while still remaining within the rate-cap limits.

On the Friday morning Livingstone confronted McDonnell with these numbers and accused him of using his position as finance chairman to conceal the GLC's true financial position. The two men argued about the validity of the figures. It was to be their last conversation for about six months.

Meanwhile Livingstone began to realise that another aspect of the no-rate strategy was in danger of collapse. He had learned that the London boroughs were falling back on more feebly worded motions for the following week. By saying they found it impossible to approve a rate 'at that stage', they were to avoid the strong language which might have set them immediately outside the law.

Livingstone thought this combination of circumstances put the GLC Labour group in an impossible position. In his view the only financial uncertainty was how much growth could be achieved and how quickly it could be implemented after budget day. So Labour councillors were being asked to risk surcharge and disqualification when the borough councillors who were egging them on were not yet taking similar risks. Livingstone's view was that the majority of his group would not wear it. He therefore set about activating an escape route. While still urging borough councillors to join the GLC in all-out no-rate illegality, he instructed Race to work up the legal growth package. This fall-back position could have allowed the GLC to argue, like

Merseyside and South Yorkshire, that it had achieved the 'bottom line' of party conference policy – avoiding making cuts.

Livingstone's response outraged McDonnell, who had been working to ensure that the no-rate option could carry in the council if it carried in the Labour group. Labour had a majority of only four. So, if the Tories believed they had a legal responsibility to vote through the maximum rate, it was likely that they could attract enough votes from the Labour right to get a majority. To counter this, McDonnell secured a legal opinion which suggested that the Tories could vote against the maximum, without risk of surcharge, if they had previously recommended a lower figure. The Tories seized on this idea with glee. So McDonnell thought he could achieve an impasse in the council chamber where no party or faction had a majority for any legal rate proposal. All it needed was that most of the group should abide by conference policy.

The dispute fomented over the pre-budget weekend at the annual conference of the London Labour Party. Livingstone continued to speak for the illegal no-rate option, but argued that the London boroughs should firm up their resolution for the following Thursday to ensure that they went illegal at the same time. Ted Knight, leader of Lambeth and Livingstone's co-editor on *Labour Herald*, told delegates: 'Quite frankly, it is a bit late for some comrades to realise that there are problems.'

On the Monday, the GLC Labour group met to decide what to do. Livingstone presented what became known as the 'Reg Race budget', the reworking of the Stonefrost package to produce the appearance of growth. Race made the £30 million Stonefrost cut 'disappear' by pointing out that £30 million of savings would inevitably be achieved through increased efficiency, the effects of the Abolition Bill on the staff vacancy rate and ministers' decisions to block some spending projects. He then suggested a couple of extra creative accounting devices to provide for £24 million 'growth'. McDonnell called it a cuts budget which assumed that the council's campaign against abolition would fail. He alleged that some of the creative accounting techniques could only have been used with confidence if there had been a deal with the Department of the Environment.

Livingstone urged the group to continue its no-rate stance, but to fall back on the Reg Race budget if it became the only alternative to a Tory budget. His advice was rejected. The group voted by 24 to 18 to back an alternative proposal from Mike Ward, the soft-left industry committee chairman, to stop fudging and go immediately for the Reg Race option.

The next day, Tuesday, the fur began to fly in public. At an extraordinary press conference, Livingstone accused McDonnell of misleading his colleagues about the GLC's financial position. McDonnell in turn slated Livingstone for betraying London Labour Party policy and for 'bottling out'.

On the Wednesday, the TUC organised a national demonstration against rate-capping, including a march through London to the GLC car park. There the TUC general secretary, Norman Willis, was taunted by a handful of activists who hurled tin cans and pieces of wood at him and called him 'scab' on the grounds that he had failed to give adequate support to Arthur Scargill during the extended miners' strike, then drawing towards its collapse. This context of defeat for the left and its feelings of betrayal were important ingredients in the political fall-out of the eventual rate-capping debacle.

Then came the budget meetings of Thursday March 7th. The GLC council chamber was shared with ILEA, which was due to hold its session first. Its leader, Frances Morrell, continued to argue that ILEA should refuse to set a rate. She was supported by Livingstone. Both of them, however, approved amendments to the spending estimates to ensure that no cuts were necessary if, somehow, the rate got through. (This was ILEA's equivalent to the Reg Race fall-back position at the GLC.)

The outcome was inevitable. With Morrell and Livingstone still arguing for defiance, enough Labour moderates went into the

Under pressure: Ken Livingstone during the GLC rate-capping crisis, March 9th 1985 (*Guardian, Martin Argles*)

division lobbies with the Tories to ensure that a legal rate was passed. It was the first victory for Patrick Jenkin. Around the country the other Labour rebel councils did what they had promised. ILEA had failed to deliver, but both Morrell and Livingstone could claim that their voting record showed they had not 'betrayed'.

The ILEA meeting lasted so long that the GLC budget debate was postponed until the next day, Friday. Then began a marathon 23-hour debate which lasted into the early hours of the Saturday morning and again through most of Sunday. It ended within seconds of the 8 p.m. deadline which Stonefrost, the director-general, ruled was the last moment before the councillors were plunged into illegality.

The detail was tedious, but the drama was electrifying. Tory motions to cut £130 million from the base budget and reduce the rate precept from the maximum 36.5p in the pound to 27p in the pound were defeated by the united vote of the Labour group. So were attempts by the Liberal–SDP Alliance to propose more modest prunings. But every time the Reg Race budget was put forward at least eight Labour left members voted against it. They included McDonnell, Tony Banks and Paul Boateng (councillors who either were or were about to become Labour MPs). Throughout the Friday night Livingstone continued to vote against making a rate and argued for the Reg Race spending estimates only as a fall-back position. But over the Saturday he received a series of warnings from the Labour right that if he could not carry the Reg Race budget, they would vote for whatever legal alternative became available. During the Sunday afternoon he was forced into a tactical switch. Under barracking from hard-left activists in the public gallery, he said it had become clear there was no majority on the council for refusing to fix a rate and that it was essential to avoid the possibility of a Tory cuts budget. He begged colleagues on the Labour left for their support, declaring: 'We have no right to put on the line other people's jobs.' But McDonnell's group would not budge, arguing that Livingstone was betraying the clear mandate of the London Labour Party conference and dealing a potentially lethal blow to the strategy of other rebel councils.

Along the marbled corridors outside the council chamber, it was possible to imagine the echo of the laugh of Livingstone's predecessor, Sir Reg Goodwin. In 1975 Livingstone led the revolt against Goodwin's 'betrayal'. In 1985 McDonnell led the revolt against Livingstone. This time, however, the voting arithmetic was more complex and the political stakes were far higher. The Labour councillors were not only dicing with their reputations, but also with their futures. They were within minutes of the deadline after which they could be surcharged and their families even bankrupted. Bankrupts cannot be MPs.

It was at this stage that Livingstone, having lost control of part of his left wing, came close to losing the support of his right. By then the Tories had gradually increased their rate proposal from 27p to 33p. Their leader, Alan Greengross, pointed out to potential Labour defectors that this could keep them within the law for the political price of only £20 million less spending. (Readers are advised not to try to make these various numbers add up: the sums all involved a complex calculation on the size of government grant and the amount of creative accounting acceptable at different spending levels.)

About 18 members of the Labour right, welded into a coherent voting bloc for probably the first time since Livingstone's defeat of Andrew McIntosh for the GLC leadership in 1981, were poised to back Greengross's proposal. Appalled at the Livingstone administration's chaos and alarmed at imminent illegality, they were ready to vote with the Tories. If they had, it is very hard to see how the Livingstone administration could have survived.

It was probably only the intervention of Larry Whitty, shortly to take over as the Labour Party's general secretary, which saved some vestige of unity. During an adjournment, he appealed to the right faction's loyalty to the party and persuaded them not to vote for the Greengross package. Give the Reg Race budget one final chance, he pleaded. The appeal worked with the right, but similar efforts by the NEC member Audrey Wise to cajole the left went unheeded. With the 8 p.m. deadline fast approaching, the Reg Race option was again put forward, but ten members of the Labour left voted against, securing its defeat. In addition to McDonnell, Banks and Boateng, they were Dave Wetzel, Lesley Hammond, Deirdre Wood, Charlie Rossi, Bryn Davies, Paul Moore and Jenni Fletcher.

It was left to a Labour right-winger, Barry Stead, to move the final solution of a formula midway between the Greengross and Reg Race packages. This was passed by the Labour right, the Tories and the Liberal–SDP Alliance. Livingstone, McDonnell and most of the Labour group voted against. The result was announced. Eight o'clock struck. The recriminations began.

As it turned out, the budget was more than ample for the council to get through the following year. But the political reality at the time was that the GLC, having campaigned against the impossibility of living within the government's 36.5p rate-cap, ended up by setting a rate of only 33.8p. There was no disguising that the affair had been a total shambles.

The recriminations reverberated for months afterwards. Given irreconcilable conflicts over fact, it is impossible to give an impartial verdict on whether Livingstone or McDonnell had a superior claim to moral rectitude. What was clear was that in the end McDonnell preferred the certainty of sticking to London Labour Party policy rather than taking the opportunity to achieve the biggest budget possible in the circumstances. He was consistent, but the result of his consistency nearly achieved the collapse of the administration. Livingstone preferred to make the best of a bad job.

To choose between them it is necessary to answer the question: is it more important that socialists never betray their mandate or that they recognise, when the chips are down, that politics is about the art of the possible? McDonnell's objective became impossible because the Labour right could not stomach illegality, not only for reasons of personal danger, but also because of their conviction that the parliamentary route to socialism demanded respect for the law. Yet McDonnell could argue that Livingstone made the right's retreat easier by encouraging the preparation of the Reg Race fall-back position.

Livingstone claimed immediately after the final vote that he would not be ready to stay in office if jobs and services were cut. 'I would not be prepared to act as a front person to provide a veneer of socialist respectability to a cuts programme,' he said. We may never know whether that really was his sticking-point. In the following year, as before, the GLC's problem was that it could not spend the money fast enough.

There was one more quote from that post-vote press conference which must have sounded rich to veterans of the Goodwin administration. 'The Labour Party is a broad church,' said Livingstone, 'but it is sometimes difficult getting its members in the same congregation.' How would Livingstone, the rebel of

1975, have behaved in 1985 if someone else had been leader? How would McDonnell have behaved if he had been leader himself? And what would have been the response of Neil Kinnock, a continuous critic of the no-rate option, if he had been a young councillor instead of leader of his party? Was it too cynical to suggest that there appeared to be natural cycles and rhythms in the careers of Labour politicians?

Other rate-capped councils maintained their defiance after the collapse of resistance at the GLC. Their tactics were explained by Margaret Hodge, then left-wing leader of Islington borough council, but later to become a Blairite moderniser who was promoted to be an education and employment minister in 1998. Writing the lead story in the April 1985 issue of *London Labour Briefing*, she criticised the 'appalling manner' in which the GLC retreated.

> Our objective remains to call for collective negotiations with government. We demand the return of the monies of which we have been robbed, so that we can provide existing services and respond to new and growing needs without imposing further massive rate rises. We also seek to set aside the Rates Act so that we protect our democratic right to determine local budgets ... All the London Labour Councils in the frontline have established structures which enable Councillors to take full financial control away from the officers. This will allow us to maintain our commitment to meet our bills for wages and services as a first priority ... Some interesting options present themselves. Should we pay our preceptors, especially the GLC and the Metropolitan Police? Should we withhold our payments to government for PAYE, VAT and the employers' contribution to National Insurance? Should we postpone payment for utilities (gas an electricity) and insurances? What should we do about meeting our interest payments on debt? ... Our aim must be to strengthen and support all our comrades who are in the

frontline, so that we can enjoy the widest possible support for a campaign which could inflict massive damage on this government and which is so crucial in the struggle to protect public services at the local level.

The no-rate tactic lasted through the spring and early summer, but one by one the authorities all ended up setting a legal rate. In several cases, the leaders were forced to resign. They included the London borough of Haringey, where Bernie Grant took over as Britain's first black council leader, soon to assume the mantle of the media hate figure, 'Barmy Bernie', for his derogatory comments about the police after riots on his authority's Broadwater Farm estate.

The two councils which stuck out the longest were Lambeth and Liverpool, where Labour councillors were disqualified and surcharged. The no-rate tactic also led directly to a major political upheaval in Liverpool, resulting in expulsion from the Labour Party of the council's deputy leader, Derek Hatton, and other prominent supporters of the Militant Tendency.

So, in Livingstone's defence, it could be said that he was merely sharing in a very difficult political problem and that his administration survived better than most. The most serious charge against him was his apparent lack of preparation. Coping with the politics of rate-capping was clearly the biggest hurdle he faced at the time. So why did he only 'discover' the GLC's true financial position a week before budget day? Was it, as he claims and McDonnell denies, that he was misled by his deputy? Did he trust him too much? Or was he just caught on the hop by failing to do his political homework on the major issue of the day? The episode confirmed the view that Livingstone is a practical politician concerned with keeping and using power rather than striking ideological postures. But it dented his image for political competence.

The consequences were immediate. Livingstone withdrew from the editorial board of *Labour Herald* (and was replaced by

McDonnell). He was vilified in the organs of the hard left. And he entered a period where, for a time at least, straddling the mutually hostile factions of hard and soft left became impossible. And all this was happening at the worst possible moment for Livingstone in his bid to achieve his ambition of a parliamentary seat. It is time to journey back into the vicious political backwaters of Brent East.

Most of the constituency's Labour activists had been outraged at the way the Party's National Executive determined, at the start of the 1983 general election campaign, that Reg Freeson, not Ken Livingstone, would be their parliamentary candidate. Livingstone invited the entire constituency GC (general committee) to his 38th birthday party in County Hall a week after polling day and was assured they would pick him next time. He says he told them he would like the nomination, but advised them not to commit themselves. His only request was that they should organise the selection as soon as possible under party rules, so that if he failed to get Brent East he would have a chance to look elsewhere. This they did. But, as ill luck would have it, the ward selection process was due to start in the week after the GLC budget debacle. It lasted through the period in which Livingstone was being portrayed in the organs of the left as an out-and-out villain because of his rate-capping retreat.

The effect was to swell the numbers of the hard-left faction that had never seen Livingstone as their first choice. They chose Diane Abbott, a black woman journalist who happened to be working at the time in the GLC press office. Why was it, they asked, that the white male traitor Livingstone, who spoke so movingly about the need to increase the numbers of black and women candidates, thought himself fit to be chosen in preference to Abbott?

In the event Livingstone won the nomination of nine of the constituency's 11 wards, where the predominant feeling was that Freeson's survival as Labour candidate in 1983 was a wrong that had to be reversed. But the actual selection was to be made by the

LONDON LABOUR 40p BRIEFING

No 48   APRIL 1985

RATECAPPED COUNCILS DEFIANT:

UNITY CAN WIN!

by MARGARET HODGE (Leader, Islington Council)

March 7th was a night to remember. The press reports on March 8th completely failed to reflect the spirit of confidence and unity which was expressed at the budget meetings of 15 Labour controlled councils, where a clear decision was taken to collectively resist the Government's attempts to cut services and jobs. Those of us who participated in those historic meetings were given a wonderful morale boost by the overwhelming support we received from thousands in our workforces and in our communities as we launched our struggle for local democracy. The mood at those meetings strengthened our resolve to fight attempts to destroy local government and slash services at the local level.

When we embarked on this campaign last July, many of us realised that our tactic was unlikely to be appropriate for the upper tier authorities. What we could not predict, was the appalling manner in which the leadership in London would manage their retreat and the deliberate attempt to bring the boroughs down with them.

The collapse of ILEA and the GLC has obviously damaged our cause; but the effect need not be lasting. There are 15 local authorities, representing over 13 million people, most of whom live in the deprived urban areas, who have taken a united stand.

GREAT ACHIEVEMENT

Our real position remains strong for the Government will not defeat local councils if they remain united. It is a great achievement that as many as 15 councils have stuck together so far. A few more may peel away, but as long as a sufficient core of authorities resolve to act collectively, our campaign can lead to victory.

There are 9 London boroughs which

CONTINUED ON PAGE 2

Demonstration against rate-capping, March 6th.   John Chapman

LABOUR—TAKE THE POWER!

Labour councillors hang tough after the GLC's resistance collapsed, *London Labour Briefing*, April 1985

210 Turn Again Livingstone

constituency GC, where Livingstone's enemies were clustered. The acid test came at its meeting on April 28th 1985. On the first ballot the left split. Livingstone got 31 votes, Abbott got 26, and there were 18 votes for other candidates. Livingstone estimates that the hard-left vote against him had increased by about ten as a result of the rate-capping row. On the second and final ballot, the right-wingers swung over to Livingstone who got 50 votes to Abbott's 25. Perhaps they thought that if he was under such flak from the hard left, he could not be all that bad.

The decision was endorsed by the NEC and Livingstone became prospective parliamentary candidate for Brent East. Suggestions continued that Freeson might stand against him as independent Labour, but it seemed a safe bet that Livingstone would at last become an MP. This did not mean that Livingstone had Brent East under control. Later that year he announced his intention to stand for the treasurership of the Labour Party at the annual conference in Bournemouth. Although he thought he had sounded out the views of his constituency officers, the GC passed a humiliating motion instructing him to withdraw. It was the left's first chance to trip him up. As time went by the sheer stridency of the hard left's criticism began to cause other erstwhile critics to become more supportive. He recalls that at one meeting, for example, a member described him as a rabid dog and said she could not feel safe in the same room as him. On another occasion Livingstone says that his criticism of the constituency secretary was described as an act of injustice against the left which ranked in its severity with the Sharpeville massacre, the crushing of the miners' strike, and the Vietnam war. Such was the comradeship of Brent East socialism.

Lest we forget, the story of the GLC's campaign against the Abolition Bill had not yet reached the final shoot-out in the House of Lords when the rate-capping crisis struck. After the trauma, a shell-shocked campaign team (minus McDonnell) got back to the job of vetting advertisements, pumping out propaganda and hoping that no one had noticed the budget fiasco. Surprisingly it seemed that very few people had.

The Abolition Bill passed its report stage in the Commons with a government majority of 124 and with only a rump of 19 Tory back-bench rebels voting against it. But the opinion polls showed support for the GLC was still strong and sympathetic peers remained eager for a fight when the bill reached the Lords in April.

On the first day of the committee stage, the government's majority slumped to four on a wrecking amendment providing for a directly elected successor to the GLC. On subsequent days the government suffered four defeats on amendments covering waste disposal, highways, conservation and the future of ILEA. The opposition plan was to identify so many London-wide functions which had to be preserved that the case for an elected authority would become unanswerable.

The climax of this gambit was due to come on Ascot Gold Cup day when many Tory peers could be expected to go to the races and so miss voting on the key amendment to set up a directly elected authority to oversee these London-wide services. It nearly worked. Many Tory peers decamped to Ascot, but the government organised a four-hour filibuster by those who remained to ensure that the racegoers were back in time for the vote. It was the GLC's last chance. In spite of some slim majorities, the government got the bill through its report stage without further damage and later reversed the more awkward Lords amendments in the Commons. When the bill came back to the Lords for the second time, the peers' opposition crumbled. On July 15th the government got a majority of 64 to snuff out the last flicker of resistance.

The bill received its royal assent the next day, leaving the GLC with just over eight months before its final extinction. The time was used for rearguard guerrilla action to channel as much money as possible into favoured schemes and to help Labour-controlled London boroughs set up joint arrangements to continue GLC

Don't stop loving me: Livingstone presents the newly restored statue of Eros as the GLC's parting gift to Londoners (*Guardian, Frank Martin*)

initiatives, such as the units for women, ethnic minorities and monitoring of the Metropolitan Police. (Even in the last week attempts were made to cock a final £76 million snook at the government by signing contracts for future housing repair work through a financial intermediary called Satman.)

On March 31st 1986 the streets around County Hall were thronged with Londoners paying their last respects. No doubt many were just there to enjoy the carnival atmosphere, the pop concert and the fireworks which had been contributed at ratepayers' expense. But deeper emotions were also stirred. That night brought the end of the institution of elected London-wide local government, which had lasted in different forms since 1889. First the LCC and then the GLC had been accused of being remote, unwieldy bureaucracies. But, at the point of death, the council had won the love of wide sections of the people it served. On the County Hall terrace there was hardly a dry eye as Big Ben struck midnight and the GLC flag was lowered for the last time.

As security personnel cleared the building and made it safe for the so-called London Residuary Body which would start the next morning on the task of winding up the council's affairs, a final cameo scene was played out in Livingstone's leader's office. He had gone there with a few colleagues for a last drink while he finished clearing out his drawers. His personal paintings and posters were still on the walls and he was asked if he wanted them carried out. He refused because they were in GLC frames which did not belong to him. Better leave them there, he said. As friends remonstrated and started removing the pictures from the utility council frames, there was a moment of insight into Livingstone's morality. Here was a man who was happy to spend millions of pounds of ratepayers' money on politically motivated advertising campaigns and the like, but he was not prepared to snitch for himself a few shoddy picture frames. The company departed into the night.

9 Destination Wilderness

If Livingstone had been a more conventional Labour politician or straightforward careerist, he would have been well placed to move on from abolition of the GLC to a comfortable and probably powerful parliamentary career. In spite of the tensions in Brent East, he had won the nomination to be the official Labour candidate and was poised to become an MP within a year or two, whenever Mrs Thatcher called the election. It was entirely predictable that he would have a rocky apprenticeship when he reached the House of Commons, where his lippy style and support for causes such as gay rights and Irish nationalism had won few friends among the party's bedrock back-benchers from Scotland and the north. Many thought his campaigning at the GLC amounted to little more than selfish posturing that did permanent damage to local government's reputation and Labour's electoral chances. For the most part, they felt uneasy with the rainbow of exotic causes that he espoused and envious of the extent of his fame and media exposure. For loyal Labour MPs toiling through those long years in opposition, there were few opportunities to gain the attention that Livingstone had been able to command at the snap of his fingers at the GLC. They were itching to put the whippersnapper in his place.

But there were plenty of reasons why he might have been able to surmount this hostility when he reached the national arena. Few of his contemporaries had as much experience at running things in the hurly-burly of political office. Those who did – such as David Blunkett, leader of Sheffield – did not have to linger long on the back-benches before becoming party spokesmen. A left-wing background was no impediment to advancement in

Neil Kinnock's Labour Party, as long as it was accompanied by a willingness to play with the team to defeat the Tories and restore Labour to government. And Livingstone possessed a clutch of personal attributes that would have made him a good member of that team if that had been how he chose to play it. They included self-assurance, a capacity for hard work, an articulacy and self-deprecating wit that made him a star media performer, a sharp tactical sense and proven resilience under fire.

All that was required was for him to abandon some of his friends on the outer fringes of the left, tone down the way he expressed his passion for Irish unity and concentrate a bit more on mainstream policy and a bit less on questions of sexual orientation. Plenty of other left-wingers emerging from municipal politics at about this time accomplished that sort of transition at varying speeds through from the mid-1980s to the mid-1990s. Livingstone was better placed than many of them in those months after abolition of the GLC to begin the process of domesticating himself in the eyes of the Labour leadership in readiness for arrival in Parliament. He had not chosen to break with his hard-left friends, but they had broken decisively with him during the rate-capping crisis in 1985.

As a result he was being driven towards the (initially welcoming) arms of the Labour Co-ordinating Committee, a grassroots activist group on the centre left. With Peter Hain and other LCC colleagues, he began working to form the basis of a broad left-leaning coalition that could become the driving force of the Parliamentary Labour Party after the next election. They organised teach-ins for about 50 prospective Labour candidates who were likely to be in the new intake, familiarising them with the routines they needed to know to play a full part in the PLP's key decisions over the first few months. In November 1986 he was elected to the LCC executive.

But Livingstone did not progress far on that hesitant journey towards the centre. Within three or four years of GLC abolition, he was to become a marginalised figure on the hard left of the

PLP, consorting again with Trotskyist groups and written off as a serious candidate for senior positions in the party. When more than a decade later the leadership contemplated opinion polls favouring Livingstone as Labour's candidate to be mayor of London, their hostility was based as much on what he did after the GLC as during it. The questions to be asked in the next stage of the story are whether he deserved that rejection; and whether his march back into the wilderness was a deliberate move or the unsought consequence of a failure by the party leadership to harness the skills of a troublesome rising star.

In the days that followed abolition on March 31st 1986, there was little time for depression about loss of the trappings of office. He was technically unemployed until he entered Parliament in June 1987 and had to adjust to functioning without the high-powered support services that organised his diary and had provided a constant political radar system since he seized the GLC leadership in 1981. But he remembers those 15 months as a time of personal liberation when he took back control of his life. On the day after abolition he plunged into a campaign to wrest control of Westminster borough council from the Conservatives.

This was something of a grudge match for Labour. Westminster was led by Lady (later Dame Shirley) Porter, the Tesco supermarket heiress who was ranked by *Vogue* magazine as the 20th-wealthiest woman in Europe. An ardent Thatcherite, she had been responsible for instructing her council to mount a series of legal challenges against GLC policy decisions. Livingstone's constituency was Paddington in north Westminster and he was closely involved in plans hatched about 18 months before the local elections in May 1986 to give Lady Porter her come-uppance.

'We realised that 1986 was likely to be a good year for Labour and we could win 27 of the 60 seats on the council. Another two seats were likely to be won by ratepayers' candidates, genuine independents who hated the Tories. All we needed was to win two of the six seats in the three least safe of the remaining Tory wards to take away their majority. So we selected our best candidates for those key seats and put all our effort there.'

Years later, recalling the GLC aftermath, Livingstone still gets excited by the memory of canvassing those wards. 'We thought we could take the Tories by surprise. We knew we'd only be able to do it once, but we were working on the assumption that they were lax locally and would put their efforts into defending more marginal seats. They woke up to what was going on only about 10 days before polling day ... They had a terrible scare.' The tactic failed. Although Labour gained an extra 12 seats, the Conservatives hung on with an overall majority of four. But the seeds had been sown for a scandal that would come to tarnish the image of Conservative local government. To avoid a repeat of the 1986 election scare, Lady Porter's administration developed a policy of selling off council housing cheaply in marginal wards, with the intention of replacing Labour-voting tenants with home-owners who were more likely to vote Tory. The district auditor later concluded that she was guilty of 'wilful misconduct' and 'disgraceful and improper gerrymandering'. The courts ordered her and a colleague to recompense the ratepayers of Westminster from their own pockets by paying a £27 million surcharge, the largest in the history of local government. Livingstone says: 'We thought we had failed and we were very depressed. We didn't realise that we'd triggered a ticking time-bomb that would cause so much embarrassment to the Tories.'

During the following year before the general election was called, he spent about three months abroad mostly on trips in his capacity as former leader of the GLC. His destinations included Australia (at the invitation of the Communist/Green coalition on Sydney district council after it was abolished to stop its obstruction of property development), Israel (at the invitation of Mapam, a left party in the Labour coalition) and Zimbabwe (to attend the opening of a Marxist school run by the pro-Moscow supporters of Joshua Nkomo). He also took the best holiday of his life, a five-week Himalayan trek to the Everest base-camp with his partner Kate Allen and their friend Merle Amory, leader of Brent council. The potential financial worries of unemployment were dispelled when the publisher Collins paid a £60,000 advance for his autobiography. He chose the title *If Voting Changed Anything, They'd Abolish It*, an old anarchist slogan that chimed well with the experience of the GLC.

But the main thrust of Livingstone's activity during this period was a political project to influence the direction Labour would take after the election. Analysis of the allegiances of candidates selected to fight winnable seats suggested that there would be a left majority among Labour MPs for the first time in the party's history. If the soft-left Tribunites could be persuaded to unite with the hard-left Campaign Group, there was an opportunity to halt Neil Kinnock's march to the centre ground and stake out a more radical socialist alternative to Thatcherite Conservatism.

Livingstone set out the strategy in an article in *Tribune* (where he had started a long-running monthly column in October 1985). In the issue of July 25th 1986 he wrote: 'Since the 1983 election we have seen a whole series of radical policies adopted by one Labour conference after another, but the vicious and damaging splits on the Left have enabled the old guard in the PLP [Parliamentary Labour Party] to sail on as though Jim Callaghan [prime minister 1976–79] were still running the Labour Party. That will change after the next election … The next PLP is likely to be: Right 27 per cent, Centre 16 per cent, Tribune Group and allies 41 per cent and Campaign Group 16 per cent.' He said the figures would not change by more than 2 percentage points unless Labour won a landslide election victory. Livingstone warned: 'It is quite clear that if the present divisions and personality clashes on the Left are perpetrated into the next PLP, it is likely to lead to the emergence of a Tribune/Centre working majority.'

Livingstone's project was to glue back the left alliance inside and outside Parliament that had carried through the party's constitutional changes of 1979–80, but fractured after it narrowly

failed to win Tony Benn the deputy leadership in 1981. He
worked with Labour Left Liaison, an umbrella grouping of
activists, which he described as the 'extra-parliamentary wing' of
the Campaign group.

The alliance was not open-ended on the left. In his *Tribune*
column on November 28th 1986 he was caustic about the 'bitter
experiences with Militant and its undemocratic tactics'. But the
campaign to win left control of the PLP allowed him to rebuild
relationships with parts of the left that had reviled him after the
rate-capping fiasco. In a further column on February 20th 1987 he
set out the bones of a policy programme around which the left
could unite after the election. Its 11 points included: no watering
down of party policy on nuclear disarmament; breaking Europe
free from subordination to the military and economic interests of
America; supporting all liberation struggles and economic links
with progressive Third World nations; toughening control of the
financial sector of the economy with specific policies for the
direction and control of capital; strengthening anti-discrimination
legislation; ending 'witch-hunts' within the party; and securing an
amnesty for convicted miners and surcharged councillors.

Livingstone now acknowledges that his political analysis at that
time was wrong. He believed then that the left was poised to gain,
whatever the outcome of the general election.

> I thought the party would move to the left if Kinnock won.
> Or we could get rid of Kinnock if we lost. I thought a
> Kinnock government would be abysmally bad and the left
> would grow very strong, very rapidly. What I wasn't aware
> of then was the classic pattern of 1931, 1951 and 1979. You
> get a surge to the left after the Labour Party loses power, but
> after about two years it begins to ebb. The longer the party
> is in opposition, the more right-wing it becomes. There's
> never a point after that first wave of anger about why we lost
> that the left then comes back. The left either has to take
> power immediately or gradually slip as its position gets eroded.

That slippage was evident within weeks of polling day on June 11th 1987. Mrs Thatcher was returned to Downing Street with a Commons majority of 101 and Livingstone had a close shave in Brent East where the Labour majority shrank from 4,834 to 1,653, a swing to the Conservatives of 4.1 per cent, one of the worst results in the country for Labour. Nationally there was a swing to Labour of 1.2 per cent in England, 4.5 per cent in Wales and 5.8 per cent in Scotland. But across Greater London there was a slight swing to the Conservatives, averaging less than 0.1 per cent in the inner boroughs and 0.8 per cent in the outer areas. Other Labour candidates who did badly in London included Bernie Grant, the left leader of Haringey council, who suffered a 6.8 per cent swing to the Conservatives in Tottenham.

Party managers decided that Labour was being dragged down by southern voters' rejection of the 'loony-left' antics of Livingstone and his pals on the London borough councils. That analysis was challenged by the big academic study of the campaign in which psephologists John Curtice and Michael Steed concluded that the main factor explaining Labour's comparatively poor showing throughout the London metropolitan area (including the commuter belt extending well outside Greater London) was 'the attraction of Thatcherite Conservatism to some 1983 Alliance voters'.* Nationally there was 'no evidence of a general unwillingness to vote for left-wing Labour candidates' and for every case of left-wingers doing particularly badly, 'the Labour left could quote a counter-example'. But that was not the perception of the Labour leadership after a campaign in which the Tories tried to make maximum propaganda impact from attacks on the 'loony-left' threat behind Kinnock's reassuring smile, including old quotations from Livingstone in a Tory party political broadcast. The possibly misleading conclusion was drawn that the GLC's popularity at the time of its abolition was due to

---

The British General Election of 1987, David Butler and Dennis Kavanagh, Macmillan, 1988.

its skillfully deployed advertising budget and had nothing to do with London voters' positive view of Livingstone.

In fact he was (for him) remarkably restrained during the 1987 campaign and said little the tabloids could use as ammunition against Labour. He attracted attention shortly before the election was called by giving an interview to *Woman's Own* in which he said everyone was bisexual. 'I don't believe there is anyone who could not honestly say at some time of their life they have not been attracted to someone of the same sex', he said. At a Lesbian and Gay Rights conference in Camden Town Hall on May 23rd he strayed outside the official line to promise legislation against discrimination on grounds of sexual orientation in the next Parliament. This came the day after a somewhat implausible front-page lead story in the *Daily Express*, headlined 'OUR CONSPIRACY, BY RED KEN', which purported to disclose how the hard left would hijack Labour after the election. 'Fighting this election is the largest collection of left-wing nasties West of the Berlin Wall. Kinnock will be their prisoner in the Commons', the paper concluded on June 9th. But such media excesses were not his fault this time. There was not enough coming out of the Livingstone quote factory during the campaign to merit criticism for indiscipline. Confusion among the front-bench team about taxation policy was far more likely to have brought the party into disrepute than indiscretions from Brent East.

Livingstone's explanation of his poor personal result in Brent East was that he shared the fate of candidates taking over the seats of de-selected Labour MPs.

> If you get rid of a sitting Labour MP, a lot of his supporters abstain. We went through the 1987 campaign without previous canvassing records for the constituency because the former agent would not let me have them ... Reg Freeson [his de-selected predecessor] did not stand against me, but a lot of the Labour voters who supported him voted Tory or abstained. I reckon that deselection of a sitting MP costs the

local party about 10 per cent of its vote. The same thing
happened in that election to Bernie Grant in Tottenham and
Diane Abbott in Hackney North, who both succeeded
deselected Labour MPs.

Livingstone thought the reason for Labour's relatively poor
showing in London and the south-east as a whole was that the
region had not suffered so badly from economic recession, but
party managers blamed the negative image of 'loony-left' Labour
councils. At the following general election in 1992 Livingstone
consolidated his hold on the seat, gaining a majority of 5,949 on a
swing to Labour that was double the Greater London average. In
1997 he increased that majority to 15,882. But his 1987 result was
too close for comfort.

The national party was shell-shocked by the dreadfulness of its
electoral defeat. In spite of a brilliantly organised campaign and
professional image-building by the party's communications
director, Peter Mandelson, Labour ended up with 40 fewer seats
than in 1979. Across southern England the Alliance (Liberals and
Social Democrats) came second to the Tories in most
constituencies. Kinnock moved swiftly to stop the party
disintegrating into a prolonged bout of recrimination. At the first
meeting of the PLP on June 17th, he called for unity 'to begin the
campaign to win the next election now'. A review of policies to
appeal to the 'breadth of the people' would be 'deliberate and
practical, not spasmodic or self-indulgent.' He was also at this
time signalling the changes to party rules for selecting
parliamentary candidates to give every member a direct vote
instead of relying on constituency committees on which the left
often had an advantage. There was little doubt that Kinnock
intended to take a grip, moving Labour further towards the centre
and shedding as much as possible of the ideological baggage that
he thought had made it unelectable.

Plenty of prominent figures in the party were nervous about
the pace and scope of this movement, but opposed to any shift

back to Bennite leftism. It was Kinnock's political skill that persistently over the next few years forced most of them to choose to go further down the 'modernising' road than many of them could have envisaged at the outset.

When the Tribune MPs met later that month, John Prescott, David Blunkett and the group's officers backed a deal with Campaign Group MPs to secure the left majority in the Shadow Cabinet that Livingstone had been wanting. But the proposal collapsed after impassioned speeches by three of Tribune's rising stars. They were (in order of seniority at the time) Jack Straw, Gordon Brown and Tony Blair. Straw said that no Tribune member of the Shadow Cabinet should be beholden to anyone from the anti-Kinnock left. He would never himself vote for Campaign candidates and thought it dishonest to reach the Shadow Cabinet using their support. The joint slate collapsed and Kinnock went on to run the party with a broad coalition of support stretching from Tribune to the right, marginalising the left. Senior figures on the centre-right of the party, including John Smith (the future leader) and Jack Cunningham, kept their Shadow Cabinet places.

As Livingstone now sees it: 'That was the decisive moment – the only time in its life that the PLP had a left majority. The Tribune Group looked at the prospect of leading the party and half of them ran promptly in the other direction. After that it's been a slow drift to the right.' But why didn't he join in that drift and accept, as so many of his left-wing colleagues went on to do, that Kinnock's electoral approach was at best correct or at worst inevitable? Labour MPs were not penalised for voting the 'wrong' way at Tribune in the summer of 1987. When Labour eventually took office 10 years later, John Prescott was deputy prime minister and David Blunkett was education and employment secretary. Other names that have cropped up in this story as leading lights of the somewhat harder left were also members of the ministerial team. What happened to those GLC leftists who refused to set a rate when Livingstone was forced to compromise in 1985? One of them was Tony Banks, who became sports minister in 1997. Another was Paul Boateng, minister for health. Peter Hain, one of Livingstone's closest political chums in 1987, became minister for Wales in 1997 and was trusted by the leadership to handle the complex politics of devolution.

Livingstone maintains that he did not join this drift to the centre because he recognised where it would end up and could not accept that 'because I am still a socialist'. He had deep-seated policy differences with Kinnock and the party leaders who followed him, notably on management of the economy, defence and Ireland. But his friends thought there were also personal factors at play. If Livingstone was going to achieve a powerful position on the national stage, he had to take the left route because hostility towards him from the Kinnock camp was so intense. There might have been a chance for 'cuddly Ken' to be rehabilitated during the campaign against GLC abolition, but by June 1987 it was too late – or maybe too early.

During the GLC period Kinnock had seen Livingstone as the prime exponent of a style of municipal politics that was ruining Labour's chances by fuelling the Tory tabloids' campaign to portray the party as a creature of the 'loony left'. He contrasted his own self-discipline with Livingstone's laxity in shooting from the lip. It must have been profoundly frustrating that Livingstone, a mere council leader with a publicity budget bigger than the national party's, should have been getting consistently more coverage than himself. Those who thought Kinnock suffered from a deep personal insecurity, imagined that he might feel threatened by an outsider who was supplanting him in the affections of the left and was being portrayed by the media as an eventual challenger and successor.

'Neil felt massively resentful about what Ken was doing,' says Bill Bush, Livingstone's chief of staff at the GLC and now head of the BBC's policy research unit. 'There were several occasions when they spoke directly or through go-betweens. It was absolutely clear that Ken could be allowed associate membership of the family [the inner party circle], but only if he showed complete loyalty – 99 per cent would not do.' Even after the rate-capping fiasco and Livingstone's split with the hard left, that degree of loyalty was never forthcoming. 'He thought that if he did nine things the leadership approved of, there would be room for one they didn't. Politics isn't like that. They won't remember or care about the nine. What they care about is the one,' says Bush. John Carr, a Kinnock loyalist and former chair of the GLC's staff committee, recalls attending the meeting of senior insiders who planned the 1987 campaign rallies and media events. 'My suggestion that Ken could do something to help was ruled out because he was not trusted. They said it was impossible. Neil hated him.'

In later years after Tony Blair became prime minister, the view in Downing Street was that Kinnock had missed a golden opportunity to tame Livingstone by giving him a job. But according to those closest to Kinnock, there was never any moment when that would have made political sense. 'We saw him as a poseur, not a realistic politician. Ken wasn't thinking strategically about London ... And he didn't understand the contempt and anger that almost all the Labour MPs felt about his GLC leadership', says one of Kinnock's close associates. According to this view, Kinnock would have gained no political benefit from bringing Livingstone into his team to set against the political costs of doing so. 'That wasn't insecurity. Neil's uncertainties had nothing to do with Ken in any way ... If Ken had knuckled down, possibly something would have been done for him. But he had to decide to behave ... Ken believed he was a political figure to be reckoned with, but Neil never saw it like that. There was a mismatch.'

Although Livingstone was restrained during the 1987 campaign, he justified the leadership's suspicion by putting the knife into Kinnock within minutes of the first results being declared.

Say no to no desk: Ken Livingstone says he will work from home until he gets office facilities at the Commons, April 28th 1988 *(PA)*

Escaping briefly from his party minder, he told BBC television that Labour's poor showing was the result of what he saw as Kinnock's weak and misguided leadership. The BBC programme cut away to a shot of Kinnock at home in Bedwelty watching Livingstone rubbishing him at his moment of greatest vulnerability as the results confirmed the worst predictions of the exit polls. In a score or more of interviews later that night, Livingstone reverted to a blander analysis, but the damage was done.

Part of his punishment for this and other past misdeeds was, what he saw as, a somewhat petty campaign against him by the party whips when he took his seat in the Commons in June 1987. It was made clear to the new intake of leftish MPs that they would do their careers no good if they had dealings with him. Ray Powell, the Labour deputy chief whip responsible for MPs' office facilities, stopped him getting a desk or phone until long after every other Labour MP was properly accommodated. Although the appalling under-funding of parliamentary office facilities left many MPs with inadequate space to do their job, Livingstone had little doubt that he was being victimised. In January 1988 he said: 'Parliament is worse than I thought it would be. It's like working in the Natural History Museum, except not all the exhibits are stuffed.' This was not the classic approach to win friends and influence people, but his resentment was understandable. In protest at the lack of facilities, he worked from home from spring 1988 until summer 1989; this was his justification for a poor voting record in the Commons at that time.

Whoever was at fault, the upshot was that Livingstone was despised by the leadership and ostracised by many of his new colleagues in Parliament. After the failure to achieve a joint left slate for the Shadow Cabinet elections, it is little wonder that he turned back to his old friends on the left: no alternative loyalist career path was available. At that stage he still harboured a strong ambition to lead the party and the first step towards that goal was to establish himself as the heir apparent to Tony Benn and Dennis Skinner as leader of the left. As he puts it: 'My objective was to gain a pivotal role in determining the strategy of the left. I had to secure the hard-left as a base and move out from there.'

For a while that strategy seemed to be working rather well. He managed to mobilise personal support from the hard-left Campaign for Labour Party Democracy (CLPD) without at first losing the backing of his soft-left friends on the Labour Co-ordinating Committee (LCC). By the start of the party conference in Brighton in September 1987, grassroots activists from both these rival organisations were campaigning for him to be elected to the constituency section of the party's ruling National Executive Committee.

The result was a sensation. At a conference that was meant to be the platform for Kinnock's next great push towards the centre (including the first signals that he would drop the policy of unilateral nuclear disarmament in favour of a multilateral

Sitting pretty: Ken Livingstone on Brighton beach during the Labour conference
when he gained a seat on the National Executive, September 30th 1987
(*Guardian, E. Hamilton West*)

approach), the left-winger Livingstone stormed on to the
constituency section of the NEC at his first attempt. He got
385,000 votes, taking fourth place in the poll behind David
Blunkett, Tony Benn and Dennis Skinner. The others elected in
lower positions were Bryan Gould, Jo Richardson and Michael
Meacher. Those who narrowly missed a seat included the left-
wingers Audrey Wise and Diane Abbott (Livingstone's adversary
for the Brent East nomination in 1985). Gerald Kaufman, Robin
Cook and other candidates followed behind with less than half
Livingstone's vote. He told journalists: 'I am stunned. There has
been such a campaign of vilification against me that I did not
expect to get on.'

Stunned, but not silent. He told a conference fringe meeting
that any attempt by Kinnock to abandon Labour's non-nuclear
defence policy 'would lead to civil war inside the party which
would render it unelectable.' Denis Healey, the former shadow

foreign secretary, riposted: 'I don't think the movement will forgive anyone who tries to exploit the difficulties of the argument for personal political advantage.' Speaking on behalf of the NEC, Tony Clarke condemned 'aspiring immature parliamentarians who jump on bandwagons'. He said Livingstone's refusal to accept advice to avoid that inflammatory language was 'disgraceful and immature and beneath the dignity of a parliamentarian'. Livingstone said his intervention stopped the conference moving further away from a non-nuclear policy, but the multilateral approach was subsequently adopted.

Those exchanges set the character for the debate inside and outside the NEC over the next two years as Kinnock, with a cast-iron majority of votes from the union and women's section, drove through his fundamental policy review. Livingstone mounted a rearguard action to maintain the party's socialist values, but the leadership thought he was indulging in a blatant form of careerist oppositionalism. The grassroots majority eventually sided with Kinnock in aching desperation to achieve electoral success. They tired of seeing Livingstone before and after every NEC meeting arguing the toss about almost every right-wing initiative that came along.

Livingstone says the vehemence of his opposition was based on the assumption that Kinnock could never win power. He thought Kinnock would be sacked once Labour's centre and right realised he could not get an overall majority at the next election. When Tony Benn mounted a token challenge for the leadership in 1988, Livingstone privately approached John Smith, to ask him to throw his hat into the ring. 'I told him he had a duty to get rid of Kinnock. My soundings in the Campaign group showed they would switch to Smith or abstain in a second round of voting after Benn had been knocked out in the first. There was not a single vote for Kinnock. The view of the Campaign group was that they would rather win with Smith than lose with Kinnock. He [Smith] was very friendly, but said he could not do it.'

Livingstone says he twice tried to raise the issue of Kinnock's

bad poll ratings at meetings of the NEC and once with Tribune
MPs. But even colleagues who accepted that Kinnock was a
liability thought it was pointless to say so because the leader's
position was unassailable.

> We went through 1987–92 refusing to look at the polls or
> have an honest debate about the problem of Neil's
> leadership. If we'd have got rid of Kinnock and had Smith, I
> think we'd have won in 1992. In 1992, the public didn't like
> our tax policy and they didn't like Kinnock. We could have
> carried one of those burdens, but we couldn't carry both.
> People would have voted for our tax policy if Smith was our
> leader, but would not vote for us with two albatrosses
> around our necks.

When Livingstone started on the NEC, he asked to be put on the
defence committee so that he could fight to preserve the policy of
unilateral nuclear disarmament. But he was happy to be given his
second preference, the economic policy committee.

> It was a deliberate choice. I'm attracted to what the problem
> is. When I was on Lambeth council, the biggest problem was
> housing and so that's what I specialised in. At the GLC it was
> transport. The biggest problem facing national governments
> is the economy. There's no point coming to parliament and
> just being a councillor translated to the national stage. Your
> responsibility as an MP is to make sure the economy works,
> not run local government. After the narrow victory in Brent,
> I needed time to spend on the constituency and so there was
> time only for one other thing. The 1964 and 1974 Labour
> governments clearly failed because they didn't get the
> economy right. It's the overwhelming issue. If you are an
> MP, all the other things are nice and interesting, but unless
> you have an idea of what to do on the economy, you are
> totally dependent on someone else to tell you what to do.

That was the start of a passionate interest in economics that has tended to crowd out other issues more suited to his populist political skills. Over the following ten years he had plenty of opportunities to become the parliamentary voice of London, articulating the problems caused by the Thatcher administration's ill-considered decision to abolish the GLC without replacing it with something better. Instead, he virtually ignored that subject and began work on turning himself into an economic theoretician. Some of his friends helped with this task. Others thought he was making a wrong turn because he would never be as good an intellectual as he was a streetwise political operator.

He started delving into the subject after the 1987 election when he attended the Ariel Road group of radical economists, discussions led by Robin Murray and other former GLC advisers named after the road in Kilburn where they met. His tuition became more intensive in July 1987 when he appointed John Ross as his researcher at the Commons. Ross was an economic historian and former leading light of Socialist Action, a group of former members of the International Marxist Group who decided to abandon their separate Trotskyite identity and work inside the Labour Party.

> We talked three or four times a week and he [Ross] explained what was happening in the national and international economy. He said you could never trust the Treasury's statistics and needed your own database. So I spent £35,000 for a five-year lease on what was then the biggest computer in private hands in Britain. We set up an enormous database about all the main world economies since 1860 and others since 1960, updating it each month with the latest statistics and reports from the OECD, the World Bank and the Treasury.

Livingstone funded the first two years of the lease with income from a television commercial for cheese: he promoted Red

Leicester and the former Tory prime minister, Sir Edward Heath, did a companion plug for Blue Stilton. He also ploughed in earnings from promotions of Poundstretcher shops and animal-friendly paintbrushes, but rejected invitations to sponsor alcohol or Captain Birdseye waffles. British Coal wanted to advertise the warming effect of an open fire by filming a frosty Edwina Currie melting into Livingstone's arms for a kiss in front of the hearth. But that was turned down by both politicians. When the advertising income dried up, he ran the computer on fees raised from newspaper articles and after-dinner speaking engagements, usually addressing gatherings of well-heeled capitalists.

Livingstone says it took two years of concentrating on economics for him to feel confident in the subject. The result of that work was the alternative economic strategy that he set out in *Livingstone's Labour – a Programme for the Nineties* (Unwin Hyman, 1989). It said the main reason for Britain's economic decline in relation to international competitors was a persistent lack of investment in productive capacity. For 150 years a disproportionate share of national investment had gone abroad. Governments of all parties had bowed to the interests of the City of London, trying to maintain an overvalued pound and thereby further weakening British manufacturers' ability to compete in world markets.

To fill the investment gap, a Labour government should divert £9 billion of excess spending on defence towards rebuilding the productive economic base and intervene to direct the flow of private investment into industry. There should be a new structure of company law, similar to the one in West Germany where companies could take long-term investment decisions without fear of hostile takeover. Financial institutions should be obliged to use a certain share of their assets to fund the modernisation of British industry. Workers should be given a lot more power over their companies' key decisions because – with their jobs at stake – they had a better long-term perspective. 'We should give the workforce in each firm a power of veto over all investment plans and the power to initiate an alternative strategy', he said.

Livingstone's proposals included prudent control of the money supply to avoid inflation and a firm promise not to increase the tax burden on the bottom two-thirds of earners. He was critical of old-style centralised public ownership, preferring to work through regional enterprise boards. The programme emphasised the importance of backing the new growth sectors of information technology and biotechnology. He has since moderated some of these policies, arguing that it would be better to create incentives for domestic investment through changes in company and tax law rather than direct controls over what firms are allowed to do. But his analysis of the problems of under-investment and his approach to monetary and fiscal policy has stayed much the same.

These ideas put him in conflict with the majority on the NEC because they undermined the arguments of John Smith, the shadow chancellor, that the economy could be put right without threatening vested interests in the City. Smith was proposing 'supply-side socialism' to regenerate manufacturing industry by investing more in training, research and infrastructure. Livingstone kept asking awkward questions about how Labour would find the money to do this without raising taxes on middle-earners or expanding the money supply by over-borrowing. Bryan Gould, the shadow trade and industry secretary, who chaired the NEC's economic review, shared some of Livingstone's concerns, but not his style of expressing them or his interventionist solutions.

Although Livingstone wanted to cause bother for the leadership on the economy and defence, his most controversial media exposure was on Ireland. After abolition of the GLC he continued to speak and write frequently on the subject and his partisanship came under fierce attack from John Hume, leader of the Social Democratic and Labour Party in Northern Ireland. In an article in *Tribune* in December 1986, Hume accused Livingstone of 'leftist imperialism' for championing Sinn Fein activists who rejected for Ireland the socialist policies and freedoms that the Labour left wanted for Britain. Livingstone defended Sinn Fein's left-wing credentials and said that Hume's piece 'surpassed in dishonesty the worst outpourings of the disinformation and propaganda unit of British military intelligence in Ireland' (*Tribune*, January 9th 1987). He later said that his attitude towards Hume at the time was influenced by a perception that he was getting ready to back Mrs Thatcher in the 1987 election.

Livingstone caused a sensation with his maiden speech in the Commons on July 7th. Setting aside the convention that honourable members ease their way into Parliament with uncontroversial remarks about the merits of their constituency and the excellence (truthful or otherwise) of its previous MP, he launched into a series of detailed allegations about political assassinations by MI5 officers in Ireland in the 1970s. He made specific allegations against the late Capt Robert Nairac, a British SAS officer who was posthumously awarded the George Cross after being murdered in Northern Ireland. Nairac, he said, was involved in the killing of three innocent Roman Catholic members of the Miami Showband in 1975, with the aim of destabilising a ceasefire negotiated between Labour ministers and the IRA. The speech was based on information provided by Fred Holroyd and Colin Wallace, two former army intelligence officers who were alleging a complex conspiracy, including an attempt by the security services to blackmail Protestant extremists associated with a sex scandal at the Kincora boys' home. Livingstone caused uproar on the Tory benches when he linked the MI5 dirty tricks operation to Airey Neave, one of Mrs Thatcher's closest political friends and her spokesman on Northern Ireland before he was killed by an Irish National Liberation Army car bomb in the Commons car park in 1979. The shock-waves generated by the attack on Neave dominated prime minister's question time on the following day. Kinnock attacked Thatcher for abusing parliamentary rules to gain political capital out of the affair, but described Livingstone's allegations as 'probably unfair'. Robert Nairac's father said: 'It is a pity

Livingstone's backside is not nearer my boot.' It may be assumed that Kinnock shared that sentiment and was furious at the distraction from the party modernisation programme that was his major priority at the time.

Livingstone still believes that the allegations about Nairac and Neave could have seriously embarrassed Thatcher if the Labour front bench had pursued them with vigour. He says he might well have picked another issue for his maiden speech if the media had not ignored his attempts to raise the matter in other ways. 'At the start I was still unsure whether Wallace was a charlatan, but Thatcher was evasive ... Normally in the House of Commons she was totally confident. But on that occasion she was crouched and shifty and didn't make eye contact. She never said I was wrong.'

Livingstone followed up the speech with 360 parliamentary questions over the next two years. His single-mindedness attracted widespread derision as an example of political dottiness. But it contributed to pressure for an inquiry, leading to an admission by the Ministry of Defence that Wallace and the intelligence services had engaged in a covert black propaganda campaign, code-named Clockwork Orange. The MoD admitted operating to destabilise the IRA, but refused to comment on evidence provided by Wallace that it was also engaged in smearing leading Labour politicians.

The stridency of Livingstone's position on Northern Ireland contributed to a final break with his soft-left friends in the Labour Co-ordinating Committee (LCC). Although he had their support for the NEC elections in 1987, they were already by then coming to terms with Kinnock's call for maximum loyalty. In September 1987 the LCC executive overwhelmingly rejected his call for closer links with the hard-liners in Labour Left Liaison. In November, he was voted off the LCC executive along with most other advocates of the left unity strategy. Later that month, he was told at an LCC meeting that metaphorically he had 'blood on his hands' if he still supported Sinn Fein after a Remembrance Day bombing at Enniskillen that killed eleven people.

In response to questions about that meeting, he told Independent Radio: 'The IRA's campaign of violence will eventually win. I do not think anybody seriously believes that they won't eventually get their own way. As with other colonial situations we have been involved in, Britain will eventually go…To carry on as we are, not negotiating and not actually ending the conflict … seems to me to be the worst of all possible worlds' (November 16th). The timing of this intervention amid continuing public shock at the Enniskillen outrage caused probably the biggest media outcry against his position on Ireland. Two days later Kinnock was applauded after a speech to the PLP in which he described Livingstone's approach as 'facile'. Pulling out of Northern Ireland would increase the slaughter there, in the Republic and in mainland Britain. The IRA was not a liberation army. 'They, like the other paramilitaries, are a few hundred armed gangsters who commit political atrocities and spend the rest of their time in graft, corruption and protection rackets, ruling by fear because they've got guns,' the leader said. The Campaign Group promptly issued a statement calling for the withdrawal of British troops. The row rumbled on for weeks, upsetting plans by Kevin McNamara, the party's Northern Ireland spokesman, to finesse a consensus around a new policy for long-term Irish unity by consent.

In the *Guardian* on November 19th, Hugo Young accused Livingstone of 'staggering incompetence'. By seeking to shock and provoking predictable condemnation in the media, he stifled legitimate debate and undermined his stated objectives, he said. The *Sun* was more trenchant in a leader on November 30th. 'He is in every sense an enemy of the people. A creature of poisonous malice who has no place in Parliament, no place in public life, no place in any civilized society … Mr Kinnock should insist on his expulsion. Right now.'

Outspokenness on Ireland and drip-feed criticism of Kinnock's policy reviews put Livingstone at risk of de-selection in Brent East. In April 1988 his hard-left supporters lost control of party posts in the constituency to soft-left and non-aligned members who included leading Brent councillors. Tensions exploded that summer when the soft-left majority on the council made emergency cuts of £17 million and raised council rents by £7 a week. In exasperation at having to defend the Labour council to aggrieved constituents, he likened its regime to that of Pol Pot in Kampuchea. But, in the absence of a strong local challenger, he was reselected in September 1989, with 64 per cent of the constituency party vote.

He was not so fortunate at national level. At the party conference in Brighton in October, he lost his seat on the national executive to John Prescott. Livingstone's vote slumped to 284,000, 122,000 less than the year before, equivalent to loss of support from more than 100 constituencies. Although part of that decline could be explained by changes in voting procedures encouraging constituencies to ballot all their members about who to support, the result was interpreted as a verdict on his political conduct. The last straw for Kinnock had come in May 1989 when the NEC approved the policy review and Livingstone said it had failed to work out how it would pay for its economic programme. Whether or not that analysis was correct, it played into the hands of Conservative attempts to discredit the policies. The LCC said it specifically asked people not to vote for Livingstone because of his sectarian behaviour on the NEC. 'Providing ready-made quotes for the Tory press against the party has not gone down well with ordinary party activists', it said.

> That was the end of my ambition to lead the party. It died quite specifically as they announced I'd been kicked off the NEC. I realised then that my strategy of trying to reunite the left was going nowhere because the soft left was losing its confidence. Neil Kinnock was doing so badly in those two years after the 1987 election that there was always a chance of some great upheaval and someone like John Smith

coming to power. Then we'd have been in a more traditional position of the left wing pushing a more receptive leadership. But when I got kicked off the NEC, it began to dawn on us that we were about to see a horrendous shift to the right in the party. Benn and Skinner had been in the top three positions in the constituency section of the NEC for years, but suddenly their vote plummeted as well. You could see they [the Kinnockites] were going to be able to get rid of us all, which in the end they did. It wasn't until Blair became leader of the party that things started to shift back to the left again a bit.

Livingstone acknowledges that for the next few years he no longer had a clear political strategy for advancing either the left or his own political career. 'The slump in the economy after the 1989 election led me to believe that Labour would win the 1992 election. Kinnock would screw it up and things would start to move to the left again. All we could do was hang on in there.' A month before losing the NEC seat Livingstone and his partner Kate Allen bought a house at Cricklewood in his constituency. As the political tides turned against him, he retreated (figuratively and literally) to cultivate his garden and find consolation in its pond life. 'We called it the Neil Kinnock memorial garden because if he'd given me a job, we'd never have been able to get it finished.'

Deprived of the opportunities of office, Livingstone devoted the non-horticultural part of his efforts to founding the *Socialist Economic Bulletin*. Its first issue was published in March 1990. Using data from his giant computer model of the world economy and the analytic skills of John Ross, he developed the small circulation bulletin as an intellectual sounding-board for an alternative economic strategy. By plotting current data against the patterns of previous economic cycles, they forecast future trends. He claims their predictions were consistently more accurate than those produced on the official Treasury model. Ross left Britain

Ken Livingstone at home in Cricklewood preparing the pond for his 'Neil Kinnock memorial garden', February 27th 1990 (*Guardian, Graham Turner*)

in 1992 to work in Moscow as an adviser to Russian trades unions, but Livingstone continues to employ him to update and analyse the model on a part-time consultancy basis. As computer technology advanced, the economic data was copied on to a powerful laptop, allowing Ross to advise Livingstone by fax or e-mail from wherever he went in Russia. The operation, funded by income from Livingstone's freelance writing and speaking engagements, was channelled through Localaction Ltd, a company set up in 1986 to handle the proceeds of his first book. One of the richer ironies of the later years was that bankers and commodity brokers were paying Livingstone to make after-dinner speeches that were larded with economic analysis produced in this way. The high priests of British capitalism were inadvertently funding the development of Livingstone's socialism and kept asking him back because they liked his jokes.

Livingstone's media profile was diminished after he lost his seat on the NEC, but his stormy past guaranteed him a permanent

On the general election campaign trail in 1992 (*Guardian, John Readon*)

walk-on role in the national political soap opera. For example, his conviction for refusal to pay a £470 poll-tax bill was reported in the national press in March 1991 when similar acts of defiance by hundreds of protesters around the country were not mentioned. After promising on grounds of trades union solidarity that he would never write for papers owned by Rupert Murdoch, he decided to gain publicity for his views (and more income for the bulletin) by taking up the offer of a regular column in the *Sun*.

His assumption at the time was that the left was going through a hiatus until Labour won the 1992 election.

> When we didn't win it, then came the point of real depression. Not just for me. The entire PLP that summer was devastated. None of us believed the Tories would win a majority. We thought that at worst we'd get a hung parliament and Labour would start cosying up to the Liberals. We began to have nightmares that the Tories were going to be in forever. Remember those pictures of

Kinnock: how it looked like he was dying. We were all like
that. I got psoriasis, which is a stress disorder. I had patches
of dry skin like Michael Gambon in the 'Singing Detective'.
I'd had a small outbreak in the run-up to abolition of the
GLC, but this was much worse. The whole PLP was in a
collective manic depression. And then along came the ERM
debacle and normal politics resumed: Britain evicted from
ERM, Livingstone's psoriasis cured. We went through
almost an entire parliament with the government in double-
digit deficit in the polls, waiting for the next election.

During this period Livingstone became the effective standard-
bearer of the Campaign group of Labour MPs, but not really its
leader. At no point could they have been described as
Livingstonite in the way that previous generations of left-wingers
were known as Bevanite or Bennite. His independence of ideas
and style always set him apart from the rest. They gave him
support when the occasion demanded it, but did not owe him
personal loyalty.

When Kinnock stood down after losing the 1992 election, it
was Livingstone rather than Tony Benn or Dennis Skinner who
was the Campaign group's candidate in a bid for the party
leadership. Rule changes stopped candidates being eligible for the
party ballot to choose a new leader if they could not get
nominations from at least 20 per cent of Labour MPs. He was
knocked out when he could assemble only 13 of the 55 required.
John Smith took over as leader with overwhelming party support.

Although Smith was identified with the right wing of the
party, he was regarded by Livingstone as a huge improvement on
the originally left-wing Kinnock. In part this was a reflection of
Smith's more tolerant approach, rooted in the broad church
traditions of the Scottish Labour Party. Smith was also more
enthusiastic about the party's trades union links and less captivated
by the black arts of Peter Mandelson and his spin-doctoring
chums. One of the key issues that defined Smith's position

through much of his political career was support for Britain's membership of the European Community and on that he had Livingstone's enthusiastic support. Livingstone assumed that he would have become a part of Labour's ministerial team if Smith had lived long enough to win office. 'He'd undoubtedly have sought to govern by bringing the left in. He wasn't planning to use us in the run-up to the election, but he had no problem with left-wingers who were pro-Europe.'

That was not to be. After Smith died in 1994, Livingstone mounted another token bid for the leadership, but again failed to gain enough MP nominations to get on to the ballot paper. Tony Blair became leader and went on to push through a further round of policy and organisational reforms, wooing middle-class voters by eliminating any vestiges of socialist fundamentalism that they might find threatening.

Although Livingstone objected to the continuing rightward drift, he was less vicious in his personal criticism of Blair than he had been against Kinnock.

> I thought he was a nice young man who hadn't been prepared for leadership and hadn't thought where he stood on the great global issues. He'd always been able to master a brief, but he'd never branched out to develop a world view. And he wasn't around a lot because he was always rushing home to change his kids' nappies. So he was going to have a very steep learning curve. I assumed all that rubbish about New Labour was just something he said to win the election. I didn't think he believed in it. Knowing what most Labour MPs and party members and union leaders were like, I knew they didn't either.

Livingstone accepted that he had become entirely marginalised. It was futile for the left to imagine that it could do anything for the time being to combat Blair's ascendancy over a party thirsting for election victory after four parliaments in opposition. But he was convinced the Blairites would ultimately fail when their approach was tested by the crises of government and they found they did not have the answers to the deep-seated problems of industrial under-investment. He decided his job was to prepare the ground by working out policies to which the party could turn when trouble struck. With a leap of political imagination, he compared himself with Sir Keith Joseph, the Conservative thinker who challenged the centrist drift of the Heath government in the early 1970s and became the intellectual father of Thatcherism. 'I was doing what Keith Joseph did in 1973–75, challenging the ideas that don't work. All my effort went into the *Socialist Economic Bulletin*, working out an economic strategy, because I assumed the party would eventually want one.'

The Joseph parallel would probably have struck most Labour Party members as far-fetched. Livingstone was still too much of a political street-fighter to be a convincing theoretician and he was unable or unwilling to cut himself off from narrow disputes that flared up sporadically among the left-wing groups whose company he kept. One example was his acrimonious battle against Marc Wadsworth in 1994 for leadership of the Anti-Racist Alliance, culminating in a messy court action. Another came four years later when he tabled a vitriolic motion on the Commons order paper supporting the sacking of John Haylett as editor of the *Morning Star*, but withdrew it when other Campaign group MPs backed Haylett. Whatever the rights and wrongs of these particular disputes, his partisan involvement in the micro-politics of the left did not help establish the reputation he sought as an independent thinker with his eye on the big economic picture.

He says that his willingness to take a stand against fellow left-wingers when he thinks they are wrong should be regarded as a political virtue.

> The hard left have always been wary of me and they still are because at the end of the day I'm interested in governing. And that sometimes means you have to say no to people.

Tony Benn never gets involved in these rows. His line is that there are no enemies on the left. I take the view that, if they are putting forward something mad or damaging, you need to tell them that at times. So I don't particularly expect to be loved by them and it's not going to happen.

A more specific charge raised against him from sections of the left was that his willingness to row with some groups was linked to an over-close relationship with others. More specifically it has been suggested that he got organisational support from Socialist Action and relied on economic analysis sent from Moscow by its former Marxist theoretician, John Ross.

Livingstone retains the services of Ross on a part-time contract, but asserts that he has always had total personal control of the views expressed in *Socialist Economic Bulletin*.

I would love to have organisational support, but it has not been offered. Why should it be when I disagree with them on so many of the main issues? Socialist Action was totally opposed to intervention in Bosnia, while I was the first to call for the bombing of Serbia and the intervention of NATO ground troops to drive Milosevic back. I am totally in favour of proportional representation, but they support first-past-the-post. I am totally committed to European monetary union and Socialist Action is totally opposed.

In the 1980s the smear against me was that I was the tool of the WRP [Workers Revolutionary Party] ... Now it's said that I'm the tool of Socialist Action. The truth is that I am prepared to work with people when there is political agreement. I'll agree on some issues and not on others. The CLPD has supported me in elections for Labour's NEC, but its major campaigns are against PR and Europe. If Tony Blair is doing the right thing, as he has done on Ireland, I'll support him.

It is likely that Blair knew little and cared less about Livingstone's complicated relationships with these various hard-left groupings. During subsequent briefings against Livingstone by the party's spin doctors, it was always his up-front behaviour on the national stage that was identified as the problem, not his behind-the-scenes relationships with left-wingers who were in some sense beyond the pale.

As the 1997 general election approached, the two men had at least one meeting which Livingstone refuses to discuss on the grounds that private conversations should remain confidential. Senior Blairite MPs, who acted as intermediaries, think the leader was preparing to offer him a job. One, who was unwilling to be quoted by name, said: 'I was a go-between. I had conversations with Ken and told him there were overtures for him to come in from the cold so that the party could make better use of his talents. He went in to see Tony two or three times. My understanding was that he was offered a junior ministerial post, but wanted more.' Livingstone denies this version of events. 'I was never offered a job. Had I been offered one, I would have accepted,' he says.

Perhaps if Labour had won the 1997 election with a more slender majority, Livingstone would have been brought into Blair's first administration. But the landslide was so massive that there was no need to balance the ministerial team to retain the support of left-wing MPs in the Commons' division lobbies. With a Labour majority of 178 seats, the Campaign group of 36 MPs and 6 MEPs was marginalised and Livingstone had the dismal prospect of yet another parliament on the back-benches, preaching his economic gospel from the wilderness. That did not mean he thought of giving up. As he puts it:

> When Blair became leader it was even more important for
> the left to hang on inside the party and keep the ideas
> flowing. This is absolutely the low point of the left. So much
> of its ideological base has been destroyed by events and at the

same time there are no areas in which new leaders of the left can emerge. You don't get promoted to the front bench if you show any signs of leftism. You can't rise through local government any more. So increasingly we have a pool of people growing old together. They watch us. We've all got electronic tags. They know where we are and what we are doing. The next leader of the left will be somebody they least suspect. It will be the Tony Benn of the time – somebody that has been loyal, who's been trusted, who's been promoted. Somewhere today on those government benches, there is be somebody who will either cynically see a space and move into it or, as with Benn, become radicalised by the experience of office.

That might have been nearly the end of the story if Livingstone's career had not yet again been rescued by the mistakes of his political adversaries. The first was by Peter Mandelson, the master spin-doctor who wanted to be regarded as a politician in his own right. In May 1997 Mandelson was appointed minister without portfolio in the Cabinet Office, a powerful job at the centre of government that confirmed his image as a backroom fixer instead of allowing him to develop a departmental profile. Without consulting Blair, he put his name forward in July as a candidate for the seat vacated by Gordon Brown on the constituency section of the party's national executive. It was to be the last of the old-style beauty contests before rule changes to exclude MPs from representing the constituencies. Jack Straw, the home secretary, had been the obvious replacement for Brown, but he stepped aside to allow Mandelson an easy ride.

Livingstone had stood unsuccessfully for the NEC every year since being knocked off in 1989. He got 58,593 votes in 1996 when he was one place away from regaining a seat, but he thinks he would have lost again in 1997 if Straw had been the candidate instead of the unloved Mandelson. Even at the high noon of Blairite domination when party members were basking in their long-awaited electoral success, there were limits to how far they could be expected to show gratitude and loyalty to the leader's favourites. Livingstone stormed through with 83,669 votes to Mandelson's 68,023. His immediate comment was: 'Blair's no fool. He'll look at this and recognise it's a bit of a prod from the rank and file of the party to say: you haven't got a blank cheque; you're there to do better; you're always there to do better.' A few days later he celebrated his victory with a vintage denunciation of what he called the party's Millbank Tendency. 'There are a lot of truly ghastly people gathered around Blair, like lice on the back of a hedgehog and they have their own agenda,' he told the *New Statesman.*

   Mandelson's error of judgment in contesting the NEC elections restored Livingstone to the political limelight. A longer-lasting tactical mistake was made by Tony Blair when he pushed through plans to create a powerful directly elected mayor of London without recognising that he was inventing the vehicle on which Livingstone would re-emerge as a heavyweight political force. As the next chapter will show, the mayoral proposal produced a groundswell of popular support for Livingstone that nobody would have known existed otherwise. Against his instincts, he was pushed back on to the battleground of London politics.

10 Mayor's Nest

The plan to create a directly elected mayor for London was a late addition to Labour's long campaign to remedy problems caused by abolition of the GLC. It was always a democratic outrage that the capital was being deprived of one form of city-wide elected authority without any other being put in its place. But the public perception that loss of the council was doing real damage to the city's strategic interests took several years to take hold.

During the fight to save the council, Livingstone and his colleagues had predicted that the city would fall into administrative chaos when the council's powers were dispersed to the boroughs and an almost incomprehensible network of joint committees, quangos and government officials. But in spite of the tears and foreboding when the GLC flag was lowered for the last time in March 1986, the transition was remarkably smooth.

Conservative ministers were desperate to prove to a sceptical London public that the new arrangements worked better and more cheaply. In the rate support grant settlement for 1986/87 they diverted more than £200 million of extra Treasury funding into the capital to give the illusion that the changes were producing savings for the ratepayers. As a result the annual rate bills on some of the most desirable homes in the city shrank by up to £1,000. Spending on the GLC's priority programmes was broadly maintained, including subsidies to maintain fares and passenger volumes on London Transport.

In an effort to convince Londoners that they were losing nothing from the new arrangements, ministers even ensured that grants for voluntary bodies were protected. The government and Tory press had spent years attacking Livingstone for profligate and politically inspired funding of a ragbag of minority interests, but more of these groups had their grants renewed in 1986/87 than in any previous annual cycle. According to the *London Government Handbook*,* only 93 out of more than 2,500 bodies supported by the GLC were denied financial support. The richest of ironies came the following year when Labour and Conservative representatives on the London Boroughs Grants Scheme, set up to handle this matter after abolition, failed to agree a budget. To avoid a breakdown of voluntary activity in the capital, Tory ministers forced the Tory councillors to compromise at a figure close to the former GLC spending level.

The administrative handover was also painless. GLC officers spent the final months before abolition working with the successor organisations and the London Residuary Body to secure bureaucratic continuity.† Livingstone played a part in this by doing everything possible to co-operate to protect as many jobs and services as possible. Few Londoners ever understood the labyrinthine network of quangos and committees, but for the first few years they seemed to work. Many of the Labour borough leaders grew in stature and confidence, not wanting to return to the old days of playing second fiddle to County Hall.

It was always going to be hard for borough nominees and civil servants to take over the GLC's strategic planning role. That job could not be performed effectively without decisive political direction and sufficient authority to drive through a London-wide vision against local vested interests. But the GLC had never made much of an impact as a land-use planning authority. Its strategies took years to negotiate with the boroughs and tended to be torn up before they could be implemented, whenever political control at County Hall changed hands and a different policy was

---

**London Government Handbook*, Michael Hebbert and Tony Travers (eds.), Cassell, 1988.

†*Dismantlers: The London Residuary Body*, Michael Hebbert and Ann Dickins Edge, London School of Economics, 1994.

wanted. As the Lawson boom gathered pace and regional policies to move big offices out of London was abandoned, the capital's economy was allowed to let rip and most of its people seemed for a while to prosper. For the first time in a generation, the London economy grew more quickly than the UK as a whole.

There was never a consensus about whether GLC abolition saved money. Arguably, the transfer of all non-strategic services to the boroughs ought to have streamlined the system and improved efficiency. But, as the years went by, the problems associated with abolition became more noticeable than the benefits. Some of the boroughs struggled to fulfil their responsibilities because they lacked the necessary financial, managerial and political resources. The subsequent abolition of the Inner London Education Authority in 1990 contributed to a collapse in public confidence in comprehensive education in some of the capital's inner city areas where schools could not cope with the problems of multiple deprivation. By the late 1980s, it became commonplace to hear people complaining that the city was going to the dogs.

One of the more memorable examples was an article by the political journalist Peter Kellner explaining why his family moved to Cambridgeshire to escape the squalor and breakdown of services in the capital city. 'London's fabric is rotting ... human beings are forced to travel on the Underground in conditions that would be banned if we were animals ... Londoners are more likely to be assaulted, burgled and run over than anyone else in mainland Britain, and the capital's villains are less likely to be caught ... That catalogue of London hazards is incomplete [without mentioning] increased begging, vagrancy, rubbish in the streets, uncleaned pavements, the stress, the smells, the noise' he wrote (*Independent*, August 7th 1989).

Few if any of those problems could be attributed to abolition of the GLC, although many were linked to other aspects of the government's policies, including lack of investment in public infrastructure, cuts in benefit and mental health initiatives that contributed to growing numbers of young homeless people. In fact the public squalor got worse at the same time as the city grew in wealth. Its population began to rise in the late 1980s for the first time since 1939. So it was hard to argue that abolition of the GLC caused a collapse. What it did was to remove the democratic forum where these social problems could be debated and London-wide strategies devised so that pressure could be applied on the government and other relevant organisations to deliver solutions. Opinion polls consistently showed that Londoners missed the GLC and wanted a replacement assembly so that somebody could be held accountable for how the capital was run.

Labour and the Liberal Democrats both went into the 1992 election, as they had in 1987, proposing a new city-wide local authority with responsibility for strategic planning, police, fire and public transport within the old GLC boundaries. They said they did not want to recreate the large GLC bureaucracy and argued for a streamlined body to articulate the views of Londoners and provide democratic accountability for the delivery of London-wide services. In response, the Conservatives continued to reject any thought of recreating a London authority, but promised to beef up the ministerial and civil service arrangements for handling the capital's affairs.

After winning the election, John Major appointed a Cabinet subcommittee for London to co-ordinate the work of all the Whitehall departments with a hand in its affairs. When John Gummer took over as environment secretary in 1993, he was specifically designated minister for London and undertook more visible advocacy of its interests. Working through a new government office for London, he began to take some of the political decisions that had been lacking in the Balkanised system after GLC abolition. According to Tony Travers, head of the LSE's Greater London Group and no fan of the Conservative record on handling the capital's affairs, the strategic planning guidance for London produced by Gummer in 1995 was 'the clearest ever and more capable of implementation than anything produced by the GLC'.

Major appointed Steven Norris as minister for transport in London and he, between celebrated affairs, did some useful work on co-ordinating the different bodies responsible for Underground, buses, suburban railways, trunk roads, local roads, parking, traffic regulation, taxis, airports and waterways. The government also encouraged partnerships to promote the capital, such as the London First initiative involving leading businesses, boroughs and voluntary groups.

But these were sticking plasters to hold together an unsatisfactory piece of Heath Robinson machinery for governing the capital. In an analysis of the system going into the 1997 election, Tony Travers and George Jones of the LSE concluded: 'London is a city with much government, but little political power.' As an example they quoted a collective failure to solve congestion problems that were increasing numbers of cars in traffic jams, worsening pollution and damaging Londoners' health. The responsibility for building and maintaining roads was split between the Highways Agency and the boroughs. Funding was determined by the Department of Transport and the boroughs. A government-appointed traffic director had a duty to improve the regulation and efficiency of major roads. Parking was a borough responsibility, although there was a London-wide committee to regulate some aspects. The Metropolitan Police, responsible to the Home Office, had some traffic-regulation functions. Bridges and tunnels across and under the River Thames fell within the control of a number of boroughs. The privatised utilities had the right to dig up roads and might do so in emergencies without prior notification. So many bodies were dabbling in control of London's roads that it was impossible for any one organisation to achieve co-ordination. 'Fragmentation of government – and the lack of effective political power that goes with such a system – is now worse than in the past. The recent creation of new London-wide committees and boards, the growth of new Whitehall involvement and the rapid development of partnerships together suggest there is a power vacuum.'*

Labour's ideas for filling that vacuum were set out in a series of policy documents in the years leading up to the 1997 election. The party said in *Working Together for London* in 1994 that London was 'the only capital city in western Europe with no democratic city government and no city-wide strategy.' It called for an elected Greater London Authority to give a sense of direction, provide a voice to carry weight in Whitehall and Europe, and eliminate duplication of effort by bringing £8.4 billion of spending by unaccountable quangos into an efficient single structure. 'The Tories are unable to deal with London's problems because they don't trust Londoners ... They took away Londoners' right to vote for the GLC because they could not face opposition', it complained.

On April 10th 1996 Labour published *A Voice for London*, a consultation document preparing for the election manifesto. It gave a bit more detail about its plans for a streamlined authority with a small number of top calibre senior officers working in partnership with the boroughs without overlapping their functions. The GLA would promote economic, transport, planning, environmental and law-and-order strategies as well as help raise funds for investment in jobs. 'It will not generally be involved in the direct provision of services. Even services for which we suggest it should be responsible, like the fire brigade and the Metropolitan Police, would, under our proposals, be run by boards at arms' length from the authority,' it said.

This was the first official party document to include a suggestion that London might benefit from having an elected mayor with executive powers. The idea looked as if it had been thrown in towards the end almost as an afterthought and hedged about with caveats. 'Such an approach would be quite new in Britain, changing the role of the elected assembly and its individual members and leaving one person in a much more

---

The New Government of London, Joseph Rowntree Foundation, York, 1997.

powerful position than has been customary. We invite Londoners' views,' it said. In fact the uncertainty of presentation was the result of an unresolved argument between Tony Blair and Frank Dobson about the viability of the mayoral approach.

Dobson, former leader of Camden council, was the shadow environment secretary and shadow minister for London responsible for this area of policy. According to party insiders, he was firmly opposed to the concept of a directly elected mayor, which Blair had floated in February 1996 in his John Smith Memorial Lecture. Dobson thought it would put too much power in the hands of one individual and would threaten the traditional pattern of local government. He also pointed out that there was negligible support in the Labour Party for such an experiment. He fought a rearguard action to bend Blair towards accepting an indirectly elected mayor, giving that title to the leader of the largest party group on the GLA, who would be constrained by the need to retain its support.

But Blair was enthusiastic for direct election of the mayor because he thought London needed the strong leadership that was enjoyed by other big competitor cities such as New York under Mayor Rudolph Giuliani. Blair had never been a Labour councillor and was unsympathetic to traditions of local democracy that he thought were a breeding ground for corruption and well past their sell-by date. He was disillusioned with the nineteenth-century committee structure of local authorities and was working towards a more fundamental shake-up of local government to establish smaller executives, giving elected councillors a more focused, scrutinising role. He recognised that a strong London mayor might sometimes provide an uncomfortable challenge to a prime minister, even if both jobs were filled by compatible Labour politicians. But he thought that tension was appropriate and in keeping with Labour's other plans for extensive devolution of powers to Scotland and Wales.

The disagreement between Blair and Dobson was never properly resolved. Just seven days after publication of the party's agnostic policy document, the Labour leader pre-empted further discussion with a barnstorming keynote speech at a public debate staged by the *Evening Standard* on London in the 21st century. He told an audience of 2,500 people in Westminster's Central Hall that a directly elected mayor would be a spur for the renewal of local democracy. 'Strong civic leadership could help restore some of the much-needed civic pride in London. It could provide vision and direction for London's future, someone to drive the development of the city, to pull together the partnerships needed to make things happen.' He said London was a great city that needed 'a galvanising, powerful vision of its future' and concluded: 'For a vision, there does need to be a voice.'

Although Blair stuck to the line that he was presenting the idea for consultation, he spoke for it so forcefully that the speech effectively quashed Dobson's resistance. A party leader riding high in the opinion polls within a year or so of a general election can do that sort of thing. But the consequence was that the proposal went into Labour's 1997 manifesto promising 'a new deal for London, with a strategic authority and a mayor, each directly elected', without any of the details being worked up by party officials or shadow ministers. Dobson loyally did his best to sell the package to MPs and the party's London executive, but everybody knew his heart was not in it.

The party conducted a limited consultation exercise, including a conference at the University of London on June 17th 1996 at which constituency and union delegates raised doubts about direct election of the mayor, among a mishmash of other concerns. But no votes were allowed and no effort was made to produce a report on the results of consultation before the manifesto was produced.

Civil servants preparing for Labour's certain victory with sheaves of policy documents on almost every other aspect of business had nothing to help them get ready for the complex legislation that would be required to establish the new pattern of London government. They were able to get up to speed quickly enough after the election when Nick Raynsford was appointed minister for London and got down to the job of crafting the detail of the policy. But lack of preparation before the election was to prove a more lasting political problem because it meant that there was never any serious attempt to build a consensus in the London Labour Party. Nobody battled with the leader, but nobody did the work. A radical departure from the British local-government tradition was imposed from the top down by a leader who had no political roots in local-council politics. The mayoral plan was to be a rare example of devolution without any evidence of support from those who were supposed to benefit.

Blair did not pluck the idea of having a powerful London mayor from out of the blue. In a sense it had been floating around since Henry Fitz Ailwyn became the first Lord Mayor in the late twelfth century. Michael Heseltine, during his spell on the Tory backbenches in the late 1980s, argued for elected mayors to revive the civic pride of the Victorian era. The proposal was periodically advanced as a solution to London's specific difficulties by a number of individuals. They included Tony Banks, Labour MP for Newham and last chairman of the GLC, Margaret Hodge, Labour MP for Barking and former leader of Islington council and – perhaps most influentially – the journalist Simon Jenkins and senior editorial staff on the *Evening Standard*.

But there was no blueprint available and no international model that was exactly suitable for London to pluck off the shelf when the Labour government started work. The problem of Dobson's lack of enthusiasm for the mayoral project was solved by promoting him from the environment brief he held in opposition to the higher-profile health portfolio, with responsibility for rescuing the NHS. As health secretary, he became one of the most obviously competent early stars of the Blair administration. John Prescott took over Cabinet responsibility for the mayoral project as part of a wide-ranging brief covering a combined Department of the Environment Transport and the Regions, which he combined with his role as deputy prime minister. Although

Prescott might have been expected to share Dobson's traditionalist suspicion of Blairite tinkering with local democracy, he saw the London package as a way of building momentum for his own dream of establishing regional government in other parts of England. So he became a committed supporter, but left the detailed work to Raynsford. Blair kept in touch with the project through Pat McFadden, the constitutional specialist in his Downing Street policy unit.

Raynsford, the MP for Greenwich and former director of a housing charity, was an enthusiast for the concept of a super-slim strategic authority. As a London politician, he had seen how the fuzzy division of responsibilities between the GLC and boroughs produced conflict between tiers of local government.

> The GLC had significant achievements, but it often appeared to be an unnecessary tier of bureaucracy ... Nobody who understood local government in London could have objected if the Thatcher government had brought forward a reform package to streamline and modernise. What was monstrous about her decision was that she abolished the council leaving an appalling vacuum from which London suffered for 12 years, leaving it at a serious disadvantage against other world cities in an increasingly competitive climate.

As an example of the damage done, he quotes an episode in 1993 when civil servants in Brussels called him as opposition spokesman to ask if he could help co-ordinate the London bid for EU regional assistance grants. They said the borough bids were too unrealistic and disorganised to be taken seriously. Conservative ministers refused Raynsford's offer of help and London lost millions of pounds of aid for its deprived areas.

Just over five weeks after the election, in a Commons debate on the governance of London, Raynsford set out the principles on which the strategic authority would work. Livingstone cheekily responded with a speech of 'comradely advice on the weak spots' of the government's plan. Many of his points echoed those made before the election by Dobson while trying to stop Blair going down the mayoral road. Livingstone warned against putting too much power in the hands of one individual. He said the American experience showed how strong mayors with control of contracts and appointments were the focus of corruption and pressure from organised crime, especially the mafia. It was far safer to have a leader kept under control by the constant scrutiny of assembly members of all parties. 'If we are honest, my party knows that there is no overwhelming support for a separately elected mayor in the London Labour Party, among London Labour borough leaders, or among Labour Members [of Parliament].' There had been massive pressure not to rock the boat before the general election. 'So we all went along with it; we did not make a fuss; it was what the leader wanted. But we must get it right: the leader may be wrong.' He appealed for a multiple-choice referendum, giving Londoners the opportunity to decide whether or not there should be a mayor as well as an elected authority, whether the new assembly should have tax-raising powers, and whether elections should be by proportional representation.

In the post-election honeymoon when Blair was at his peak party popularity, the speech was strikingly acerbic. It included a warning against 'the disease of manifestoitis' (slavish adherence to an election commitment of the sort that damaged the Thatcher government when it forced through abolition of the GLC against the better judgment of most Conservatives). And it concluded that failure to give the London assembly adequate revenue-raising powers would leave it 'with no more independence than the Vichy regime in France under the Nazis'. With the Treasury in control, 'the mayor would have no more authority than Marshal Pétain, which is not what we want.' It may safely be assumed that, at this stage, Livingstone was not looking for the job.

Of course his intervention made not a blind bit of difference.

When the government presented its plans in a Green Paper, *New Leadership for London*, in July 1997, it adopted a genuinely consultative approach, asking 61 open questions about the detail of how the new system would work. But it left no room for doubt that there would be 'a strong executive mayor' and 'a small assembly of 24–32 members', a lot fewer than previously envisaged.

Interested parties were given until October 24th to submit reactions to the Green Paper. Just 12 days before that deadline, the Greater London Labour Party held a regional consultation conference at the University of London Union. Its chairman, Jim Fitzpatrick, Labour MP for Poplar and Canning Town, told delegates at the opening plenary session that there would be an opportunity for expression of views, but no votes because they were not mandated by their constituencies, unions and affiliated societies.

After protest from the floor, he agreed that the various workshop groups discussing different aspects of the Green Paper could submit resolutions to the closing plenary if they had strong views. Livingstone addressed the workshop on the mayor and assembly, delivering a passionate attack on concentration of power in the hands of a directly elected mayor. It voted by a 2:1 majority that the assembly should elect the mayor, that it should have tax-varying powers and that there should be a multiple-choice referendum to give Londoners the final say on these issues. At the final plenary session, Fitzpatrick refused to put the views of the workshops to the vote, arguing that they were merely indicative and not couched as formal resolutions. Livingstone's allies maintain that a vote at that stage would have firmly rejected the plan for a directly elected mayor. His Blairite opponents say the outcome was never so clear-cut, since nearly all the left-wingers packed the workshop on mayoral issues and they might not have had the numbers to win a plenary vote.

Eight days later and just four days before the deadline for consultations, the subject was discussed by the regional executive.

Although it was to the left of the party leadership on most issues, it included representatives of London MPs, unions and council leaders who did not share the hard-left sentiments of the constituency delegates. Left-wingers pressed the demand for a multiple-choice referendum, but this was defeated by 15 votes to five. Fitzpatrick said the implication of the vote was that the executive now backed the idea of a directly elected mayor.

Livingstone's supporters later claimed that this ruling was a non sequitur and that no London party body ever had an opportunity to say yes or no to the mayoral proposal. Fitzpatrick says he was merely following the rules. 'There was no skulduggery. I made it clear that if the [multiple-choice] proposition passed, we would be in conflict with the manifesto and the NEC. If it failed, we would be in support of the proposition put forward [by the government]. The challenge fell and so the status quo pertained.' The consequence was that the government escaped official party criticism in spite of the activists' misgivings.

The southern and eastern regional council of the TUC was irritated by the Green Paper's failure to mention the unions' role as partners in London's economic regeneration. It submitted a critical response calling for the mayor to be the leader of the largest party in a bigger and more inclusive assembly. On October 23rd the Greater London Association of Trades Councils said its soundings across the capital showed that the people wanted an assembly with tax-varying powers, but not an over-powerful directly elected mayor. Livingstone commented: 'Basically what Tony [Blair] is saying is that Londoners should not be trusted when it comes to their own city. I find that overwhelmingly embarrassing for him personally. I know of only four Labour London MPs who support this idea. Most others say privately that the idea is absolutely barmy, but they don't want to rock the boat.'

This use of the word 'barmy' to describe the mayoral plan was later claimed by Livingstone's opponents to be a key reason why he could not be considered suitable for the job. They said Labour would be handing a propaganda gift to the Tories if it ran a candidate who was so contemptuous of the job. But at the time ministers concentrated on claiming that their proposals were widely accepted. Legislation was passed to establish a referendum in which Londoners would be asked a simple question, which was whether or not they approved a package deal for a strategic authority under a directly elected mayor and assembly.

However, in terms of the party's internal democratic machinery, that could not be the end of the matter. At some stage there had to be a properly constituted conference of the regional party at which formal resolutions were likely to be passed condemning the government's mayoral plans. The conference was scheduled for March 1998 in the run-up to the campaign for the referendum and local elections in May, the most embarrassing time for hostile votes showing that party members did not support the proposition that the electorate was being asked to approve.

Terry Ashton, general secretary of the London party, wrote to the constituencies on December 5th 1997 informing them: 'In our search for a venue big enough to take the annual meeting we were unable to find a suitable date and place before the referendum and London borough elections on 7 May. Rather than having an unsuitable venue and given the huge resources that organising the annual meeting takes, I decided instead to switch to a later date and more suitable venue.' The meeting was to be held on June 13th and 14th at Queen Mary and Westfield College, Mile End Road. The reason he gave for postponement began to look threadbare when the *Evening Standard* established that the college's facilities were available for hire on the weekend when the conference was originally due to be held as well as on other weekends in February and March.

London party officials say they now regret not being franker about the real reasons for postponement. They deny it was motivated by desire to muzzle debate within the London party until after the referendum was safely completed. According to this explanation, the main factor forcing deferral of the conference was acute staffing pressure in the small regional office made up of eight people, including clerical assistants. They were all due lots of time off because they had not been able to take holidays earlier in the year when maximum effort was being put in to fight the general election and the Uxbridge parliamentary by-election at the end of July. The problem was compounded in mid-October when Piers Merchant resigned as Tory MP for Beckenham, obliging the staff to decamp to the constituency to fight the by-election called for November 20th. If they were to be allowed to take their holiday entitlements, there would be no time to do the work needed to stage an effective regional conference before campaigning started for the local elections and referendum in May 1998. But nobody wanted to admit staffing shortages for fear of ridicule by other political parties.

An added bonus to be gained by postponement was that regional conferences held after March would be conducted under the new rules agreed by the party conference in October 1997 under the Partnership in Power programme. Instead of grinding through the old diet of composites of resolutions submitted by constituency parties, unions and affiliates, there would be workshops and debates on the key policy issues identified by the national party. Ashton liked the idea that London would be the first region to adopt the new style. 'Of course it was more helpful to have the regional conference after the referendum rather than before, when the left would have carried on having an argument which they had already lost. But it suits the left to ignore the fact that political parties do not have huge resources. That was the reason for postponement, not some conspiracy,' said one party official.

Whatever the motivation, the upshot was that the regional party never got the chance to influence the shape of the government's plans to re-establish a London-wide democratic authority. And that omission seemed especially glaring since the proposal was meant to be part of a programme of devolution. London would get a mayor, but the London party would not be allowed to have a say in the matter. Government powers would be devolved, but the Labour Party would continue to be ruled from the centre.

Maybe Tony Blair and the party centralists had a surer feel of what ordinary electors wanted. The scheme was eventually approved by 72 per cent of Londoners voting in the referendum in May 1998. Although turnout was only 35 per cent, ministers were reassured by canvassing reports suggesting that the mayoral plan was a vote-winner, boosting Labour's successes in the borough elections on the same day. In spite of continuing rumblings of concern among party activists, the government was able to claim that its plans were legitimised by the will of the people.

When the regional conference was eventually held in June 1998 it was too late for party delegates to do anything to change the government's plans for a directly elected mayor. So attention turned to the method of picking the party's candidate. The Unison and GMB delegations, responding to press speculation that Labour's national executive wanted to make the final choice, submitted resolutions for the decision to be taken by a ballot of all London party members.

Five constituency parties, trying to pre-empt any attempt to stop left-wingers getting through to the ballot, proposed rules to ensure that popular candidates were included on the shortlist. After a lot of procedural wrangling, delegates overwhelmingly carried a composite resolution combining these demands. It said that the selection should be through a One Member One Vote ballot of London party members and all candidates nominated by at least 10 London constituencies 'will automatically be short-listed so that their names will appear on the ballot papers to select Labour's candidate'. The decision could not be binding because party rules put the NEC in charge of candidate selection procedures. But the sovereign body of the London party laid down a marker that its members wanted direct control of the selection process. They would not accept any attempt by the national or regional executives to weed out candidates unacceptable to the party leadership. Guess who they had in mind?

By that stage Livingstone was being widely touted as the popular favourite to be Labour's candidate for mayor. He had not organised to get himself into that position and was initially reluctant to run, partly because he thought the mayoralty was ill conceived and partly because it looked like a dodgy personal career move.

After eight years in the wilderness, he was at last beginning to regain political momentum at Westminster. His unexpected triumph against Peter Mandelson in the 1997 NEC elections went some way towards restoring his credibility as a character to be reckoned with in the party. And he wanted to use that position to fight his corner on a range of national issues. Bashing Gordon Brown's handling of the economy came top of these priorities; running again for local office looked at first like a distracting waste of time.

Perhaps because he was always an outsider, people still tended to think of Livingstone as a young pretender to office. But he would be nearly 59 by the end of the mayor's first term and nearly 63 if he completed a second stint. In all probability the party would decide that a Labour mayor could not stay on as a Labour MP because it frowned on dual mandates. For example, Labour MEPs were not allowed to seek re-election to the European Parliament if they managed to get themselves elected to Westminster, an approach that seriously weakened opportunities for the two parliaments to integrate their scrutiny of EU business. A similar procedure was likely to be invoked to stop Mayor Livingstone standing again in Brent East at the next general election. When the job was done, he would have to go tramping round the candidate selection circuit to find another seat against competition from people whom the party leadership would find more amenable. So there would be all sorts of problems re-entering the parliamentary arena if he left it to run London. He had been there, done that and could probably no longer squeeze into the T-shirt.

What changed his mind was the evidence of the opinion polls. As soon as Tony Blair proposed the election of an executive mayor, the media started asking who it might be. And the people of London cast their minds back to the GLC and called for the return of Livingstone. The first poll was conducted by MORI for the *Evening Standard* in November 1996. A sample of more than 1,000 voters were shown a list of hypothetical candidates, including figures from the business world whom Blair had suggested might be the best people to bring administrative flair to handling the capital's affairs. Richard Branson, the Virgin entrepreneur with a laid-back personal style and attractive enthusiasm for doomed ballooning expeditions, came top with 26 per cent support. Livingstone was second with 18 per cent and Betty Boothroyd, Speaker of the House of Commons, was third with 17 per cent. Other Labour politicians trailing behind included Glenda Jackson, the former Oscar-winning actress with 14 per cent, Tony Banks with 9 per cent and Bernie Grant with 3 per cent. For the Conservatives, Lord Archer got 7 per cent and, for the Liberal Democrats, Simon Hughes got 6 per cent.

The poll may have been more akin to showbiz than serious politics, but it set the tone for a series of samplings over the next two years in which Livingstone always emerged as the top Labour candidate and most likely to beat the Tories. He was consistently the favourite among party members and Labour voters, as well as being the Labour candidate most likely to attract the supporters of other parties.

The Labour leadership got an even more alarming signal in April 1998, just a week before the referendum, when a poll by NOP for the *Evening Standard* showed that the voters would disapprove of any moves to block a Livingstone candidacy. The public was asked: 'If Labour's candidate were chosen by ballot of all Labour Party members in London, do you think the Labour leadership would be right or wrong to prevent Livingstone from standing?' The answer was that 16 per cent thought it would be right, 74 per cent thought it would be wrong and 10 per cent

We're no lame ducks: Lord Archer and Ken Livingstone defy their respective party leaders in a bid to become mayoral candidates, December 10th 1997 (*Guardian, Martin Argles*)

didn't know. The majority against blocking Livingstone was slightly larger among Labour supporters, 78 per cent of whom thought it would be wrong.

For the Blairite party managers, this result conjured up a

nightmare. Livingstone was the front-runner to become Labour's candidate if the selection were to be conducted by an open ballot of London party members. As candidate, he would be the most likely to beat the Tories and win the mayoralty for Labour. Indeed he was so likely to win that he would probably frighten off the ablest Conservative candidate, Chris Patten, the former Cabinet minister and last British governor of Hong Kong. If Patten was interested in resuming a political career and aiming for leadership of his party after William Hague failed at the next general election, he would not want to risk the stain of being beaten by Livingstone in London.

For Blair at the height of his powers, the prospect of allowing the unreliable Livingstone to achieve the limelight of office as mayor was unthinkable. London might need a voice, but the idea of handing the megaphone to an oppositionalist who might damage New Labour's prospects of winning a powerful second term seemed wholly absurd. He would have to be stopped, but the *Evening Standard*'s April 1998 poll showed the danger of stopping him. An overwhelming majority of Labour supporters in London thought that would be wrong and there was a danger that some might hold that view strongly enough to deprive the party of their votes in the mayoral election. The stakes were rising.

Livingstone agreed with much of this analysis, although not the part that pigeonholed him as an inveterate oppositionalist. Through 1997, he regarded the mayoral polls as an amusing boost to his personal standing, something to be encouraged, but not to be taken seriously as a reason for committing himself to run. As late as February 1998 he was telling journalists that he ruled himself out because he wanted to 'stay in national politics'. But the briefing against him by the party's spin-doctors whetted his appetite for a fight. He began to think that the issues of party democracy raised by the mayoral policy were at least as important for the immediate future of the Labour left as his efforts at economic analysis. By the time the government's White Paper on 'modernising the governance of London' was published in March

1998, his political adrenalin was flowing. As he put it during interviews for this book: 'You suddenly find yourself thinking: what would I do to tackle racism in the Metropolitan Police and how could I push through a high-speed bus lane strategy? Suddenly you know you are hooked.'

The White Paper, *A Mayor and Assembly for London*, was launched by John Prescott on March 25th 1998. It promised 'a powerful directly-elected mayor' with 'exceptional influence going well beyond the specific statutory and financial powers of the office'. The boroughs would continue to deliver the same full range of local services, but the mayor would have 'sweeping new powers' over transport and economic development, and 'hands-on responsibility' for strategic planning and the environment. He or she would make appointments to new devolved authorities with policy control over the Metropolitan Police and fire service. The mayor would play a leading part in developing the capital's tourism, culture and sport, and would have a general duty to promote the health of Londoners (although the NHS would remain under central-government control). With these devolved powers would come a £3.3 billion annual budget, funded largely by the Treasury.

The document emphasised the strength of the mayor's mandate from up to 5 million electors: the individual who won the post would have got more personal votes than anyone else in British politics. It would be a full-time job with a substantial salary, mooted at £90,000 a year. 'We expect the Mayor to become a high profile figure who will speak out on London's behalf and be listened to... This will change the face of London politics,' the White Paper said. Livingstone immediately responded by thanking Prescott for 'placing before Londoners this exciting and radical new job opportunity'.

Party spokesmen say they were restrained in briefing against Livingstone until they were stung into action by his effrontery that day, when he stole the publicity from the government on the presentation of a key plank in the Labour manifesto. Jim

Fitzpatrick, chairman of the London party, says it was 'breathtaking' that Livingstone should have the gall to lay claim to a job that he had been consistently arguing against. 'He attacks the proposal and then says he'll do it. And everyone is supposed to say: we forgot about you Ken, but of course you can. He wants the very people he has been challenging to trust him with a budget of more than £3 billion and 20,000 staff. It doesn't make sense. That's why he'll have difficulty persuading a selection panel that he should go before London party members as a candidate.'

The government inserted a number of checks and balances to stop any holder of the office getting seriously out of control. To maintain accountability, the mayor's exercise of power would be scrutinised by an assembly of 25 members, elected to serve over the same four-year term. To reduce scope for the mayor to use pork-barrel techniques to buy off members by favouring their particular areas, 11 would be elected on a London-wide mandate and 14 for large newly formed constituencies straddling borough boundaries. The assembly would call the mayor to account at a monthly public question time and in an annual state of London debate. 'The mayor must be given the means to deliver on his or her promises without frivolous or destructive intervention. But the assembly must be able to scrutinise the mayor's activities and at the last resort must be able to change the mayor's budget.' It could do that if two-thirds voted against.

Given the arrangements proposed for the mayoral and assembly elections, it seemed unlikely that any halfway competent mayor would have any problem getting business through the assembly. The mayor was to be elected by an unusual form of proportional representation designed to stop minor party candidates winning the job on the second-preference votes of their larger rivals. Like tying your shoelaces, the supplementary vote system will be easier to follow in practice than describe in theory. The likely upshot – in all but exceptional landslide years – was that the winner would be a Labour or Conservative candidate who could attract the second preferences of centre-party supporters and independent voters. It would be extraordinary if either Labour or the Conservatives failed to win at least a third of the assembly seats in an election on the same day as the mayoral contest. So the mayor would have to lose the support of fellow party members on the assembly to encounter the two-thirds blocking majority needed to stop the budget. (The assembly elections were to be fought under a different method of proportional representation, the additional member system involving a mixture of first-past-the-post and topping up with candidates on party lists. All this might leave the voters baffled, but there should be little to trouble the mayor.)

More serious constraints on the power of the office stemmed from the government's reluctance to release its detailed grip on public spending. Although the mayor was being 'given' a £3.3 billion annual budget, ministers would set a floor for each of its main headings and a ceiling for total current expenditure. So the mayor would have limited room for manoeuvre and no power to raise a separate tax on Londoners (although parking levies and anti-congestion charges on motorists might provide some financial leeway). Ministers would also keep a tight control on capital spending and borrowing. The arrangements would 'seek to minimise the scope for conflict with central government'. That would mean no repeat of that episode of defiance mentioned in Chapter 2 when Peter Mandelson's grandfather, Herbert Morrison, ignored a Whitehall veto on building Waterloo bridge and charged the cost to the ratepayers.

There were also to be limits on the mayor's capacity to hire and fire. The White Paper estimated that the mayor and assembly would need a combined staff of 250 and an annual budget of about £20 million to cover their central services, less than 1 per cent of the total budget. The government would keep a reserve power to stop this amount expanding. Within the headquarters total, the mayor would be expected to run a personal office of about a dozen people, including a chief of staff, senior policy experts and a couple of political advisers. The tightness of that arrangement implied that most of the work to prepare and implement London-wide strategies would be done by the operating organisations: Transport for London, the London Development Agency, Metropolitan Police and the fire service. Although the mayor would have powers of appointment to the authorities running these services, the White Paper suggested board members should be non-political, with security of tenure even after a new mayor was elected.

These financial and managerial controls were designed to stop the mayor and assembly slipping back into the bad old bureaucratic ways of the GLC. But the unintended side effect was to eliminate the objections that some people might have had to Livingstone getting the job. In a final ironic twist the government decided that the London-wide body would not be given responsibility for handing out grants to London-wide voluntary bodies. That would remain under the control of a committee of borough nominees.

As Livingstone sees it: 'If London was being given the powers available to the *Länder* [the regional authorities in Germany], the two main attacks against me by the Tories would be that I'd increase the taxes and give all the money to lesbians. But the government is saying I can't tax and I can't fund local organisations. In the two areas of weakness that I'd have had to contend with in a rough old campaign, I've been saved by Tony Blair.'

His analysis of the White Paper, in a series of interviews for this book, is that the government is giving too much power to the mayor and too little to the London authority. He sees this reform of London government as a tentative first step towards a European model of regional democracy in which real power is devolved from Whitehall.

> Eventually it will grow into something akin to the *Länder*
> system in Germany, but they are nervous. The British state is
> so centralised and the Labour Party has always been a

centralising party, based on the idea that we could elect a government that would impose change from above and make a better life for all. It was only when Mrs Thatcher's abuse of central power became so stark that people started talking about the need for devolution. That influenced the municipal radicalism of the early 1980s and mobilised the middle-class concerns of *Guardian* readers and Charter 88. Back in 1974, nobody was talking about the British constitution. Nobody cared a toss. Now there is a view that we need to have a whole series of checks and balances so that we could never have a Thatcher experience again. That was the core of all this, plus looking at Europe and thinking things work better there with decentralisation.

The Labour Party is halfway caught up with that, but not wholly persuaded. Blair hasn't got any local-government experience himself and is disparaging about it. He's worried that devolution could go horribly wrong if power goes to local authorities because he thinks that might mean people like Bernie Grant [left-wing Labour MP and former leader of Haringey] running the show. So he took up this idea of having a mayor like they do in the United States – somebody with a close relationship with big businesses in the area, somebody who was not bound by a party caucus system. He thought the job would attract the best and brightest from the world of business – people who would give up great corporate jobs to work for the community. Of course the problem is that people who run a big business have real power and they are not going to come in here and flog their way through all the procedures of consultation and listening to Londoners.

So the White Paper was a mishmash of conflicting ideas. They wanted a devolved, decentralised Britain run by people who wouldn't give them problems – a contradiction in terms. And it was a move towards a more American-style of politics that is about individuals rather than parties with ideologies and history. Around Blair there are so many of these ghastly young lobbyists and researchers who deeply regret they weren't born in America and working in the White House. They think Britain is second-rate and want to be somewhere between Hollywood and Washington with loads of glamour, loads of publicity, loads of sex and no serious politics. I find that concept repellent.

My proposal would have been that the leader of the largest party in the assembly becomes the mayor. That was Chirac's position in Paris: he was never directly elected. My worry is that it's going to be too easy under the government's scheme for any half-way cynical, manipulative mayor to keep the assembly sweet.

The mayor could be sure of getting the annual budget through unless it was blocked by a two-thirds majority agreeing an alternative.

That means that you carry your budget as long as you keep just nine of the 25 assembly members in your pocket. And that's just ridiculous. You may read the proposals and see the checks and balances and constraints, but you're not a politician. I looked at it and thought – that's how you could buy off this person and that person.

The mayor appoints all the posts on committees. Imagine that you have just got elected as a member of the assembly. You've got this bloody big constituency that covers two or three boroughs and you have to deliver things for them. You'll want the mayor to come and do events in your area and you'll want to be on a particular committee. That's all in the mayor's gift. How many of these assembly members are going to say: up yours, mayor? The only sort of person likely to do that would be somebody like me. As we know that isn't a normal character trait.

The mayor has such preponderant powers. For example,

there will have to be an outside assessor to advise on appointments, but it's left to the mayor to decide whether to take that advice. I'm saying there are real problems here, but I am the person you can trust because I'm not going to steal from the voters. I didn't when I was at the GLC. If you have too great a concentration of powers, it's best to have someone in that job who is always sceptical and amused rather than avaricious.'

Best also, thinks Livingstone, to have a mayor of sufficient independence of mind to be trusted by Londoners to fight for their interests rather than act as a pro-consul representing the interests of national party bosses.

People want someone who is not a clone. Increasingly the public want somebody who will speak up for them. Perhaps more damaging than any short-term problems with the economy will be the long-term perception that this is a government that just wants to control everything. Working-class people who probably thought I was an evil little shit when I was running the GLC now come up to me in the street and give their support because they see me as my own man. That's what people want. In a world in which the parties are virtually identical and the policies don't change very much after the biggest election landslide in this century, I suppose people start thinking rather more about the individual candidate and their personal style.

Those comments reach to the heart of the problems perceived by Labour's high command about allowing Livingstone to run for the job. In the space of a few paragraphs he has criticised the proposals for reforming London government, raised doubts about the powers of the mayoral office that he seeks, questioned the prime minister's lack of political experience, rubbished his party's senior advisers and proclaimed that his own popular support is based on his unwillingness to remain obedient. His unreliability would have been even starker if he had been talking about the Chancellor's 'disastrous' economic policy, a theme on which he persistently expounds at length to anyone who will listen.

In spite of all that, he maintains that Blair would have nothing to fear and a lot to gain from having Livingstone as mayor.

> You seem not to have noticed that I don't score points against Blair. I know that if Blair fails, we won't get another Labour government in my lifetime. We have to make sure that Tony succeeds. My view is that he is going to change. Look at any prime minister after their first year in office and then look at them again five or six years later. They've all changed their policies and their style. During Harold Wilson's first government, he was totally interfering at every stage and at every level. He didn't trust and he didn't delegate. By his second term, he'd stepped back. The same will happen with Blair. Right now he's running something for the first time in his life with no preparatory experience. Barristers don't run anything. He didn't even run anything in his student union days. He wasn't involved in all the knockabout politics, as a lot of others were. So the first time he was running something, he was running the country. He's bound at this stage to want to keep a very tight control. As events keep whacking away and things go wrong and international problems arise, he'll loosen his grip on a lot of the detail to concentrate on the things that are essential to his survival. That means Europe and Emu. It means macro-economic policy and his relationship with America. You come back in four years' time and Blair will not be worried about what is happening in Newcastle or with the mayor of London.

But, even on this analysis, surely Blair could not be indifferent to the dangers of having a high-profile mayor who was contemptuous of the government's economic policy. 'That's Gordon Brown's policy, not Blair's. You may well find if things go badly wrong that there won't be a Chancellor Brown. No other prime minister has devolved economic policy to the chancellor to this degree. You can already see the tensions. People in Blair's circle complain that the information coming to them from the Treasury is not as full as it should be. A slant is put on it. This is not going to last.'

Some may find this line of argument somewhat slippery. With or without Brown as chancellor, Blair seems hardly likely to adopt the economic policies advocated by Livingstone's *Socialist Economic Bulletin*. But Livingstone has a more reassuring explanation of the reasons why his conduct as mayor would not be a threat to the Prime Minister. He says he knows that quite simply he would fail in the mayoral job if he tried to use it as a platform for attacking a Labour government. A balance would have to be struck between standing up to ministers on issues of direct importance to London and working with them – and with the borough leaders and other interest groups – to achieve agreement for getting things done.

> People want someone who will speak up for London, who will not be a rubber-stamp for central government. You can't create this post and assume some party hack can be shoe-horned in, who will spend four years telling Londoners why it's very difficult for the government to do anything more for them. That just can't work.
>
> The question is how the criticism is made. Would it be part of a constructive debate? Or would it be the sort of broadside attack that we launched on all sections of the Conservative government's policy in the GLC era? The answer is that the way you approach your own government would be totally different to the way you approach the opposition.
>
> I know that some Labour people are saying they would be

more comfortable with Chris Patten as mayor than Livingstone. They wouldn't actually. Patten still wishes to lead the Tory party and, if he was elected mayor, he would be needing to demonstrate to his supporters that he was going to harry the government and grind them into the dirt right up to election day. That's inevitable if your opponents run the system. But if you did that to your own government, your own party would get rid of you. It wouldn't need Blair to do it. Your own party would say: we didn't put you in there to have a civil war against the government. We put you in there to try and make it work.

Inevitably there would be arguments and the most important of these over the next few years would be over London's share of resources. There was a wide cross-party consensus in the capital that it was not receiving back enough of the money it raised in taxes to meet its public spending needs. But there were powerful forces within the Cabinet arguing for a redistribution of resources the other way. John Prescott and David Blunkett were pushing hard for a better deal for what they regarded as Labour heartlands of the north that had been starved of cash during 18 years of Tory rule. A successful mayor would have to mobilise a London alliance around a consensus package about what the city ought to get back from central government.

That did not imply a confrontation with Blair. Labour held 58 seats in London and half were marginal. Blair would be sympathetic to London's claim on resources and would want the mayor to deliver positive achievements before the next general election. So there was scope for a normal process of political negotiation. There could not and would not be a repeat of the abnormal confrontation of the GLC period when the Thatcher government made compromise impossible by threatening to withdraw all the council's grants if it carried out the policies on which it was elected.

This does not amount to a pledge by Livingstone of political obedience. Even if there could have been a deal between him and Blair, he would not have been able to change his character. It is scarcely credible that he could have got through four years as mayor without coming out with plenty of juicy quotes which the Conservatives could use to make mischief. But Livingstone maintains that his conduct would have been within the boundaries of what Blair could handle.

> This is not Kinnock. Blair has this incredible public-school confidence which they all get by the age of eight. I remember going to Harrow School. After I'd done my speech there were all these 15–16 year olds having dinner with me, sitting round saying what they'd do if they were chancellor of the exchequer – how they'd change this or that tax law. Totally self-confident. That's what Blair's got. You can see it in meetings of the Parliamentary Labour Party when they all turn against him, which happens more frequently that it did with other leaders early in their term. The left doesn't attack him because that wins him support. But some of the others often make strong personal criticisms. It happened over the Oratory [the London grant-maintained school where the Blairs send their sons], over Harriet Harman [defended by Blair after she decided to send a son to a selective grammar school] and on trades union issues.
>
> Kinnock used to go purple in the face, bellow, rant and question the maturity and sometimes even the manhood of his critics. He didn't have Blair's confidence. He felt any criticism about policy was a personal attack and so there was a terrible atmosphere at the top of the party. But Blair gets up and says something self-deprecatory with a little bit of humour, hoping we won't be offended by whatever it is he's done. And everyone moves on. He doesn't go home at night and fester and hate you.

The message being relayed to the prime minister was that the political pain of having Livingstone as mayor would be a lot less than the pain that would result from using the power of the party machine to stop him running. Blair might not like having a left-winger in that position, but the deal Livingstone was offering was a lot more palatable than a mutiny in the London party and loss of the mayoral election.

'The polls show a huge bedrock of support out there. If they are seen to fiddle the system to block me, I think the Tories would run with that as an issue and we'd lose. Whoever was the Labour candidate would get a poisoned chalice. The polls show that 78 per cent of Londoners think it would be wrong to stop me. It's amazing the issue has that level of public recognition.'

Livingstone's view is that Labour cannot rely on winning London. It has been a swing city over the years, often moving ahead of the national trend. For example, in February 1974 and May 1997 it had a bigger than average swing to Labour and in May 1979 a bigger swing to the Tories. In the local elections in 1998 Labour got 45 per cent, Tories 38. To win the mayoral race, the Labour candidate will need to pull over the first- or second-preference votes of Liberal Democrats.

> I don't think there's someone they haven't found yet who's going to score better than me in the polls. They've run every conceivable name and most of them didn't get into double figures... Blair has to think of the consequences of ignoring that scale of public opinion. Suppose he ignores it and we lose. The defeat will be hung round his neck for years. He'd then have an antagonistic mayor who'd use the position to attack the government. That would sink the whole regional government project. It would be a searing experience for Labour if it set up regional bodies in London and Scotland and then lost the elections.
>
> If they'd seen where all this was leading, they'd never have started down this road. If they'd had an assembly but no mayor, they could easily have controlled who got elected.

They could have seriously vetted the panel of candidates and whoever Blair wanted would have been elected as their leader. That was the system I was advocating. It would have given him exactly what he wanted. Isn't life full of wonderful ironies?

I could never have got to be leader of a London assembly. I couldn't even have got on to it as a member. They could still have gone around saying Ken Livingstone wasn't that popular after all. But they went for a high-profile directly elected mayor and so the *Evening Standard* commissioned the polls that have demonstrated how much support I have.

But that does not mean the people are voting for Livingstone's version of socialism in preference to Blair's. The prime minister enjoys excellent poll ratings stretching well beyond Livingstone's local fiefdom. 'People want him to work. They don't want to slip back to the Tories. The average person in Britain is unhappy that there hasn't been more change. They are prepared to pay more tax for a little bit more public spending. So Blair's doing about half what they want and they'd like him to do more. But they want him to win. They want him to grow in office.'

In August 1998 Livingstone wrote to Blair to present his case for a political deal. The accepted wisdom among the chattering classes was that Blair would not touch Livingstone with a barge-pole. It was common knowledge that the London Labour party board was preparing the procedures that could be used to stop Livingstone getting on to the short-list if Blair said that was what he wanted to be done. So was Livingstone's talk of an accommodation merely a tactic to feign reasonableness so that he could condemn Blair even more forcefully when his mayoral bid was blocked?

There was one strong piece of evidence that Livingstone genuinely believed a deal was on the cards. If he has had a meeting with the prime minister, he would not say a word about what transpired. It seemed that he still had enough faith in the possibility of a deal to want to avoid careless talk that might ruin it. The issue of who would be Labour's candidate for the mayoral race was turning into a cliffhanger.

11 Conclusion

As the crowds streamed in for the first 'Let Ken Stand' rally at Westminster Central Hall on February 15th 1999, an old man in a red anorak introduced himself to the waiting journalists. John Ryan, aged 71, had been Livingstone's English teacher at Tulse Hill comprehensive. He fondly recalled his former pupil's performance when the class stood on their desks to declaim passages from Shakespeare's *Henry V*. But Ryan was not attending the rally merely out of sentiment. When he came to the microphone towards the end of the meeting, he had a message for the Brent East MP's supporters. 'I worry when I hear the name Tony Blair mentioned here this evening. Please don't set Ken against the government. We want Ken as mayor, but not a mayor having a war with our own government,' he said.

The warning was appropriate and the retired teacher spoke for thousands of Labour loyalists who want the party to be a broad church able to accommodate the very different talents and appeal of a Blair and a Livingstone. But his plea was not as well received as the comments of Livingstone supporters who viewed his mayoral bid as an opportunity to strike back at what they saw as the Blairites' abandonment of socialist values. The bigger cheers went to another member of the audience, the comedian and columnist Mark Steel, when he urged people to vote for Livingstone 'because we want to blow a great big hole in their rancid, weasely New Labour project.'

The question overhanging the final chapter of this book is whether the teacher was justified in believing that a Mayor Livingstone could work with a Blair government. Or is that wishful thinking? Will this story have a much uglier ending, with

Livingstone rebelling against a decision to block his candidacy by standing as an independent against the official Labour party candidate?

As the rally got under way in the hall where Blair first announced the mayoral plan less than three years before, Livingstone positioned himself as his old teacher recommended. His speech did not attack Blair, although as usual it was peppered with non-Blairite language and ideas. This was vintage Livingstone, keeping faith with the left, but reaching out to the politically uncommitted with a mixture of fun and an appeal to people's sense of fair play. It is worth pausing to observe his style to try to understand how it works.

Livingstone's speech began with a strong statement of support for workers in the RMT union who called a two-day strike against threatened changes to their terms of employment when management of the London Underground is handed over to a public-private partnership. The strike coincided with the rally and was expected to reduce attendance. As it turned out, so many people turned up that the meeting had to be switched at the last minute from a smaller hall to the main auditorium. About 1,500 people attended and they contributed £3,300 when a collection was taken for the 'Ken Livingstone's Right to Stand' fund.

'People are striking because they fear that the changes to the Underground will put their jobs, wages and conditions at risk. I don't want to see services in London paid for on the cheap by cutting the wages and conditions of the people who run the service,' he said. This was not a sanitised Livingstone abandoning his political allies to make a populist appeal to the commuters on whose votes he would eventually depend if he wanted to win the election to be mayor. At this stage of the campaign, he needed those allies more than ever to build up an organisation for the selection battle ahead. On the platform beside him were celebrities to appeal to a wider audience – the comedian Jo Brand who chaired the meeting, and the novelist Beryl Bainbridge who said she was backing Livingstone because he was one of the few politicians who answered questions, told the truth, didn't fudge and didn't talk in clichés. But beside them also were Peter Tatchell, the gay rights campaigner, Lee Jasper, chair of the National Black Alliance, Barry Camfield, regional secretary of the Transport and General Workers Union, and Diane Abbott, left-wing Labour MP for Hackney North. In reaching out for support from the middle ground, Livingstone still relied on the organisational strength of the left and was willing to let that show.

The rally was as good an example as any of how he pulls off the trick of staying loyal to his roots while appealing to people from across the political spectrum who would never dream of aligning themselves with the activists on his platform. Livingstone's recipe is a mixture of nostalgia, anti-establishment knockabout, a relatively short list of popular policies and a gift for language that sugars his ideological commitment with a great sense of fun.

The nostalgia came in Livingstone's statement of pride in his record at the GLC. He called it, with typical self-mockery, 'that brief shining apex of civilisation' and went on to list policies that were attacked at the time as examples of crazy left-wing excess, but are now part of New Labour orthodoxy. 'I'm proud of what we did ... cutting the fares to get people back on public transport, intervening to try to create jobs to put people back to work, saying that the police should be democratically accountable to Londoners, saying you weren't going to end the war in Ireland without talking, that if you wanted to stop the killing in Ireland you had to sit down and talk to the people doing the killing to bring about agreement ... I can't see why people don't want me to stand for mayor when it seems to me that the Labour government has taken all these policies forward. They have almost become mainstream.'

There were echoes of his campaign to save the GLC in his attack on Labour spin-doctors for briefing against his mayoral bid. He fought against the Thatcher government because it was denying Londoners the right to vote about the future of their council. Now the Labour Party was preparing to deny its London members the right to vote on whether he should be their mayoral candidate. On both occasions, Livingstone's grievance about infringements to the democratic process became a stronger weapon than the policies for which he stood. He accused party spokesmen of 'months and months of off-the-record statements and unattributable briefings ... and not a single sentence has been about the policies I'm advocating. It's all personal abuse.' The growth of spin doctoring 'has degraded the whole currency of politics in Britain and America.'

But what were the policies on which he would want the mayoral election to be fought? Cutting fares again is not a solution to the current problems of London Transport. You cannot squeeze more people on to the Tube until there is investment to increase its capacity. But quick action is needed to make the service more passenger-friendly. That requires bringing back conductors on the buses and guards on the Underground. To get the buses moving there should be a bus lane on every main road inside the Circle Line. There is no excuse for a filthy public transport system. Mayor Livingstone would order the buses to be properly cleaned 'so you don't have to go to the dry cleaners after every time you travel'. Mayor Livingstone would make sure this happened because he would forswear the use of chauffeur-driven cars and use public transport. When the time came to renew the contracts of London Transport managers, they would lose their chauffeurs too and begin to learn a bit more about the service they ran by using it as passengers.

This was hardly a costed strategy for public transport, but for a politician running for office it made the beginnings of a potent populist agenda. As did his concern about the pollution that was causing half the children living on major roads to develop asthma; and about traffic management policies that contributed a mounting death toll among cyclists and pedestrians. A 20mph speed limit on residential roads was his suggested solution.

Other commitments included changing police regulations in the light of the Stephen Lawrence inquiry to make it a dismissable offence for a police officer to refuse to co-operate with an investigation into a fellow officer. And at the heart of Livingstone's programme would be the question of London's money. The city is one of the wealthiest in Europe, but it contains some of the worst poverty in Britain. In some areas unemployment is more than 40 per cent. Yet from every £100 raised in taxation from Londoners, only £75 comes back to London in spending by central government. The other £25 is syphoned off to help other areas of the country. 'I will sit down with the Social Exclusion Unit to mobilise resources to tackle this poverty. You can't create a London worth living in, if a quarter of the people are living in poverty and denied the life chances they have every right to expect,' he said.

There was nothing especially novel or left wing about this policy mix – nor about the fuller version of his putative manifesto which is reproduced in the Appendix. Prospective candidates from any of the main parties could have come up with something similar. Livingstone's particular gift was the language in which he wrapped his ideas. We knew he wasn't serious when he suggested psychometric testing to pick the most vicious and unpleasant people for 'a Taliban class of traffic wardens' to enforce the bus lane policy. 'They will operate Sharia law. Drive in a bus lane and you lose your arm,' he said. Everyone laughed, but people left the meeting remembering the bus lane policy better than they would have done if it had been presented with a battery of statistics.

These are the skills that boosted his popularity in the opinion polls and made him favourite to win a selection contest to become Labour's mayoral candidate if he was allowed on to the ballot paper. But would he get that chance? The procedures for stopping him, described in the Introduction, were not yet finally bolted into place by the time of the rally. In November 1998, the London regional party board had agreed to 're-forward' the motion from the regional conference in June that would have provided an automatic place on the shortlist for any candidate gaining the nominations of ten constituency parties. However, alongside that, the board suggested an alternative procedure. Potential candidates would be entitled to nominate themselves for mayor or membership of the Greater London Assembly. Their merits would be considered by a selection panel, including representatives from the regional party and the national executive. The panel would draw up a long list of contenders and then narrow it down to a shortlist. To reach that decision it would be entitled to summon the aspiring candidates for an interview that could include hostile questioning of the sort they might encounter during a mayoral campaign – testing their suitability for office and record of party loyalty. The final selection would be made by the London party as a whole in a one-member-one-vote ballot, but party members would get to choose only from the list of names approved by the panel. The regional board also recommended that 'additional relevant training' should be offered where possible to the candidates. It called for an appeals panel to handle disputes and a code of conduct for candidates together with a financial limit on what they could spend in pursuit of the nomination.

In January 1999 the national executive accepted this approach for picking candidates for the assembly, but postponed a decision on the mayoral selection procedure. There was continuing argument about the best way of stopping Livingstone among ministers and London MPs who wanted to avoid having him as mayor. Was it coincidence that two ministers who came out publicly with conflicting points of view were Paul Boateng and Tony Banks? As GLC councillors in 1985 they both voted for continued defiance of the law when Livingstone was forced to back a legal budget to keep his administration from collapse. Now Boateng was writing in the *Evening Standard*: 'Good old Ken, some say. I am not one of them. Opposition would be total and waged as much in the press and media as in the party.' And Banks was telling viewers of BBC 1's *Question Time* that Livingstone was a good friend who ought to be on the shortlist because the 69,000 members of the Labour Party in London had the right to vote on the matter and 'because I want, maybe, to have the opportunity of trying to beat him.'

A third rate-capping rebel was also playing a part in the drama. John McDonnell, the GLC chairman of finance who denounced Livingstone for 'bottling out' by voting to fix a rate, was now Labour MP for Hayes and Harlington and working behind the scenes as one of the main organisers of Livingstone's mayoral bid. He took responsibility for setting up a network in the constituencies. Neil Pearson, the actor best known for his performance in *Drop the Dead Donkey*, led a drive to attract funds and other support from celebrities who were immediately dubbed by the press as Luvvies for Livingstone. Harry Barlow, a former GLC press officer who runs an advertising agency, handled the promotional material. Livingstone says that he also got help from Mark Seddon, editor of *Tribune* and individuals from various left-wing groups, but none of these were formally represented in his campaign team.

Officials of the London regional party frowned on Livingstone's decision to set up an organisation and run public meetings. They thought his sources of funding were questionable and they said he was breaking the spirit of rules intended to limit the amount aspiring candidates could spend on seeking the nomination. In fact these rules had not been agreed by the time of his Central Hall rally and would not come into force until the NEC made a formal decision on the whole mayoral selection procedure. Livingstone said there was nothing sinister about his funding because the cost of hiring the hall and advertising the meeting in the *Evening Standard* was covered several times over by donations from supporters. These arrived mostly in small amounts from individuals responding to the advertisement and articles about the rally, but larger sums were also raised 'in the theatre community'. By the end of February 1999, total receipts topped £25,000. Another rally was planned at the Hackney Empire theatre in March, featuring the singer Billy Bragg and a cast of celebrities.

Whoever takes the eventual decision about whether Livingstone should be allowed to run, there is plenty of evidence in this book to help them make up their minds. But a few pointers may be helpful. At least eight allegations against Livingstone have been made by various critics over recent months to suggest that he is unfit to be the Labour candidate. First, that his record as leader of the GLC from 1981 to 1986 showed that he would do the job badly, preferring oppositionalism to sound administration. Second, that his vicious attacks on Neil Kinnock – particularly during Livingstone's first period on the party's NEC from 1987 to 1989 – were an unforgivable breach of party discipline, making him unsuitable for high office. Third, that his intermittent friendships with Trotskyite groups inside and outside the Labour Party were inappropriate for a democratic socialist. Fourth, that the security services had something unpleasant about him on their files. Fifth, that his failure to respond to olive branches offered by Blair before and after the 1997 election soured their personal relationship, making it impossible for them to do business together as mayor and prime minister. Sixth, that Livingstone's criticism of some of the policies and leading personalities of the Blair government went beyond the boundaries of legitimate internal party debate. Seventh, that he was not a credible candidate because he said on October 23rd 1997 that the proposal to have a directly elected mayor of London was 'barmy'. And finally, that if he did get elected as Labour mayor, he would use the megaphone of office to attack the New Labour project instead of working with Blair to secure the best possible deal for Londoners.

The evidence from Downing Street suggests that the prime minister is not troubled by the first five of these allegations. The source quoted in the introduction to this book indicated that Blair would have offered Livingstone a ministerial job if he had behaved more loyally after the 1997 general election. This implies that he does not regard anything that Livingstone did or said before 1997 as unforgivable. There are others in the party who are less tolerant, especially those who worked closely with Kinnock in the 1980s. But Blair takes a mature view of what he would regard as past indiscretions. If previous association with Trotskyites was a bar to senior positions in the Labour Party, he would never have appointed some of his Cabinet colleagues to their present positions.

The *Sunday Times* reported on November 15th 1998 that the central secretariat of MI5 passed a summary of a file on Livingstone to Downing Street immediately after the 1997 general election, raising questions about his contacts with Sinn Fein, some as recently as 1996. Livingstone's reaction was that he would be amazed if he were not on any MI5 list of subversives, given his history of criticising the organisation. But the view in Downing Street, which plays host to Sinn Fein representatives itself these days, is that the security issue was not a factor in consideration of Livingstone's bid to be mayor and was never even discussed. 'We are talking about a fairly defined job. The mayor is hardly being put in charge of MI5', the source said.

It is not entirely clear how big was the olive branch offered by Blair to Livingstone in 1997, since neither side will talk about their private discussions and Livingstone does not even admit they took place. But Downing Street provides no support for the theory that they could not do business in future because Blair feels spurned by Livingstone's rejection of his overtures. The source quoted in the Introduction saying 'Tony likes him' and 'was not slighted' seems to dispose of that as an argument.

Even if the prime minister is prepared to forget the past, an assessment of Livingstone's record at the GLC is still relevant to the question of whether he would make a good mayor. So, before dealing with the last three allegations against him, it is important to draw some conclusions about his performance as council leader. Some of his attributes are obvious from the account of that period in this book. They include an exceptional ability to articulate a political vision and resilience under fire. At the defining moment of his administration during the rate-capping crisis of 1985, he showed he was more interested in exercising power than maintaining his left-wing credentials. He was also a smart and energetic administrator. Since that may not have come across in the account of the hurly-burly of those GLC years, it is worth quoting the views of the two officials who worked most closely with him at the time. Bill Bush, his chief of staff at the GLC and now head of the BBC's policy research unit, says: 'He was an astonishingly good bureaucrat. He read papers fast and got the point. On the big issues I don't remember him ever being bounced by officials into an ill-considered decision. He got through a lot because he was good at delegating. He built up trust with the people working closely with him and made them want to do things for him. That made him phenomenally productive. If we made a mistake, he would say so privately, but take responsibility in public. So we'd die in the last ditch for him and work ludicrous hours and take shocking risks, because the deal was that he'd back us up ... He was mayoral in the way he worked at the GLC. One of the flaws in the mayoral proposal now is that the job requires a larger than life personality with good media skills. They seem to have played to his strengths.'

Maurice Stonefrost, the council's director-general, agrees about Livingstone's astuteness, but has reservations over his management style. 'There is no doubt whatsoever about the quickness with which he would absorb an issue and understand all the angles. He made a great virtue of delegating to his colleagues, letting them run their own parts of the operation and intervening only on occasions when politics forced him to come in, or when he chose to do so. In my view that was not good delegation in the corporate sense. I don't get the impression that he knew or wanted to know what was going on in anything other than the main issue in each of the areas. So he wasn't putting himself in a position to see that the organisation was going well.' In Stonefrost's view it will be extraordinarily difficult for any mayor to grasp the complexity of the different services for which the office will be accountable. He thinks Livingstone as mayor would be better at articulating what Londoners want than perceiving what the capital needs to compete in the international big city league.

Striking the right balance between pleasing the people and providing the conditions for business prosperity will be the mayor's most difficult political judgment. Livingstone is not the most obvious candidate for the job of persuading a merchant bank to locate its headquarters in London instead of Frankfurt or New York. But it would be wrong to conclude that he is anti-business and his after-dinner speeches at City banquets are received surprisingly well. Even the capitalists seem to like his jokes and see the sense in a public transport system that gets their staff to work on time. Surprisingly, he emerged at the top of a MORI opinion poll of 250 company directors in London commissioned by the chartered surveyors Farebrother in January 1999. Among those expressing a preference for a mayoral candidate, he got 19 per cent support, compared with 5 per cent for the next highest placed potential candidates, Lord Archer, Chris Patten and Richard Branson.

The government has helped Livingstone's claim to the job by legislating to stop the mayor following some of the policies adopted by the GLC. As he put it in Chapter 11, he would not have the power to 'increase the taxes and give all the money to lesbians', although the proposed congestion tax does give him some financial leeway. Rules limiting the mayor's office to a small team of strategic advisers would also suit his style of operation. Administration would be delegated to the controllers of service organisations such as London Transport and the Metropolitan Police. The mayor would provide London with a vision and a voice, but would not be immersed in day-to-day management of thousands of staff.

Livingstone's record as leader of the GLC does not amount to a proof that he would be the best candidate for mayor, but it certainly does not invalidate his claim to be on a Labour shortlist. If he gets there, party members may conclude that his experience of running London is an asset in comparison with some of his possible rivals who do not have a track record of political administration. It is hard to judge the GLC's overall success under his leadership because it was diverted from policy issues in mid-term to fight against abolition. But its fire brigade still put out the fires, the public transport system worked and the Thames did not flood.

So what about the other three allegations against Livingstone that came closer to the real reasons why Blair was considering blocking his candidacy? Livingstone could claim that the mayoral plan developed into something less 'barmy' than many Labour MPs thought it was in October 1997. But the remark would haunt Labour if he were to become the party's candidate. Party officials imagined London covered in Tory posters asking the voters if they really wanted a mayor who thought the job was barmy. Blair also had to consider how his long-term political strategy could be damaged if Livingstone survived this electoral test and became London's mayor. Some of Livingstone's riper criticism of New Labour ideas and personalities since the 1997 election provided a warning of what might be in store. Even if Mayor Livingstone honoured his commitment to work with the Government on London issues, he could at any moment use the megaphone of office to comment on party business, challenging every step along Blair's path towards political realignment. And he would be living, troublesome proof that non-Blairite candidates could win high-profile elections.

These are real worries for the prime minister and he cannot be blamed for wanting the party to have a more amenable candidate without so many downside risks. But was the political pain of having Livingstone as mayor worse than the pain of blocking him and being portrayed as an anti-democratic control freak? This was meant to be an experiment in devolution and the mayor was meant to be able to stand up for Londoners in negotiations with the government. Could people believe that devolution was genuine if the most popular Labour candidate were to be vetted out of the race by a small committee of party figures, most of whom could be expected to follow any guidance emanating from Downing Street?

The downside risks of having Livingstone as the Labour candidate were not about confidential matters that could not be aired in public. Quite the opposite. They concerned his all too public unwillingness to sing the leader's tune. Party members in London were in a better position to decide if that was what they wanted than Blair or his vetting panel.

Paradoxically, the prime minister's most persuasive answer to accusations that he was a control freak would have been to point out that he had allowed the situation to get completely out of control. He failed to quash Livingstone's mayoral bid before it built up steam in 1999. He did not give early backing behind the scenes to an alternative candidate because he did not know who that person should be. As time wore on, the names of increasingly senior Labour politicians were floated in the press. It was suggested that Frank Dobson might have the political weight to see off Livingstone, although he seemed most reluctant to give up his Cabinet position as health secretary. Then came the enticing prospect of Mo Mowlam, the Northern Ireland secretary, entering the ring. Her massive popularity in the party might allow her to overtake the front-runner Livingstone. Yet it was hard to understand why a fast-rising politician from the north-east of England should want to leave Parliament to run a city where she never felt at home. The speculation was endless. But, pending the declaration of a heavyweight Blairite candidate the spin-doctors' briefing against Livingstone was largely counter-productive. Whatever the outcome, there will be a huge post-mortem in the party's high command about who was to blame for allowing the issue to get so out of hand.

Blair could have taken some useful lessons from his friend Bill Clinton who would never have allowed the selection of a troublesome Democrat as a mayoral candidate to become a political worry for the US presidency. Clinton would have shrugged his shoulders and wished good luck to anyone winning a local party nomination. In the US federal system, they understood devolution. By importing the idea of directly elected city mayors without understanding the implications for party management, Blair was bound to get in a muddle. He had similar problems with devolution in Scotland and Wales.

It would be simple enough to end this book with a judgment that Blair should follow the logic of his commitment to devolution and let London party members choose between Livingstone and rival candidates. He would be wrong to do otherwise. But an assessment of Livingstone would be incomplete without an element of speculation about what he will do next.

If he gets on Labour's shortlist and is defeated for the nomination, he will be a spent force. Having made so much of party members' right to choose, he would be obliged to live by their verdict. At the age of 55, there will be little time left for him to bounce back, although given his resilience anything is possible. But if he is blocked from the shortlist, another scenario opens up.

Livingstone is too canny to say at this stage that he might run as an independent against an official Labour candidate. It would be tantamount to courting excommunication from the party and provide Blair with a copper-bottomed excuse for keeping him off the shortlist. But some of Livingstone's political friends are convinced that he has already made the psychological leap towards accepting the possibility of a future outside the Labour Party.

There can be little doubt that his overwhelming desire is to win the Labour nomination and get the job as mayor. That would be a challenging position in its own right, probably his last chance to exercise real power. And it would provide a platform for resisting the next stages of the Blairite project. Although Livingstone is likely to honour his commitment and avoid using the office to attack government policy, he would be a trenchant critic of any attempt to weaken Labour's links with the unions or impose vetting of sitting Labour MPs to weed out the left-wing troublemakers at reselection.

But if he is blocked, what then? In those circumstances another possibility beckons. His friends say he would not stand as an independent against an official Labour candidate unless opinion polls suggested that he had a chance of winning. Splitting the Labour vote and letting the Tory candidate win would not be a satisfactory outcome. Some of his supporters believe that his personal popularity is such that he could win as an independent and that his coat-tails would be long enough to carry with him a number of independent candidates for the assembly. Only the opinion polls will tell whether that is a fantasy or a realistic prospect. He would not need to make a judgment until early in 2000.

This might be considered a strange time to break with the party he had served for more than 30 years. Blair is not likely to make his next realignment moves until after another general election and Livingstone could not expect to take other left-wing MPs and unions with him unless and until Blair did something to trigger a mutiny. So Livingstone would be short of organisational muscle and obliged to run a presidential-style campaign, using the media to project himself without much support from canvassers in the constituencies.

But Livingstone is not short of friends who are egging him on to make the most of the opportunity to delay or derail Blair's realignment project. They think a lot about a comment the prime minister is said to have made in a private chat with a group of Labour MPs about the political situation in Scotland. The problem there was that disaffected Labour people had somewhere else to go because the SNP provided them with an alternative. What would happen in England if there were an electorally credible alternative to Labour on the left? Just suppose that Livingstone could win the mayoralty as an independent. What effect would that have on Blair's image of invincibility? Could he continue to push his party further towards the centre to build relationships with the Liberal Democrats and pro-European Tories if he faced a leeching of support on his left?

Livingstone has a simple answer to this speculation. He says he is fighting to become Labour's mayoral candidate and expects Blair to allow him on to the shortlist. But the secessionist sentiment that is swirling around among his supporters will not please Livingstone's old English teacher and the continuing believers in the broad-church traditions of the party.

That may provide Blair with an opportunity. It might be easier to beat Livingstone in an above-board selection ballot if party members suspected that he was considering a break with the party. Or would Blair's long-term interests be better served by losing the mayoral election to the Conservatives if the by-product were to be a split that would break his party free from its left-wing past? He used to say that his job would not be complete until he persuaded the party to love Peter Mandelson. Perhaps persuading the party not to love Ken Livingstone is now a more realistic way forward.

The outcome will depend on choices that have not yet been made. A choice by Blair about whether to let Livingstone through on to the shortlist. Then perhaps a choice by party members about whether he should be the party candidate. Or a choice by Livingstone about whether to run as an independent. If the drama is to have a happy ending – happy, that is, for Livingstone and Labour – the decision will have to be made openly by party members. But at the time of writing it feels as if the last act may end in tears.

Appendix: Manifesto for a Mayor and Assembly for London by Ken Livingstone*

So far the debate about the new government for London has been totally dominated by the issue of which individual might be elected mayor with virtually no discussion on the powers and policies of the new mayor and assembly. The overwhelming majority of the proposals in the White Paper are a sound basis for the establishment of the new GLA. This response is a contribution to the debate on the government's White Paper in the hope that it may influence the final form of the legislation which will be introduced in this November's Queen's Speech. The comments should be read alongside the White Paper and therefore I have followed the structure of the White Paper in this response. To keep this document to a reasonable size, I have not have of course bothered to reiterate those proposals in the White Paper with which I agree.

It is important to establish from the beginning that the GLA is not the recreation of the GLC with all its inherent contradictions. Harold MacMillan's government established the Herbert Commission to report on the best method of governing London

---

*Ken Livingstone's response to the government's White Paper, published in March 1998, setting out the government's plans on 'modernising the governance of London' and promising London a directly elected mayor.

at the end of the 1950s, but largely ignored its central recommendation that the new London wide body should be genuinely regional with powerful London boroughs providing the day-to-day services such as education and housing. Because the then government did not wish to devolve any of its powers to the new body it ended up creating a big council running a quarter of a million council homes and 1200 schools. Although the new GLC had regional planning responsibilities the last word remained with the government and it was not until 1970 when Harold Wilson's government transferred control of transport to the GLC that the council finally began to be more strategic in approach rather than a service provider.

Rather than fall into the trap of recreating a council mentality with a tendency to interfere in borough decisions the first mayor and assembly must establish a framework of thinking and practices which are genuinely strategic. If it is successful the new authority will be a powerful first example of the government's desire to introduce regional government for the English regions. Some councils may switch to a mayoral system. Whilst this will have the same name, the powers will be completely different to those of the London mayor. Local mayors' powers will be primarily the local services for which councils are already responsible. Powers that the government is transferring to London's new mayor and assembly are quite specifically regional. If the new system fails in London it would be a massive setback for all those who hope to see England moving towards a more devolved system of government in line with modern trends in Europe.

The use of proportional representation to elect the mayor and assembly will undoubtedly reduce the confrontational system of politics that has been the norm in town halls. To be effective however the mayor must not only create a consensus with the 25 members of the assembly but must achieve a wider consensus with the London boroughs and public opinion so that when the mayor speaks for London he/she will speak with an authority that compels government to listen and respond. If such a consensus can be built it is more likely that the new authority will attract the best and brightest to work for and with it.

Transport
(para 5.6–5.51 in the White Paper)

Undoubtedly the biggest immediate problem on the new mayor's desk will be the abysmal state of transport in London. Congestion, pollution, and dreadful levels of poor service pose a threat not just to our health but London's attraction for international commerce. Simply breathing London's air doubles the chance of developing lung cancer and we now face the horrendous reality that half of all children who live on major roads have developed asthma.

The government's White Paper on transport is a good framework within which the mayor will work. London should be the showcase that demonstrates the government's transport policies can be both effective and popular. It is important to remember the lesson of the last Labour GLC that it is easier to make public transport more attractive rather than simply make car usage more difficult. A policy which is perceived to be 'anti-car' would merely mobilise the maximum opposition. A policy that improves public transport and attracts people back onto the system is one that would have a huge consensus behind it.

The London transport fares cut of the early 1980s led to five per cent of car users switching to public transport. The statistician George Stern recently conducted a detailed survey of passenger usage on London Transport between 1959 and 1986. His figures show that between our fares cut and the abolition of the GLC, fares were reduced by 35 per cent. This generated a 70 per cent increase in passenger miles with a resulting increase in fares revenue of 11 per cent. The objective of the mayor must be to shift the balance from car usage to public transport not lead a holy crusade against the car user.

There is no chance that Londoners will tolerate a mayor trying to shift the public back onto public transport if the mayor and assembly members are themselves swished around London in chauffeur-driven cars. The mayor must therefore give a lead by using public transport. The mayor and the assembly members must give a clear undertaking before they seek election that they will not establish a GLA car pool.

Although the new mayor must not be anti-car we must recognised that the balance in our city has shifted strongly against the safety and comfort of the pedestrian or the cyclist making this a very unpleasant city in which to walk or cycle. Over the years the death rate of motorists in accidents has declined whilst that of cyclists and pedestrians has equally dramatically increased. The mayor must therefore have the courage to take the sort of decisions recently shelved by Westminster council to pedestrianise substantial parts of the city centre and introduce a proper network of cycle routes.

The mayor must have powers to override the objections of borough councils in determining what areas of London need to be pedestrianised. Such decisions would need to be in line with the government's strategy but it is clearly unacceptable that an area like Soho has not been pedestrianised and it would undermine the entire transport strategy if councils like Westminster were able to thwart the emerging national consensus on transport.

It currently costs more to travel a mile on the tube than it does a mile in the luxury of Concorde. When the GLC reduced fares in the early 1980s it was against a background of spare capacity on the tube. This is no longer the case. Although fares should over time be reduced in real terms an immediate fares cut now would simply mean the tubes becoming more congested in the suburbs and impossible to board at inner city stations. Whilst there must be an extension of the tube system recent experience with the Jubilee Line extension shows that it would take ten years for such policies to bear fruit and Londoners need immediate improvements.

Part of the problem of congestion on the tube has been that the introduction of driver-only buses has led to increasing delays. Therefore under these conditions more and more people have switched to the tube. Increasingly the bus system is in danger of becoming a second class system for the poorest Londoners.

The mayor must therefore ensure the rapid completion of a London wide system of bus lanes and have the powers to overrule any borough such as Westminster which might wish to stop the bus lanes at its borders. But the bus lanes on their own will not be enough. Unless we can speed up the rate of boarding at bus stops the bus system will still be slow and a major contributor to transport congestion. We all frequently see buses delayed for minutes whilst the driver has to explain to tourists with a limited grasp of English that Buckingham Palace is not on their route. The reintroduction of conductors is therefore a priority. Equally, we must retain the existing Routemaster fleet until a modern Routemaster can be designed. Not only is the Routemaster the bus that Londoners wish to use, it is also a symbol of London recognised the world over.

The new mayor will also want to investigate whether the bus operators' constant attempts to reduce the number of long distance bus routes has not been a factor in driving people off the buses and onto an already crowded tube system. If that is the case the mayor must direct the new transport authority to restore long distance routes. It has also been suggested that the present system of bus route tendering could be changed in order to save up to £85 million a year if we switched from individual route tendering to large area franchising. Clearly investigating this possibility must be a top priority for the mayor.

The other way to make a rapid increase in the capacity of public transport is to look at rail operators in London. Those Londoners who have access to the tube don't need to plan their trips into London as they can expect their tube to arrive within 5–10 minutes. Those Londoners who are dependent on the rail network may only have two trains an hour and are therefore much more likely to resort to the use of their car. As rapidly as resources allow the mayor should introduce an increase in rail service frequency to eventually match the frequency of service levels on the tube. This should dramatically reduce car usage in areas such as South London.

The *Evening Standard* recently reported a survey which showed the largest increase in car usage had been amongst women. This is because of their fears over safety and the general standard of cleanliness on public transport. Before guards on the tube were removed it was quite common to see women gathered at the end of the platform knowing that they would be able to travel in a carriage with the guard. The mayor should consider the reintroduction of guards onto the tube as a safety factor.

There has clearly been a decline in cleanliness on buses, tubes and trains over the last decade. Many of the privatised cleaning services are failing to clean the system to a standard that is acceptable to Londoners. Improving cleanliness is a key part of making London an attractive city in which to move around.

The White Paper on Transport spells out that new taxes on car parking and congestion will be hypothocated for use in improving the public transport system. They would be the source of revenue to pay for the proposals outlined above. It may be that these new taxes will not come into law nationally before the creation of the GLA. If that is the case then the bill establishing the GLA must include clauses for the early introduction of these taxes in London.

Planning and economic development
(paras 5.52–5.103)
Up until 20 years ago London's wealth vis-a-vis the rest of the nation was such that all governments relocated jobs out of London. Now of the 20 most deprived council areas in Britain, fourteen are in London. Consistently the House of Commons library analysis of unemployment by constituency shows that of the 25 constituencies with the highest unemployment 10 or 11 are in London and only one in Scotland. Yet Londoners are still subsidising the rest of the country. For each pound London puts into the national exchequer we get back only 75 pence. It is clearly no longer acceptable that Londoners should be supporting a level of public spending in Gordon Brown's constituency which

if applied to London would transform all our problems by providing another £4.4 billion a year for vital investment in modernising our city. In no sense am I arguing for a reduction in public spending in Scotland, merely that the most deprived areas in London can be raised to Scottish standards.

Recent scares about a major reduction in the government grant for education services in London show that there are still civil servants blissfully ignorant of the scale of poverty in the city in which they live.

The mayor's planning powers and leadership of the new London Development Agency create the opportunity to intervene to tackle the great arc of poverty that encircles the affluent city centre. Running from Harlesden through to Newham, as far north as Tottenham and from Woolwich to Brixton on the south bank over two million people live in conditions of unemployment, educational failure, bad housing and high crime. If this area was a free standing city in its own right anywhere else in the country there would be cabinet task force to tackle the problem. Recent figures show that in 1995 whilst 36 per cent of the unemployed had been out of work for over a year, in London the figure rose to 42 per cent. Whereas in the rest of England a GP's list averages 1887, in London that figure rises to 2038. It is not surprising that infant mortality figures are higher in London than in the rest of England.

The mayor must bring together the LDA with the government's Social Exclusion Unit to rescue the Londoners trapped in this arc of poverty. Imaginative second chance education programmes and a switch of government resources to fund a major programme of investment and reconstruction are essential. The mayor should appeal to the City Corporation to back this task-force with hard cash as the City has a direct interest in creating a safe environment for inward investment. We must also recognise that for many of those people who have been out of work for over a decade or have not had a job since they left school it may be easiest to bring them back into the culture of work via a job in the public sector, coupled with training and day release so that they can acquire the skills that allow them to move on to the private sector. The GLA must make full use of the government's welfare-to-work programme to get people into real paid employment.

The government's White Paper states that the London Development Agency will not be established until the GLA is in place. In response the Association of London Government, CBI, City Corporation, London Chamber of Commerce and Industry, London First and others have come together to establish a shadow LDA. The vital preparatory work this body has undertaken will allow the mayor to move rapidly to establish the new LDA out of the shadow body.

Given the many interesting historical sites, there is a huge potential to attract tourists into inner city areas which are currently not on the normal tourist routes. The proposal of the Zoological Society for London for a public private partnership to jointly develop a world class aquarium in Newham could open up a massive increase of tourism into Britain's most deprived borough with one million tourists a day visiting the aquarium and Thames barrier as well as Greenwich. The mayor should provide the matching 50 per cent public sector funding to allow this world class project to go ahead. It is clearly ridiculous that the nation whose history has been most dependent on its maritime achievement has not got a world class aquarium on the scale of Lisbon or Osaka.

In an overall planning strategy we need to learn the lessons of the past. The Greater London Development Plan, which took a decade and half from start to finish was bureaucratic and inflexible. A city like London changes so rapidly that we need a planning strategy which can respond quickly and flexibly.

Environment
(paras 5.110–5.135)
One weakness in the government's White Paper is that although it acknowledges that the present fragmented structure of waste management in London is undermining the efforts of statutory and

306 Turn Again Livingstone

other bodies to move to new ways of dealing with municipal waste, the government does not propose making the GLA the waste disposal authority for London. The decision to break up the old GLC's waste disposal operation into five regional units was undertaken solely to make it easier to privatise the process not as the result of careful analysis on what would be best for London's environment. The government should rethink this issue with a view to once again creating an integrated waste disposal system for London. This would prevent a recurrence of the nonsense when Westminster City Council decided to switch the transportation of waste from boats on the Thames to lorries through congested streets.

The mayor's State of London Environment report proposed by the White Paper must:

- set clear air quality targets
- set realistic traffic reduction targets
- ensure that the LDA adopts and follows a sustainable design, construction and inward investment policy
- set targets for business, developers and boroughs to integrate sustainable development principles into all regeneration projects
- ensure that all current Green Belt, Metropolitan Open Land, and Sites of Special Scientific Interest are protected
- designate the Thames as a Blue Ribbon special zone with protection for shore and habitats while maintaining access for local communities
- involve people in planning by establishing a citizens' forum as part of the GLA
- ensure proper community and voluntary sector involvement in all London 'partnerships'
- tackle energy waste and fuel poverty
- set low waste/no waste targets in GLA operations including those of all its agencies and suppliers.

Police

(paras 5.136–5.167)

The new Police authority will have 23 members of whom only eleven will come from the assembly, one of whom will be the Deputy Mayor. It would clearly not be acceptable for the police authority to be chaired by somebody who has not been elected by Londoners. I therefore propose that the Deputy Mayor should automatically chair the police authority (the mayor has the option of chairing the transport authority).

There is widespread concern that as with police forces throughout the country, the public does not get value for money with the absence of modern management techniques leading to extensive hidden waste. The new police authority will have the chance to investigate the truth of these concerns and set targets to eliminate any waste thus releasing resources into front line policing.

Police have prioritised tackling more serious crime but this has led to a failure to tackle the petty crime and vandalism that does so much to disfigure London. The new Police Authority must be asked to report on what it can learn from the zero tolerance regimes in operation in cities such as New York where tackling petty crime and vandalism has helped create a climate in which it has been easier to tackle and reduce more serious crime.

The amazing revelations flowing from the Stephen Lawrence inquiry show how important it is to respond to the concerns of Police Commissioner Sir Paul Condon that it is too difficult to remove corrupt and racist police officers under present disciplinary procedures. These procedures must be changed if public confidence in the police is to return. Police officers must recognise that the powers vested in them demand a higher standard of integrity than in other areas of employment and therefore we must not allow the corrupt and racist minority to hide behind disciplinary procedures to avoid justice. The police must also recognise that it is not acceptable when an officer fails to testify against a corrupt or racist colleague. Where that happens the officer concerned must also expect to be dismissed from the force.

Culture, media and sport
(paras 5.183–5.204)
Whilst the government's White Paper contains many excellent proposals in this area of policy it does not propose to return control of the South Bank arts complex to the democratically accountable GLA. Given its location this site has the potential to be the cultural heart of London, but since the abolition of the GLC it has stagnated. The failure to proceed with the imaginative proposals to cover over the complex is unacceptable and will leave the complex in its present spiral of decline.

We must try to persuade the government to pass control of the South Bank complex to the GLA along with a revenue raising proposal to pay for the covering of the complex and a major expansion of activities throughout the site.

The government's proposals to make entry to museums free is a tremendous boost to London but it leaves both London Zoo and Kew Gardens making substantial charges for admission. Even middle income Londoners find a family visit to both institutions costly enough to be a real deterrent. The GLA should be able to provide funding for both organisations tied to a programme of increased educational use.

The money to pay for my proposals on the South Bank, Kew Gardens and London Zoo could come from a straightforward tax per passenger at Heathrow airport. The revenue collected could also fund increased levels of funding for sporting activities in London. Visitors to London would benefit from free access to London Zoo and Kew Gardens and the enhanced activities on the South Bank. This tax could be directly collected by the GLA or as a precept on the Chancellor of the Exchequer's existing tax.

Preparing for the GLA
(paras 7.1–7.8)
My major disagreements with the White Paper arise under this section. It cannot be acceptable to expect Londoners, who have been without an elected authority for twelve years, to wait

another two years before we proceed with these exciting and radical proposals. The government can learn from the experience of Mrs Thatcher who introduced first a short Bill to abolish the GLC election followed by a long Bill to tackle the detail. The government is planning to publish one omnibus Bill in November, which will be so long and detailed it is bound to take until Easter or even summer 1999 before it becomes law.

To ensure that Londoners are able to elect their new authority at the same time as the people of Wales and Scotland, the government can quite easily publish a short Bill to create the electoral process and fund the initial start up costs of the GLA whilst at the same time publishing the long Bill which will deal with all the powers and responsibilities of the GLA. This is asking no more for Londoners than the government was prepared to do for the people of Northern Ireland. Following the Easter peace accord, the government was able to get legislation on the statute book for both the referendum and the elections to the new assembly in time for the first meeting of the assembly at the end of June.

Instead of a long drawn out two year mayoral campaign which is likely to stretch Londoners' patience to the limit, a short Bill would allow Londoners to elect the GLA in May 1999.

The new body would spend the period until April 2000 setting itself up and preparing the budgets for its first full operational year of office. It could also take immediate responsibility to establish the LDA. The new authority would then have three full operational years before it faced re-election in 2003.

The government should also reconsider its decision not to have term limits for the mayor. So much of the American experience of directly elected mayors shows it gets progressively more difficult to defeat a well-dug-in incumbent who has been able to establish extensive systems of patronage. As recent experience in Paris also shows, corruption tends to flourish the longer an incumbent is able to hold onto power.

In a city that changes as rapidly as London it is hard to believe that a mayor who has served two terms will have the freshness of approach that is required to stay abreast of such a dynamic city. I therefore recommend that no mayor should serve more than two terms.

If I am lucky enough to be elected as London's first mayor and bearing in mind I have already served 5 years as leader of the GLC, I would not seek to serve more than one term.

The government's White Paper leaves it open for sitting Members of Parliament to stand for mayor and as members of the assembly whilst retaining their seats in the House of Commons. The pattern of regional government in Europe is that parliamentarians move into and out of regional and local government. If we are to attract the widest range of talent we should allow the same flexibility in London. No one suggests that the demanding task of being Chancellor of the Exchequer, Foreign Secretary, or even Prime Minister, has led to these ministers neglecting their constituency duties.

Whilst the work of mayor will be demanding there is no better forum in which the mayor's voice can be heard than the floor of the House of Commons. When the LCC was established in 1889 many members of both front benches in the Commons and the Lords held dual membership of the LCC because of the importance they attached to London government.

The second term

Establishing the GLA with the powers and responsibilities set out will be a demanding but exciting task. The new mayor must also prepare for the development of the GLA during its second term, coinciding with what will hopefully be the second term of Tony Blair's government. The mayor's final legacy at the end of the first term of the GLA must be to bequeath, after extensive public consultation, a package of recommended legislative changes that will extend and strengthen this new institution. Areas which are the most obvious candidates for consideration are as follows:

- It has long been a nonsense that further education is locked into wasteful competition for student numbers which leads to the duplication of many courses whilst neglecting vital areas of specialism. Oversight of further education in London would easily fit in with the economic development role of the GLA

- It is equally clear that the GLA should eventually become the regional health authority for London, with the boroughs taking responsibility for the provision of services at district level
- Once the GLA has established the confidence and respect of Londoners and government it would be opportune to ask for proper tax raising powers
- We also need to consider if appeals against borough's planning decisions might be to the mayor rather than to the government
- There are also areas of housing policy currently under control of the Housing Corporation which would be more logically under the control of the GLA, given its overall strategic view of London's needs.

If the GLA is a success, it will establish the pattern for regional government in England which will be the centre piece of the second term of Tony Blair's government. In that sense those elected to and those who work for the GLA have a vital responsibility to get it right and lay the foundations on which the government can proceed to build a modern decentralised and devolved European state.

Ken Livingstone

Chronology

June 17th 1945	born in his grandmother's flat in Streatham, south London
July 1962	leaves Tulse Hill Comprehensive and starts work as a lab technician at Chester Beatty cancer research unit
February 1969	joins Labour Party
1970–73	teacher training at Philippa Fawcett College in south London
May 1971	is elected to Lambeth borough council, becoming vice-chairman of housing until December 1973: continues on the council until 1978
May 1973	is elected as GLC councillor for Norwood, soon becoming vice-chairman of housing in the Labour administration under Sir Reg Goodwin
April 1975	rebels against Goodwin's housing cuts and loses his committee vice-chairmanship
June 1976	is selected as prospective parliamentary candidate for Hampstead
May 1977	is elected as GLC councillor for Hackney North: Conservatives win control of GLC under Sir Horace Cutler
May 1978	is elected to Camden borough council, becoming chairman of housing until 1980
May 1979	loses parliamentary election in Hampstead by 3,681 votes

April 1980	comes within one vote of winning leadership of GLC Labour group following the retirement of Sir Reg Goodwin
May 1981	is elected as GLC councillor for Paddington: after Labour wins 8-seat majority on council, defeats McIntosh to become leader of the council by 30 votes to 20
December 1981	Law Lords rule that cheap fares on London Transport are illegal
January 1983	GLC gets High Court backing for an alternative fares package
May 1983	Labour Party national executive blocks his bid to become parliamentary candidate for Brent East
March 1984	Conservative government publishes bill to scrap GLC elections due May 1985, as a first step towards abolishing the council
June 1984	government scraps bill after rebellion in House of Lords
November 1984	government publishes bill to abolish the GLC
March 1985	Labour group is split over rate-capping crisis, but Livingstone's administration survives
March 1986	GLC ceases to exist and its powers are dispersed to other bodies
June 1987	is elected as MP for Brent East with a majority of 1,653 votes
September 1987	wins seat on Labour national executive and uses it to mount strong opposition to Neil Kinnock's policy reforms
September 1989	loses position on national executive
April 1992	re-elected as MP for Brent East with a majority of 5,971 votes
April 1996	Tony Blair announces plan for a directly elected London mayor
May 1997	re-elected as MP for Brent East with a majority

	of 15,882 votes: remains on backbenches when Blair forms government
September 1997	defeats Peter Mandelson to win back his place on Labour's national executive for one year
March 1998	government publishes white paper on reform of London government: opinion polls showing Livingstone is most popular potential Labour candidate
May 1998	Londoners back mayoral proposal in referendum by a majority of nearly three to one on a low turnout
June 1998	London Labour Party conference says mayoral candidates nominated by 10 constituency parties should be on shortlist for ballot
November 1998	London Labour Party board recommends candidates should be vetted by a panel before shortlisting
May 2000	First mayoral elections

Glossary

Campaign for Labour Party Democracy
Established in 1973 as a pressure group to increase accountability in the Labour Party. It achieved success in 1980 by changing the Labour Party constitution to introduce an electoral college for the election of the leader of the party, and to introduce the mandatory reselection of Labour MPs. Now one of the two main organisations in the centre/left Grassroots Alliance.

Campaign Group
The Socialist Campaign Group of Labour MPs which was set up as the 'hard-left' wing of the Parliamentary Labour Party. Members include Ken Livingstone, Tony Benn and Diane Abbott. It is now chaired by John McDonnell. Publishes a monthly newspaper, *Socialist Campaign Group News*.

Chartists
Broad-left group established in the mid-1960s which gradually evolved into a hard-left faction that partly formed the basis for *London Labour Briefing*.

Constituency Labour Party (CLP)
The local Labour Party organisation in each parliamentary constituency

County Hall
Built before and after First World War as the new home of the London County Council and became the home of the GLC in 1965. It is now an aquarium and two hotels following its sale to a

Japanese corporation by Michael Portillo during John Major's government.

Greater London Authority (GLA)

The new strategic authority promised in Labour's 1997 election manifesto. It will comprise of the mayor and a 25 member assembly.

Greater London Enterprise Board (GLEB)

GLC-established agency aimed at creating and preserving jobs in London.

Greater London Council (GLC)

Elected in 1964 but formally took over from LCC one year later. It was abolished on March 31st 1986. Reg Goodwin was leader of the Labour Group from 1967-80 and leader of the council from 1973-77. Andrew McIntosh was leader of the Labour Group from 1980-81. Ken Livingstone was leader of the Labour Group and council leader from 1981-86.

Greater London Labour Party

Labour Party region covering the Greater London area, which holds a biennial conference, electing its leading body the London Board (formerly the Regional Executive Committee). Currently chaired by Jim Fitzpatrick MP.

Inner London Education Authority (ILEA)

Following abolition of the LCC in 1965 the ILEA took over responsibility for education in the former LCC area comprising the 12 inner London boroughs. Members of the GLC for the inner London boroughs formed the ILEA along with one nomination from each borough.

International Socialists

See Socialist Workers Party

Labour Co-ordinating Committee (LCC)
Initially a pressure group set up by leading Bennites in such as
Frances Morrell and Chris Mullin. It broke from the hard left and
created a 'soft-left' grouping amongst constituency activists which
rapidly became the leading 'modernising' faction. Dissolved itself
in 1999. Ken Livingstone was a member of the LCC from
1985–88 and member of the executive from 1986–87.

Labour Left Liaison
An umbrella alliance of Labour left groupings in the 1980s, with
which Ken Livingstone was closely associated. It included the
Campaign for Labour Party Democracy, Labour Women's Action
Committee, Labour CND, Labour Party Black Sections, and the
Labour Committee on Ireland.

London County Council (also LCC)
Established by the Conservative government of Lord Salisbury in
1889. It was Liberal controlled from 1889–1907, Conservative
controlled until 1934, and Labour controlled from 1934–65.

London Labour Briefing
Hard-left magazine established in 1979 by Graham Bash, Ken
Livingstone, Chris Knight and others (see *Socialist Organiser*). It
split with Livingstone over rate-capping, but is now supportive
over the London mayor. Now called *Labour Left Briefing*.

Labour Herald
Weekly left newspaper established by Ted Knight and Ken
Livingstone to unite Labour councils against the Thatcher
government.

London Labour Party
See Greater London Labour Party

Militant Tendency
Trotskyist organisation established by Ted Grant. It came to national prominence in the 1980s due to its influence over the political leadership of Liverpool City Council, and expelled by Neil Kinnock. Regularly clashed with Livingstone and his supporters over issues such as Ireland and feminism. It is now called the Socialist Party.

National Executive Committee (NEC)
Until the 1997 rule changes, this was the governing body of the Labour Party dealing with policy and organisation. Each section of the party elects representatives to the NEC, and Ken Livingstone was a member in 1987–89 and in 1997–98 when he famously defeated Peter Mandelson. MPs were barred from seeking election in the constituency section from 1998 onwards.

National Union of Public Employees (NUPE)
Public sector workers union merged with NALGO and COHSE to form the largest British trade union UNISON.

Parliamentary Labour Party (PLP)
The parliamentary group of Labour MPs

Poll tax
The final attempt by Margaret Thatcher to control local government spending was a flat rate tax levied equally on every local council resident regardless of ability to pay. Officially called the community charge, it was replaced by the council tax in 1993.

Rates
A tax on property dating back to the Middle Ages. Homes and businesses were given a 'rateable value' based on their notional rental value. Each year local councils decided how many pence per pound of rateable value were needed to finance services and billed ratepayers accordingly. In the 1980s businesses contributed about

75 per cent of local rate income in London, with owner occupiers and tenants providing the rest. Replaced by the poll tax in 1990.

Regional Executive Committee
See Greater London Labour Party

Socialist Action Review
Quarterly Marxist magazine founded in 1989 by former supporters of the International Marxist Group. It argues for unity around single issues like anti-racism and Irish unity. It frequently supported Livingstone against the right in the Labour Party but differed with him over Europe and NATO intervention in former Yugoslavia.

Socialist Campaign for Labour Victory (SCLV)
Hard-left organisation established in summer 1978 publishing *Socialist Organiser*.

Socialist Economic Bulletin
Quarterly bulletin edited and published by Ken Livingstone offering news and analysis on the economy.

Socialist Labour League (SLL)
Group of Marxists led by Gerry Healey, which were expelled from the Labour Party in the 1950s and formed the Workers Revolutionary Party in 1973.

Socialist Organiser
Former Labour left newspaper operating on an open editorial policy, taken over by Sean Matgamna's supporters in July 1979, which lead to Ken Livingstone and associates including Chris Knight, Keith Veness and Graham Bash establishing *London Labour Briefing*. It is a long-standing opponent of Livingstone. *Socialist Organiser* has now ceased to publish, having succeeded by *Workers Liberty* magazine.

Socialist Workers Party

Established by Tony Cliff as the International Socialists and is now the largest far-left group in Britain. It became the Socialist Workers Party in late 1976. Clashed with Ken Livingstone over his support for black leadership of the anti-racist movement and may stand a candidate for mayor if Livingstone is excluded.

Tribune

A weekly Labour left newspaper established by Aneurin Bevan in 1938. Its former editors include Michael Foot and Chris Mullin. Now edited by NEC member Mark Seddon. Ken Livingstone contributes a monthly column.

Tribunites

Usually refers to the Tribune Group of Labour MPs, which is not directly linked to the newspaper of the same name. Originally the left wing 'Bevanite' grouping, it became the largest group in the parliamentary Labour Party in 1987 and moved to the centre under Neil Kinnock's tenure as leader of the Labour Party.

Workers' Revolutionary Party

See Socialist Labour League.

Index